Books should be returned on or before the
last date stamped below.

13. AUG. 1980   24 FEB 1982   JUL 87 7 0

                                        −1. SEP. 1987
1 0 OCT 1980   5 NOV 1982

1 4 FEB 1981   1 3 JAN 1987   − NOV 88 1 3 1
                       17. JUN 83 8 5
                       11. FEB 84 1 8
                       −2. JUL 84   6 3
                                                AP 90 1 0 6

1 0 MAR 1981   29. AUG   4

                       28. SEP. 1984

23 MAY 1981
    3 AUG 1981   −4. FEB. 19   5

16 SEP 1981   17. FEB 86 2 6

   15 DEC 1981

Being the Odd Odessey and the
Anecdotage of a Comedian

Cyril Fletcher

BARRIE & JENKINS
COMMUNICA · EUROPA

First published in 1978 by
Barrie and Jenkins Ltd
24 Highbury Crescent London N5 1RX

ISBN 0 214 20581 9

Printed in Great Britain by The Anchor Press Ltd
and bound by Wm Brendon & Son Ltd
both of Tiptree, Essex

To my Darling Wife

'But the loveliest things of beauty God ever has shown to me,
Are her voice, and her hair, and eyes, and the dear red curve of her lips.'

John Masefield

Acknowledgements

My thanks are due to Betty for helping me to remember an d for helping with the proofs. To Esther for writing the preface – especially as she did it slap in the middle of the last series of *That's Life*, when she was so busily employed performing, producing, and writing. To the Society of Authors as the literary representative of the Estate of John Masefield and to Judith Masefield for allowing me to quote from her father's poetry. To Georgie Wood for giving permission to include his story of Harry Tate, to the BBC for allowing the use of many photographs and to others for similar permissions. To Ann Miles for her patience in deciphering my writing and typing the script, and to my mother and father, without whose co-operation none of this life story would have been possible.

Contents

Foreword

Television programmes come and go – like mayflies, they take to the air, and die again in a single day. But sometimes something is born out of a programme which has an abiding value. For me, one of the treasures I have gleaned from the series of consumer programmes called *That's Life* has been the friendship of Cyril Fletcher and his wife Betty Astell.

When you read these pages you will understand why their friendship is so precious to me. Cyril has taken part in every aspect of showbusiness – from sophisticated cabaret to pantomime, from one-man shows to radio phone-ins – but somehow he has never been touched by the jealousy or bitterness which is part of this fiercely competitive industry. He enjoys all the good things in life, good food, good wine and most of all good gardens, without succumbing to glittery, showbizzy temptations. He is a gentleman – and in the gentleness of his Sussex garden a great many of his friends have found the kind of peace and refreshment which can be desperately hard to find in theatres and television studios.

As you will also discover when you read this book, he has a fund of very funny stories. Reading the description of his mother, you can quite well see how he developed his sense of humour. Let me just add one other Cyril story. We discovered a great new British sport – lawnmower racing. Cyril agreed to take part – on a ferocious lawnmower, so huge and bone-rattling that it nearly disconnected his vertebrae. He suggested that he should drive it wearing a suitable outfit – covered with leather and studs and with a crash helmet so that he looked like a rather mature Hell's Angel. He did look extremely funny. His natural refinement clashed somewhat with all that gear. We explained the plot of our film to him, which meant he had to 'chicken out' of the race early, mow his way to the far end of a field, and be discovered there sipping a little champagne.

He stamped his leather boot in front of a crowd giggling at his crash helmet and said, 'Me? Chicken out of a race? Certainly not! Think of my image!'

Cyril never thinks of his image – never counts his lines or his close-ups. His interest is in the programme, the production, the value of his work to other people. You won't find in this book any mention of the enormous generosity he devotes to countless good causes. You also won't find any mention of the fact he drives his car terrifyingly fast, and has a passion for peppermints. But you will find the elegance of language and the constant enjoyment of life and good things, past and present, which make reading his book as enjoyable as meeting him.

Esther Rantzen

Introduction

'It is the highest praise to be able to
furnish harmless pleasure – it is as
great a power as any man may possess.' – Samuel Johnson

My idea of a perfect West End theatre musical is when the curtain rises on a glamorous chorus of beautifully dressed young ladies dancing to exciting music played by a large orchestra and inspired by a brilliant choreographer. Then, to suitably important fanfares, there will enter the Star Comedian, faultlessly tailored in white tie and tails. He tells us with perfect enunciation and style a fairly short but well-constructed very funny story. Now this story is so uproariously risible, and is so comically told, that the audience laughs solidly for an hour. The curtain falls. After the usual interval of about a quarter of an hour, the curtain rises on a spectacular but quite short dance of panache and élan executed this time by a male chorus and leading up to another imposing entrance by an exquisite vision – a comedienne of great beauty, style and perfect timing who reminds the audience of the joke told by the comedian in the first half of the show. It is such a good joke and told with such professional expertise that the audience will laugh, night after night, for another hour. Both choruses will then unite for an exciting dance lasting exactly one minute, when the comedian will join the comedienne for the finale 'walk down' and tumultuous applause.

The show will need a very good scriptwriter. So will this book; and it only has me. Those of you with stamina will read on. I know that the great British Public has stamina because it has been 'putting up' with me for forty-two years. But in spite of this long career as an entertainer on what compères describe as 'Stage, Screen, TV and Radio' there is no mention of my name in *Who's Who in the Theatre* or in any similar TV or radio handbook. Histories have been written of the music hall in wartime and on radio in its heyday; my name appears in none of them. Read a dozen or more star autobiographies of the last forty years: no mention. This is the sort of fame one has to get used to living with. So I have, I suppose, an understandable urge to write this book myself, to make sure that I *have* really existed and that I am not a figment of my mother's imagination.

I was once the guest of honour of the Radio Trades Association, and Lord

Hill, who was at that time the Chairman of the Governors of the BBC, had as President of the Association to make the speech to introduce me. I greatly enjoyed this; that such an important man should be eulogizing on behalf of the humble Fletcher. Lord Hill has a reputation for being thorough. He told at length and in detail of parts of my life and career that even I had forgotten. Wherever had such a busy man amassed such a fanfaronade of information? As he sat down I realized the impeccable fount of his knowledge. 'You got that from the BBC Obituary Department,' I said. 'Yes,' he said, 'I did.' So at least I am mentioned by them. We seem to have come to the end of this book before even starting the first chapter.

Then one day a man in a lift at the Royal Lancaster Hotel said, 'Are you Cyril Fletcher?'

'Yes,' I said, 'I am.'

He looked me up and down for what seemed quite a time, and then he said, 'Oh well! Good luck, anyway!'

1   Early Days

'The Mid-wife laid her hand upon his skull
With this prophetic blessing – be thou dull.'
– Dryden

When I read an autobiography, I like the early facts quickly and plainly written down and then the writer can flannel on as much as he likes. I was born Cyril Trevellian Fletcher in Watford, Hertfordshire, at three o'clock in the afternoon on Wednesday, 25 June 1913. My mother, I am told, was cleaning out the bath when I began my journey into the world (so I very nearly began with the rhyme about the plug-hole!). Her name was Maude Mary Fletcher, née Ginger. My father was George Trevellian Fletcher and he was the Deputy Town Clerk of Watford at that time. The venue was Hagden Lane, and I do not know the number of the house, so there will, alas, never be one of those blue plaques. I was a second child and only son, my sister Ida Mary being two years older.

*   *   *

I am a small boy of six walking down the High Street in a small town, almost a country town, Watford in 1919. ('Pleasant, homely, loving Hertfordshire,' said Charles Lamb.) It is a Wednesday, which is early closing, and the street is deserted. It is hot and sunny and everything is covered with a white dust, coming from the flint road recently covered with tarmacadam. There is a smell of past hot summers in newly sprayed tar.

At the bottom of Watford High Street there is the majestic building and frontage of Benskin's Brewery, with the high red-brick chimneys and the warm cloying scent of malt and hops of which many tiny country towns are redolent. Housemartins sweep and weave from the eaves of the houses. From the station half-way down the street come the frightening shrieks of steam engines, which, I suppose, most of us now have forgotten.

I was always rather pleased to get past the station noises, even though I had imagined that inside the station, beyond the brick façade, there was some kind of fairyland depicted by the sunny seaside posters and that somehow the sea was lapping rather magically at the foot of the station stairs. I had never seen the sea, not that I could remember, which seemed silly when it was so close and only needed the authority of some grown-up to take me down the steps. There were vast ocean-going liners down there too, according to the posters, and these went from Watford Station to the ends of the world.

I had never been down the High Street on my own. I may have done so with my sister, but never alone. I was going to tea with my Shop Granny and Grandad. They were my father's parents and kept a small grocer's at the bottom of the High Street and were always sadly irritable on a wet Saturday because they needed the trade of a good, dry, sunny Saturday to make the week worth while. The shop smelt of bacon and dry, large, white ('curiously strong' they had written on them) peppermints in bottles, soap and perhaps paraffin. It was a warm, likeable smell. All along the front of the counter was a row of biscuit tins with glass tops so that you could see the variety inside; there were piles of tinned fruit and pickles and bottles at regular intervals on the counter displayed in precarious pyramids, and in the spaces between were the white-coated figures of my grandparents.

My grandfather had a red face, quite a lot of neatly brushed and parted white hair and a white moustache neatly rolled and spiked like a sergeant-major's. He had bags under his eyes, and his eyes, blue and merry, seemed to have difficulty in peering over the bags as they also peered over half-moon-shaped gold spectacles but seemingly never through them. If it was winter, you would marvel at the puffy blue chilblains on his blue ears and nose, and cruelly on his hands, which wore mittens to prevent the chilblains but which never did.

On the other side of the shop was the bacon counter, in front of which were a dozen or so little sacks with their necks rolled down, displaying to the customer the split peas and currants and grain and rice. It was great fun to thrust your hand and arm down into the sack and play with the musty, dusty-smelling contents. But especially fascinating on the counter was the large red and silver bacon machine which clamped the bacon down with a great toothed ratchet and which then glossily flowed to and fro as the handle was turned with a lovely rasping sound of the circular knife as it cut through the falling rashers of pink and white bacon. Sometimes I was allowed to turn the handle myself, and I used to have a slight feeling of sick horror at the sharpness of the blade as it cut through the flesh of the bacon so efficiently.

Shop Granny was small and quick and had a long pointed nose and deeply sunken eyes. They were large and darkly coloured eyes – even the whites were a dark moist blue. Her hair was in a kind of fashionable pancake, held together with a hairnet and, because it was rather sparse, reinforced with hair pads which were never quite the right colour to match the natural hair and which were never quite in the right place to cover the bald patches and therefore deceived no one. She had a striking, pleasant, almost pretty face and a charming smile which could be cynical and quite wicked at times. Round the well-shaped mouth there was a slight moustache. At one of the family gatherings I had asked, 'Why has Granny got a moustache?' as it seemed an unusual ornament for a woman. The silence and dismay of the gathering was so impressive that I have never forgotten it.

These family gatherings took place at Christmas or Easter or Whitsun or on

2

August Bank Holiday (when my grandmother never failed to remark that this would be their last weekday off until Boxing Day). They never had a longer break than a Bank Holiday weekend, and they didn't retire until they were nearly into their eighties.

At the back of the shop was an office and then a courtyard which had a glass roof from which hung many baskets of ferns. There were several steps up, with a Georgian front door leading into a small Georgian house. The parlour was over-full with Victorian furniture, the centre table covered in red plush with red bobbles round the edges.The silver teaset was brought out on these occasions, and the beautiful bone china had open boat-like cups with roses on them. There were roses on the carpet and on the wallpaper. My grandmother's name was also Rose, but my grandfather called her Jo. My grandmother also called my grandfather Jo, although his names were George Trevellian, and, to add to the considerable confusion, they had a canary in a cage which hung in the glass-covered forecourt among the ferns which was also named Jo.

The family, with my grandmother and grandfather at either end of the table, consisted of my mother and father, my sister and myself, my father's two sisters and their respective husbands, although one sister and her husband were to go quite shortly to Australia.

I remember how (to recover from the gaffe of remarking on my grandmother's moustache) I gave a little sketch, playing the three parts myself, of how Jo would call Jo to hear Jo's latest song, and had Jo cleaned out the bottom of Jo's cage? 'It is as good as a pantomime having that child here,' said my grandmother rather generously, and indeed one of these family gatherings seldom passed without her saying it. I don't suppose anyone noticed it but me, but it was a remark I began to hope and wait for. I had begun to learn how to make people laugh.

There were family gatherings too upstairs in the drawing room, reached by a twisting staircase. I was usually carried up and down this staircase and would see at eye level a sampler with heavy mahogany frame made by my grandmother's grandmother, Elizabeth Bennett, in the tenth year of her age in 1839. It is all that I have now of those days.

Sundays would be sometimes spent in the drawing room. My mother, who had a very pleasant mezzo-soprano voice, would play the piano, my father the mandolin, my aunt a violin and my father would add a very nasal and tuneless tenor and sing 'Friend of Mine'. While he was singing this, I would hide my smiles in *King Albert's Book*, which had a white binding and was published during the First World War to aid gallant little Belgium. There was a picture in it by Arthur Rackham of a woebegone damsel sitting on a rounded knoll and surrounded by distant woods. Immediately behind her was a thin tapering silver birch, but so placed by the artist, and his perspective being such, that it seemed to me to be growing out of the girl's rather round shoulders. I used to imagine how difficult it would be for this girl to dress herself in the morning with this enormous tree growing out of her shoulders and how difficult it must be for her to get on a bus; and perhaps that is why she looked so sad.

These thoughts were possibly inspired by the tomb of the woman in the churchyard of the parish church at Watford who had insisted on being buried with a fig seed in her hand, and should this tiny morsel of life grow into a fig tree, then it would prove to all disbelievers that there was a God. This vigorous tree was there for us all to see, having split the tomb asunder, but, rather disappointingly for a small boy, one could not see any of her remains inside through the dark, black cracks in the shade of the tree.

My Shop Grandparents, as they were always called, were Wesleyan chapel-goers, and in consequence were held in considerable suspicion by my maternal grandfather and grandmother, who were Church of England. Being chapel, no games of any kind were allowed on a Sunday, one had to wear one's best clothes and read only 'improving books'. To produce a pack of 'Happy Family' cards, and for them to catch sight of Mrs Potts the Painter's wife, and especially Mr Bung the Brewer, produced such a storm of disapproval that they were promptly put out of reach on the mantelpiece among the Goss china.

My mother's parents, known as King Street Granny and Grandad, lived in a tiny Georgian cottage which has now been pulled down, this part of Watford having been redeveloped beyond recognition. A tiny terraced cottage, with the house on one side used as offices by solicitors and the Registrar of Births and Deaths, and the one on the other side housing a family to whom we never spoke as they were 'common' – but one could feel the warmth of their fire through the adjoining wall in the 'hall', which was a narrow passage made more narrow still by a table and a hall-stand and an aspidistra, and on the other wall a lithograph of the Duke of Wellington autographed by the great man. My mother's family were not only Church of England but also Conservative.

King Street Grandfather was bald with a large moustache and large brown protuberant eyes. He was also fat and had a violent temper which we children never saw. He was kind and attentive to us. He would sit in his armchair by the window of the living room and his enormous knee would always be a welcome perch for us. He would tell us long and involved stories and illustrate them on the margins of the *Daily Mail* with beautiful, delicate little drawings. We loved him and we loved the long hours we spent with him on his allotment by the brewery. It was here that I began my apprenticeship to gardening. He kept a few hens in a henhouse which was creosoted every year; whenever I smell creosote, I'm back there finding eggs beneath the black Minorcas – large warm white eggs. Spent hops were given free by the brewery to its employees and these were dug in assiduously by my grandfather. All the vegetables for the family were grown here and were taken home and washed and cleaned and tidied up on the large black rainwater tank by the back door. As a child it never occurred to me to know exactly what Grandfather's job was at Benskin's Brewery, but he had some kind of executive position – a sort of foreman of foremen. His office was up a ladder and his little room perched high on the wall of a vast warehouse containing hundreds of barrels – enormous barrels they seemed to me then, and when they were moved the noise was like thunder. For many years I was quite sure that thunder was the sound of God moving his beer barrels across the floor of the sky. Grandfather had to visit the brewery sometimes on a Saturday or a Sunday and I might go with him. I suppose he would check the temperatures and we would walk side by side through the silence of the warehouse past hundreds of barrels in dusty rows with yeasty froth oozing from the bungs with their bitter-sweet beery smell. Sometimes if there were festivities in Cassiobury Park, perhaps on a Bank Holiday, we would accompany our grandfather to the refreshment tents early in the morning before the gaiety began and he would go round tasting the beer, rolling it round his mouth and squirting it out under his moustache with the most enviable length – a facility I tried without success many times to emulate.

A small keg of beer was delivered every week from the brewery and installed in the dark of the scullery next to the washing copper. This was for the exclusive use of my grandmother, not my grandfather (who was a teetotal brewer). She had half a glass every day with her luncheon, which was called dinner. My King Street Granny was small and neat and tidy, always wearing black and with a black apron: a black satin apron in the afternoons and jet earrings. Her hair was very white and parted in the middle. Her collars were high and her shoes seemed always to be of black velvet. She had been an invalid for years and was looked after by my maiden aunt, Marth, who had devoted her life to keeping home for my grandparents, as so often happened in those days to the daughter who was the last off the shelf, although for some years she had been courted by a sandy-haired grocer's assistant.

King Street Granny had a sweet, kindly face and was a sweet, kindly woman, and I spent many happy afternoon hours in the gloaming at her feet, the black kettle singing on the trivet by the living-room fire. I would ask again and again to hear her two stories of how they lived at the Brewery House, Watford, and how the cat, Dusty, would bring rats into the house and lay them dead in a row on the mat in front of the fire for her approval, and how the dog – also called Dusty – would bring rats in from the brewery and lay them dead in a row on the mat in front of the fire for her approval. When I first knew her she must have been in her late fifties. At the end of her days, at over eighty, she looked exactly the same, with her dear smile and neat silver head.

But I digress: I am a small boy of six walking down Watford High Street, and because it is Wednesday, and early closing, and hot and deserted, and quiet once I get past the station, the *clop-clop* of horses' hooves behind me is all the more noticeable and I look round to see what is coming. Two gipsy caravans and a bedraggled gipsy cart are coming down the High Street. A hideous, tall, dark man with a dark-shadowed blue chin and thick gold earrings leads the first caravan, from the doorway of which lolls the unkempt head of his wife, swinging to and fro with the jolt of the caravan as if dead, half a clay pipe hanging upside down from her sleeping mouth. In the second van are two youths and on the cart several small children: stolen children I am sure. I hurriedly walk on. Not too fast; I mustn't look as if I am running away, but fast enough to keep my distance, and then hurry through the side-door to the shop and the haven of my Shop Grandparents' house where, of course, they will have left the door ajar.

I am sure they are stolen children on the cart. All gipsy children are stolen. Not only have I read so in books at home, but my mother has threatened me with the nightmare of being given to the gipsies if I misbehave.

I am getting nearer to the shop and a quick covert glance over my shoulder shows, to my terror, that they are gaining on me. I am almost running now and I can hear my heart pounding. I get to the side-door of the shop; the shop windows and door are staring blindly at me with navy-blue blinds down and the legend 'Geo: Trevellian Fletcher Grocer' in copperplate writing upon them; with lazy flies trapped in the corners. The side-door is not ajar, it is closed. I try the handle. It is locked on the inside, I can't get in. I try the handle again and kick the door with my small shoe. It will not give at all. I am sobbing now and then, with a great burst of joy, realize there is a bell. I will press the bell, and with luck, Grandfather will be down the passage and the door will be opened before the gipsies are there. They are very near now. I reach for the bell. I am only six and short for my age. The bell is too high for me to reach. Panic helps me to jump to try and ring the bell, but I can't manage it.

Tears; silent, fearful tears, course down my white cheeks. I will be stolen, I will be stolen by gipsies: yes, the man has left the caravan and is coming across the road to me. The man comes over to me, he stands over me, I can smell the stale sweat from the hairy chest and feel breath through the broken teeth as the gipsy smiles down at me. I faint.

The gipsy picks me up in his arms, quite gently, and rings the bell and tries the handle, which turns quite easily under the man's muscular grasp. He carries me up the passage to where Shop Granny, at the top of the steps, is saying, 'Is that you, Jo?'

I am now a small boy of six and a half and I am in a great rage. I am beside myself with fury and frustration. I am crying and shouting and swearing and throwing myself about and wishing my parents were dead. Perhaps it would be better if *I* were dead, then *they* will be sorry. How can I kill myself before this indignity that they are about to thrust upon me? I am to be page at a wedding, my aunt's wedding, and I am to wear a pale-beige tussore suit I have not worn for at least two years. I have been told to get into it and be quiet and get on with it or they will all be late. (A small child has great dignity which one should always respect. I have remembered this hurt vividly for over fifty years.)

I have now got into my tussore suit and my hair is neatly brushed and I have strict instructions to keep clean and look as if I am enjoying myself. The whole grown-up charade seems absurd to me. Why all this fuss about getting married? Why do they all have to dress up? Why do I have to dress up? I am then given my instructions. I am to be the only attendant and as there are no bridesmaids I have to carry my aunt's gloves, prayer book and bouquet. I already look cissy enough in my tussore suit, but now I have to hold a bunch of flowers. In front of everyone, too.

I remember arriving at the parish church. There was no time to look at the fig lady's tomb. We assembled. We walked slowly up the aisle. I was given the gloves; hurriedly taken off and with the fingers inside-out, the white prayer book and the flowers. The service, with full musical honours, was quite a long one. There seemed to be a lot of kneeling. I knelt with my arms full. My arms got very tired indeed. I can feel the dull ache of them now. I decided after some cowardly looks all round that the best thing for me to do was to put the flowers carefully on the floor and still hold the gloves and prayer book. It was the flowers that were so heavy. So I gently put them on the paving stones of the aisle in front of me.

I was quite tiny kneeling there in my tussore suit, and the grown-ups on either side seemed to tower over me. On my left-hand side, that is to say the bride's side of the aisle, and looking even larger than usual, was the largest of my aunts. She was married to my mother's brother and was also my godmother. She was not 'of the family' as she had merely married into it and was, consequently, although I had known her all my life, 'a stranger'. Her face always had a certain hauteur and she whispered from within the pendulous folds of it to my uncle, 'Cyril has thrown the flowers down.' It was the word 'thrown' which angered me. Because the flowers were making my arms ache I had quite reasonably, and gently, put them on the cold pavement in front of me. My large aunt moved her enormous form a little towards me. There was the edge of the pew, the heating grating and half the aisle between us. 'Pick those flowers up,' she hissed. I pretended not to hear. (Thrown indeed!) She tried again. I still pretended not to hear. She tried to draw my attention by striking out at me with her long glove. I took no notice. She must by then have demanded at least six times that I should pick up the flowers. I have very large brown eyes, they were even larger when I was a child as my face was smaller. I turned them on my aunt with a blank stare. She glared back in fury. I then turned my face to the front and began to break off the heads of the flowers from the bouquet and one by one stuff them down the grating. I followed my bridal aunt out of the church holding her gloves, her prayer book and a bunch of stalks.

There are two other crises I remember about this time. One concerned a small boy called Cuthbert who attended with me a small preparatory school at Watford. I tied him to a tree and then rather absent-mindedly went home to luncheon and forgot all about Cuthbert, who was a frail, delicate child, otherwise I would never have had the temerity to tie him up. During afternoon school we were making Noah's Arks out of glossy postcards with blanket stitches of wool when a message came that the headmistress wanted to see me. I suddenly remembered that Cuthbert was still tied to the tree and my heart leaped with fear. 'Leaped with fear' is the sort of phrase one would expect in an Ethel M. Dell novel, but, please believe me, I can still feel it now actually leaping or stopping a beat or whatever sudden shock causes it to do.

The only other times that I have ever known my heart do this was once when I was presenting a show, the entire finances of which were my own sole concern, with a salary list of over £1,000 a week (present-day value £10,000), asking the manager of the theatre where it was to be resident for the whole summer what our advance booking figure was the day before we opened. He said, 'Eighteen shillings and fourpence.' (It should at the worst have been £2,000.) The other occasion was when a specialist leant across my dining-room table and said, 'Your wife is very gravely ill indeed. There is a 50–50 chance.'

The other crisis or *faux pas* one might call it, but a *faux pas* has always meant 'crisis' among my relatives, was when we returned from a holiday and I found my maiden aunt nursing my cousin Andrew who was about a day old, the same week that aunt had made such a success in a series of religious tableaux as the Virgin Mary, and I asked her if the child was hers. I remember well the furious, studied quiet and my father's stifled laughter.

This was my Aunt Marth. After this Nativity performance I remember she took us to a missionary exhibition in the parish hall where there were a series of little boxes in which lead figures, rather like toy soldiers, enacted other little tableaux explaining the life of a missionary. We were shown round by a very comical curate, almost a stage curate, chinless, with a lisp, unable to pronounce his R's, the whole capped with a slight stutter. You will gather: a terribly easy person for even a child of my age to impersonate. One little box was of the mission laundry, and for light relief the comical curate pointed out a little boy at the back who was smoking a cigarette, and the impersonation of this unfortunate man showing us all round the exhibition was taken home by me and greatly enjoyed by us all.

This church that Aunt Marth frequented was very High Church indeed and I was compelled to go with her every Sunday. The theatricality of it all I greatly enjoyed. The incense was very strong and the incensory was swished towards me each time by a malevolent little choirboy whose angel face belied his intentions as the procession passed us in the aisle. This would set my eyes running, and I am sure that Aunt Marth thought that it was an outward display of my meanness (I have always been careful with money) because immediately following I would have to give up one penny of the two which was my pocket money for the week into this extraordinarily little embroidered oven glove which was shoved beneath our noses by the church warden. I am sure I should be indebted to my Aunt Marth, a very discerning woman, because she took me on two or three occasions, I would think against her personal inclination, to the Palace Theatre, Watford, to see performances of music hall. One bill was headed by Ella Shields, the male impersonator, and on it were some trapeze artists, whose dizzy paraphernalia collapsed in the middle of their performance and the girl fell with an horrific thud to be, alas, only *almost* caught by her partner; both being tragically injured.

King Street Grandfather's half-brother's widow was Great-Aunt Kate. She lived in a long Victorian street backing on to a railway – tall houses all attached to each other with semi-basements, bay windows enriched with stone lintels painted cream, but never recently, fronting the four-storeyed façade.

Great-Aunt Kate was terribly poor, her house was let off into flats and she lived only in one front room. This room was her drab world, for the poor woman suffered terribly from arthritis. She was able after she had been dressed to stagger to a chair by the almost empty grate and sit and stare in front of her unsmilingly for the rest of the day, her misshapen hands resting on her aproned lap. Her head was held up seemingly by the lace collar, strutted at either side by whalebones and decorated in front by a large brown-and-white cameo brooch. Her fleshy ears were also held up by this then fashionable contraption of white lace and whalebone and bulged over it redly on either side. Her face was red and suffused with a myriad of tiny blue veins, giving an overall purple effect. Her nose, more purple than the rest, was a bulging blob put on afterwards. The mouth was grim and turned down on either side and was sucked in at regular intervals; for there were no teeth. Her hair was white, parted in the middle with a very small bun tightly held at the back with many pins. But the thing which fascinated me so much as a small boy was a cyst on the top of her head, round which the hair was parted. It was pink and round and exactly like, and the same size as, the button in the centre of a schoolboy's cap. I could not disassociate in my schoolboy mind this odd protuberance from the button on my cap. I once asked my mother who had sewn it on.

A Miss Rouse, my great-aunt's companion, who was also dressed in black, would usher us into our great-aunt's almost empty room, iron bed on one side, armchair at the fireplace – a large white marble fireplace and on the enormous mantelpiece two pieces of Victorian china; on the one side a china chair in which sat a Victorian father with his daughter on his lap and the other side a Victorian mother with a somewhat sickly boy on her lap. The boy had bright yellow hair. Miss Rouse looked after my great-aunt and brought her the meagre meals on trays and stoked the tiny fires. She was sixty and out of Dickens.

The door would be thrown open. My sister and I would be ushered in, two small figures in this large, cold, empty room. Great-Aunt Kate, her head propped up by whalebone, her mouth dragged down at each corner, the cruelly deformed hands mute in her lap – the cruelly deformed feet on a little footstool of wool-work, was sitting there staring into and waiting for eternity.

Her cracked voice invited us in. She didn't look towards us. I stared fascinated at the 'button' on her head – I waited for her to say the dreaded words. The words which would mean that we would have to screw up every vestige of childish courage we had. The words we had been knowing that she would say as we turned the corner and saw the distant view of the tall ugly house. Looking as hideous as any eighty-year-old, half-starved, arthritic old recluse could look – she leaned forward and said, 'Kiss me, but mind me feet.'

While we are talking of relations, I am reminded of this weird man, a publican in South Africa, who for many years, throughout Hitler's war, and for years afterwards, would send people to England to look me up, 'The brother of whom I am so proud.' And these people really used to get quite annoyed when I told them that I was the only son of an only son of an only son, and therefore had no male relations whatsoever, and certainly not a brother. There was such a constant stream of these visitors from South Africa who kept looking me up, indeed, on occasion stopping me in the street to talk about this brother, that I began to get slightly suspicious of my father and wondered whether perhaps he had had a bicycle, and on some sunny evening had cycled off into the sunset and been unfaithful to my mother. But the joyous day came when one of these fans came out of the audience to me after a broadcast and told me of the sad death of my brother, but then, 'It was expected,' the man said, and I asked, 'Why?' and the man said, 'Well, he was eighty-five if he was a day.' To which I replied, 'How interesting – my father is only sixty-nine.'

Which leads me to my father ...

I never really knew my father as I was born in 1913 and he was in France by the end of 1914. There must have been leaves when he rejoined us for a short time here and there, which meant the four of us sleeping in the front room of my grandfather's house. (I can peer now through the white painted iron bars of my cot and feel the searing pain in my finger when I caught it in the collapsible side.) My father had a very prosaic legal mind. He was very diligent in his work and very honest. Lying was a heinous crime. Fairness and fair equable decisions are essential for the happiness of a child. My father was often, and oddly for a lawyer, unfair. I cannot remember ever spending one long happy day in my father's company. (My King Street Grandfather yes; halcyon days.) It didn't worry me unduly. I cannot fairly say that my father did not try. On looking back I suspect that he made one great effort. He was a great one for sea voyages. He was never wealthy enough for long sea voyages, but he would go on trips to France and Brittany and Gibraltar, Scandinavia and similar short excursions. Sometimes he would go in small cargo boats as he was an exceptionally good sailor. I am a bad sailor. 'We are going,' said my father, 'to Edinburgh and then to Dundee, and then home again by boat. There's a small cargo boat . . .' he continued. I had not been on the sea other than short rowing trips, and I was never sick in trains like my sister, so it was a fair and reasonable suggestion. And I like to imagine my father saying to himself, 'Get to know the boy – ten days on our own. Four days each way on a small boat.' I was very ill indeed on the way. It was April and cold and squally. They kept calling it 'a slight swell'. I stayed in my bunk until I overheard the captain say to my father, 'If you don't get him up on to the bridge into the air he'll die before we get to Edinburgh.' So, wrapped in blankets, I took my bowl up on to the bridge and retched my heart out from there. My two days ashore were a nightmare of apprehension. Could I not go back by train? 'It will have calmed down by the time we go home,' said my father. It was a lot rougher. When I was carried ashore at Tilbury I had to get myself home by bus and tube. The sheer joy of being ashore helped me.

I shall never forget how considerate the elderly steward-cum-cook was. (The whole ship's crew would only have numbered about eight.) He ministered to me in a very kindly way, and in spite of it being rougher on our return I did rally a little on the last day: the sheer joy of knowing there could only be a few more hours. Unfortunately, it was the cook's birthday. He decided I should have a little of his birthday cake, which he most enthusiastically pressed upon me. I had an immediate relapse. I was in bed for over a week on my return. So I never really got to know my father; even though he lived to be eighty-four.

When I was seven my father became the Town Clerk of Trowbridge, a small market town in Wiltshire. We lived on the outskirts of the town towards Bratton and we could see the Westbury White Horse from the end of the road. This end of the road, known by the locals as Up Round, was the edge of unspoilt country-side. It was also the edge of Lord Long's large country estate and there were acres of woodlands, long grassy rides, tiny Wiltshire lanes. Far, far 'from the dust and din and steam of town'. I was not a very strong child and at seven the doctor had wisely told my parents that I was to do nothing but roam in the country for three months. Here began my intense love of living in the country. It was April. Imagine April, May and June in unspoilt country at the age of seven.

> I loved the winds when I was young,
>   When life was dear to me;
> I loved the song which Nature sung,
>   Endearing liberty;
> I loved the wood, the vale, the stream,
> For there my boyhood used to dream.*

There was a tiny farm – smallholding would be a better description – just past Up Round belonging to the local milkman, Mr Grist. There were but two fields – one bordered by a stream which also blissfully trickled through the end of our garden. There were a lot of henhouses, duck pens, geese runs, hatcheries and a stable for the pony that drew the milk cart.

The milk cart had two large wheels only and in the middle of it a tall milk churn with a brightly burnished brass top to it. The milk cans were fastened to the side and to the side of the milk churns were fastened measuring ladles, also with brass handles. Mr Grist drove with a flourish of the whip at a spanking speed, and if you had the courage to jump on once he had started you were given a ride beside him. I think now with amazement of the way at the age of seven I was allowed the free run of the farmyard: either Mr Grist was a very trustful and discerning man or he was a fool. I spent hours there. Should I hear today the tiny, whistling cheep of a downy chick I am there at once fifty-odd years away. Is there any sight more sweet and moving than soft yellow ducklings waddling after the mother duck in a row, the imprints of their tiny webbed feet in the mud criss-crossed with the giant imprints of the geese and goslings? Oh, the magnificent drama of letting out into the field the turkey cock and his harem! I'll not forget the horror of trying to get them back into their house before Mr Grist returned. The comedy of the mother duck taking her ducklings for their first swim and her terrible anxiety over the swift currents sweeping them at least three feet away from her; their joy in the water; the dipping and shaking of heads; the diamond water drops in the sun; and the gathering of the ducklings around her under the dappled shade of the willow where the water shone warmly brown and blue reflecting them. We were all very young and very happy.

I helped Mr Grist to move the wire-netting arks over the fresh turf; this was

* 'The Sleep of Spring' by John Clare.

especially fun with the broody mother hen, her body in the coop and anxious head and neck, clucking for her vulnerable brood through the slats.

Sometimes I would stand still, so still, for perhaps half an hour while the busy life of the farmyard went on around me. Each animal and bird a different personality, and each one behaving differently and getting a different message and reward out of its brief existence.

The stream through Mr Grist's fields, unlike the stream through our garden, had minnows and sticklebacks. The picture above my drawing-room mantel-piece, 'Tiddlers', painted by our great friend Edward Seago and in my home now, is an exact illustration of the scene. I might be any one of the children he has so beautifully painted: any of them delving into the rocky glooms of the stream and catching the darting silver fish in our nets; any one of them grieving when the still, silver, oddly brittle husk floated with dead blind blue eye reproach-fully on the top of a scummy glass jam-jar the next morning. Ted Seago painted it exactly in 'Tiddlers', and H. E. Bates has told it exactly in his short story 'The Source of the World': small boys and streams and sunshine and the country-side.

One or two of the boys who lived in the road would sometimes walk along Greenlanes with me perhaps two miles away to a field which grew the Fragrant Orchid in prodigal abundance.

Life was not without its excitements in this little country town. Living exactly opposite to us in the road was a lunatic; dangerous at times, he would be called for and taken off in a padded van to Devizes where the nearest asylum was. Several men would overpower him and take him struggling and yelling down his short garden path to the van; there being no sedation in those days, I suppose. Then he would be banging the sides of the van as it drove him down the road out of sight. Then, some months later, apparently cured, he would be returned only for this sad excursion to be repeated again and again.

Then one day a two-wheeled hand-cart arrived and a large box was put on it and pushed off away down the road. I watched this fascinated, the whole oper-ation taking about half an hour. When I returned home my mother was furious. 'How dare you stand out there in the street watching the poor man's funeral!' I had no idea it was a funeral! Near us at Watford had been an undertaker who did things magnificently. There was a glass carriage for a hearse with mauve ostrich feathers in bunches at each corner of the roof and mauve ostrich feathers on the heads of the four glossy black horses which drew the carriage, slowly, oh so slowly, with a mute holding each prancing horse's head; while other carriages followed, drawn by similar horses. This was my idea of a funeral. There was pomp and circumstance, and one was taken away grandly; a pageant of death. How different just a deal box on a two-wheeled hand-cart pushed by one man; how was I to know?

There was another madman who lived at the opposite end of the road – a little white-haired man in a black velvet jacket and large black-and-white check trousers. He was known to us all as 'Mad Clem'. He was harmless and rather fun. We would taunt him mercilessly as only heartless children can. 'Dance,

Clem!' we would cry, and blithely, and I like to hope happily, he would do a merry Morris step or two for perhaps five minutes. He was fawn-like and as light as a feather. He may once have been a dancer.

We had dancing classes at Trowbridge Town Hall. All the boys and girls in the area would go; learning not just fox-trots and waltzes but the more complicated Lancers and Roger de Coverleys. One wore 'dancing pumps' for this – the girls' like a soft ballet shoe, the boys' black patent leather slippers with a heel and a bow on the front. My mother, in her zeal to economize, decided that as my sister had grown out of her pumps, I should wear her cast-offs as I too had grown out of mine. I can feel my outraged fury as I write. It was a perfect example of my mother's complete lack of imagination. She could not understand the indignity of her suggestion. I refused to go. In the end I had to take a carving knife and slit my sister's discarded pumps to ribbons. That way I was safe.

My father had his first motor car while we lived at Trowbridge. It was a three-wheeler Morgan with two front seats and two very small seats at the back for two small children. We were not really small by then, and it was agony squeezing in there. Driving over Salisbury Plain in the winter we would manage to go at the alarming speed of 40 miles an hour, and in an open car with the wind driving across the plain, my ears would very nearly drop off with the cold and pain.

My mother and father were members of the Trowbridge Amateur Dramatic and Operatic Society. They sang in the chorus. I can see how utterly lost and unnatural they looked as they cavorted and gambolled. *Iolanthe* it was, and my mother was a fairly immobile shepherdess. They both seemed to have very red faces as if in a state of constant embarrassment. It was caused through their inexpert use of stage make-up. There is a small part of a page-boy in the opera . . . he has only one sentence I believe – but he is dressed magnificently in Louis XIV costume with patches and a powdered wig. Geoffrey Wootten, the son of the Trowbridge grocer, was given the part. I was incensed; I felt most strongly that I had been overlooked. Such was my annoyance when the boy's mother gave me a photograph of him dressed for the part that I could not wait to get home and put it on the fire. Now, how did I know so strongly at the age of perhaps ten that the stage was to be my career and that my inborn talent for it had been unknowingly outraged? Does this indicate the truth of reincarnation – of a previous existence; a repetition of a life through eternity until one has got it right? I know I felt very strongly then that if there was a child-acting part it was mine by right. This feeling was made all the more frustrating at the time because I had no argument to put in its favour. I had no stage experience, to justify my claim. How, indeed, was I to know I was to have stage experience in the future to retrospectively justify my claim? Only the unravelling of time had done so. Stephen Spender summed up the situation when he wrote 'Who from the womb, remembered the soul's history.'

I have searched everywhere for the source of my supposed performing talent. Indeed, some critics have searched for my talent! It must have had its original spark in my mother's side of the family. My Uncle John played the banjo and ran, for fun, an amateur concert party called the Badminton Pierrots, in which my mother took part as a soprano. She was, in spite of her appearance of massive calm, terrified of performing in public. She had a very pleasant and quite power-ful mezzo-soprano voice, and had actually 'had lessons'. But when she sang her solo song in the Pierrots she dared not sing anything from memory. She always held a copy of the song in front of her and sang from that. On one occasion she left her copy of 'Curly-Headed Babby' at home. How was she to sing it without the copy? She said she would try to sing it, as long as they allowed her to hold a sheet of music in the same way that she usually did. This way she would feel familiar and happy and would not forget the words. What she had not realized was that the audience would have a sense of humour. When they realized that the young lady was singing 'Curly-Headed Babby' from a copy of Tosti's 'Good-bye' they began to giggle uncontrollably. She then forgot the words.

On the other hand she has had her successes. When Eamonn Andrews sur-prised me to appear in *This is Your Life*, my mother (aged ninety-two) was too elderly and immobile to come to the studio. So the cameras went to her and a recording was made. 'Are you there, Cyril?' her image on the set in the studio inquired of me. At the end of her little piece the audience kindly applauded. It was about a fortnight before the show was actually seen on the air. My mother saw the recording. She rang me up. 'I got the most applause,' she said.

The school I went to at Trowbridge was a tiny preparatory school owned by a Miss Lansdowne above a shoe shop in Hilperton Road. She was large, fat and jolly; yet with a certain presence; not unlike a merry Queen Mary. She was the sole staff. The ages of the pupils were from five or six to about eleven, when one was expected to pass the entrance examination to the grammar school. I learned more in my three years with this sensible, practical woman than at any other time at school. She was a firm disciplinarian, but never hit a pupil physi-cally. If one was caught talking, a large red felt tongue about a foot long was tied round one's neck. Good behaviour merited chocolate drops. She played the piano with her back to us, but she had a 'driving' mirror on the piano and knew everything that went on. She did endless pokerwork on pieces of soft leather which we used to colour and buy for Christmas presents.

I wrote a play in verse about King John when I was nine at Trowbridge. I had my first garden of my own there; and in my mind's eye I can see the four first plants I ever planted: two plants of London Pride and two of forget-me-nots. I haven't.

By now I am perhaps twelve. It is a cold day and I am sitting at the back of an open GMK tourer car at the side of my sister Ida. Because she is two years older than I am she is much larger. She was still able, in a sisterly tussle, to pick me up and fling me down. Embarrassing for a small boy. But at the moment we are sitting quietly and expectantly. There is a sense of drama about my father, who is sitting at the wheel wearing a cap, very flat and very straight on his head. He has a handsome aquiline nose, an expressive mouth, too thin a neck with a protuberant Adam's apple, a little hair and pince-nez. During the war he had sported a Charlie Chaplin moustache. His lips are set in a thin line. My parents are a happily married couple, by now he is the Clerk to the Council of Friern Barnet, a North London suburb, and we are living in a Victorian house on three floors in New Southgate, rented on a repairing lease for £80 a year.

The house has two bay windows, one on top of the other; and the attic one above is smaller and flat to the house. There is a lot of embellished stonework which has been painted cream. The house is of a hideous shade of yellow brick. The front door has two small oblong panels of stained glass of various colours and a semi-circular fanlight. This is contained in a small porch. There is a subdued shrubbery of laurel and laburnum and lime trees, and it is a cold March day. We are going to see our grandparents at Watford. (Half of the precious Saturday afternoons of my youth were spent in this way. Why did my parents always take us with them?) My father is waiting for my mother to join us. For some reason now forgotten she has decided not to go to Watford on this Saturday. She may have had a row the previous Saturday with her mother-in-law. My mother's maiden name was Ginger and the whole of her family loved rows. They thrived on rows and were really only happy when they had some jolly good family feud going.

For a woman to come from such a family as the Gingers and be as happily married as my mother showed either the depth of her love for my father, or his for her, or his extraordinary patience. They seldom rowed. But when they did my sister and I (being half Ginger) thought it was heaven. We are wondering what the outcome is going to be. We have now been sitting – rather upright in those motor cars of the 1920s – for half an hour and are very cold. My father has not uttered a word for half an hour and the back of his neck and his ears are very blue. Eventually my mother's realization that she will have to nurse all three of her family through pneumonia if we stay there a moment longer causes her to capitulate. She will have to come to Watford. But she will not capitulate without a final Ginger gesture of annoyance. She decides to slam the front door. This she does with such vigour that both panels of stained glass fall out and shatter on the patterned tiles of the Victorian garden path.

The attic of this house was given over to a lot of junk and to Cyril. I had my first aquarium up there. With the aid of a large tank of water above the aquarium, a labyrinth of rubber tubing and a carefully bent and extruded piece of glass tubing, I had made myself an attractive fountain for aerating the water. You will remember I was an absent-minded child; I was having fun with this one lunch time and then dashed off to school without turning it off. The attic bedroom with the aquarium was immediately above my parents' bedroom. The aquarium was immediately above their bed. The water went through the ceiling. The sodden ceiling landed with the water on to the parental pillows. I was suitably punished and forbidden to have water up there. So I turned the aquarium into a vivarium, and kept with the newts and toads an Italian grass snake three foot six inches long. After some months it escaped. We could not find it anywhere. About a month after the escape we moved to another house and I like to imagine that one day it let its inquiring length down the chimney and peered into the faces of the new tenants in the early hours of some summer morning.

I am a great believer in the *status quo*. I think I get this from my mother; she, finding herself alive, sees no reason to interfere with this situation and has decided to remain that way with as little disruption to her life and way of living as possible, and that is why she is still living at ninety-three. In evidence that I have inherited this trait I find that for the last forty years I have been using the same hairdresser (Mr Gittar of Simpsons, Piccadilly), the same tailor (Hawes & Curtis), and the same soap (Morny's French Fern).

Although an avid worrier, my mother gives out an atmosphere of great calm. I, on the other hand, have tried all my life to worry, without success. She has never been fat, but she has a solid look about her. Her eye is calmly tranquil, almost bovine; but when the Ginger is aroused in her they can pop out. If my mother is sitting down she stays sitting down. I recall when I was about seven (this would make my mother about thirty-four), we were on holiday, staying at a small hotel at Weston-super-Mare with quite a jolly crowd. My mother was sitting in a bathing costume on the side of the sea wall or on the jetty. This was at a time when one did not put on a bathing costume to sunbathe. They even had long sleeves to them and skirts and were usually of navy blue. It was at a time when one put on a bathing costume solely for going into the sea. So there she was, my mother, sitting on the edge of this jetty, as it were, with her arms folded in front of her around her knees. She had the odd appearance of being completely bald because of the tightly fitting pink rubber bathing helmet she was wearing; Heaven knows why, she could not even swim. Now I was in the sea bobbing up and down as one did before one learned to swim, when the Life and Soul of the Party (there is always a Life and Soul of the Party in small hotels) decided it would be amusing to push my mother off the side of the sea wall into the water. The sea closed over her head because by the jetty it was about four feet deep. My mother, still in the same sitting position and still with her arms folded around her knees, landed on the sea-bed and stayed sitting there for what seemed to me a frightfully long time. Being five foot six or seven in height, she really needed only to stand up to save her life. My father couldn't save her life, he was swimming out to sea. My father always swam out to sea. If I had not drawn the attention of some well-intentioned fellow-bather to my mother's plight she would be sitting there yet. You see, my mother accepts things; and there she was accepting the fact that somebody had pushed her into the sea and she was drowning; and if she *was* going to drown she was going to do it comfortably, sitting down.

She has this virtue of immobility. She never really went for walks. There was an occasion I remember when my mother was in the kitchen and had left the gas on in the oven for quite a time, having thought that she had lighted it. She had things simmering away happily on the top of the stove and then op n ed the door of the oven to put a cake into it. The explosion was such that the whole gas cooker was wrenched from the wall and the window blown out. The cake mixture was flattened (as in a pantomime) against the ceiling. I was blown with the kitchen door down the passage. My mother, only a little singed, was standing statue-still in the centre of the kitchen floor; she never had much in the way of eyebrows from then on.

I suppose you could say that my first date was when I was seven, but it wasn't a date, it was dates, and one was Betty Huntley and the other was Peggy Cook, and I couldn't, at the age of seven, make up my mind which one I was going to marry. So I made a date with them both. The same day and the same place and the same time. There is rarely any great success in this sort of thing. There wasn't. They both made their minds up about me. I was also in love with Joan Watson. It was because of her mother's dressing gown, which, together with a splendid burnous which Joan made me, transformed me into Rudolf Valentino as the Sheik. Our tent made from a bedspread was a bit inadequate.

The first really serious date I ever made was with my wife, Betty Astell, and although this was years later (I was twenty-six by then) I cannot help but describe here and now what was, after all, probably the most important moment in my life. As Marlowe wrote, 'Who ever loved, that loved not at first sight?' We met at a Home Guard Concert at the Colston Hall, Bristol, during the war: the autumn of 1940. Henry Hall was conducting Adrian Boult's Orchestra and Adrian Boult was conducting Henry Hall's Orchestra. Betty was one of the acts. I was also one of the acts. I followed her on the bill. You can imagine how this very beautiful girl had an audience of several thousand Home Guards eating out of the palm of her hand. They didn't want her to go. They encored her several times. My act had to follow hers, and they really didn't want me at all, even though in those days I too was young and beautiful. You might say that Betty overwhelmed the audience. I followed and underwhelmed them.

As Betty walked off the stage she had held her head in a way that I have always, and will always, love. After the show Henry Hall said to me, 'I want another guest for my *Guest Night* that I have booked you for at Exeter on Monday.' 'Do you think this girl Betty Astell would go well?' I asked. Henry didn't really need persuading because he had already seen her success, and wise showman that he is, he booked her. We spent the rehearsal together. We did the show together. Then we went back to Bristol in the train together, which was delayed for about three hours because of the bombing that night in Bristol. That evening I told Henry that I was going to marry Betty. I hadn't told her yet, and I kept forgetting to look to see if she was wearing a ring and was already married. We met another six times and got engaged, and met another six times and got married. Naturally on a train that is three hours late you get talking and we talked. We found that we both loved the country. As we parted, Betty and I said that we would meet again, she said she often went riding, and I said, 'Right, I'll come riding!' So, the next day we both went riding.

Now although I had spent a lot of my youth living in the country I had never ever been riding. I was afraid of horses. It is through my mother that I have this inherent fear of horses. Her name is Maude. Anyway, my mother, just from a small girl, only had to walk down a high street – and there were lots of horses attached to carts in my mother's youth, sort of idling about down high streets – she had only to walk down a high street and a horse would stretch out its neck and eat the shoulder out of her overcoat with its long yellow teeth. This is true – I know. She kept the coats – dozens of them through the years. I have seen them and I have even seen a horse do this to my mother. It was a strong horse and a strong coat, and neither of them gave way easily, and my mother hung about in the air a little like an enormous nose-bag dangling from the horse's mouth. They wore funny coats in those days. Not horses. Mothers. Horses had those hats on hot days with their ears sticking through.

Well, this perfectly legitimate fear of horses which my mother felt was passed on to me. I have her ears too. Well, she too has these ears, but you know what I mean.

So there was this first date with a girl who I was so much in love with that I had told Henry Hall, and it was a date to go riding. Betty had ridden frequently since she was five. She mounted her horse with divine skill and agility, dressed immaculately in riding breeches, and her horse looked perfectly normal and quite beautiful.

The horse that they led out for me was enormous and gangling and it seemed to snarl. It didn't really – it may have smiled, but whatever it did, its showed its long yellow teeth. As I got on it – I cannot say I mounted it – it bent itself double, rather quickly and sideways, and snapped at my leg. I was twitching violently with fear by now, and a providential twitch of my leg at the same time as the horse snapped saved my foot. I still have two feet, as well as my mother's ears.

Now, another of my fears is that of heights. (This I inherited from my father, but that's another story.) A horse is very high up the first time you are on it. Also there seems very little in front. If you are used to riding a bicycle, as I was, actually one belonging to my sister – but I digress. If you are used to riding a bicycle, then the handlebars are there – solidly for you to lean on; to hold on to; and steer with. With a horse it is different; no handlebars but reins, which are loose and nebulous and are no use to steer with. Not on one's first ride. And horses know if it is your first ride; and this one certainly did.

We moved off. How grand that sounds. Betty went up and down with her horse. My horse only seemed to go up as I went down and *vice versa*.

We negotiated a couple of fields. I think that is the best term to use – negotiated. You will remember my horror of heights. Well, my horse went sideways round the edge of a quarry. This was the edge of a quarry where they had dug all the stone out, and I suppose it was about sixty or seventy or even a hundred feet deep; and just a rickety, very badly in need of repair, barbed-wire fence of two or three very rusty strands was between the horse and its rider and the steep, stark precipitous edge of this quarry. Most of my ride was round the edge of the quarry.

I have only been riding once. I have lived in the country now for thirty-seven years. I have two dogs, twelve goldfish and a daughter. There is not a horse in sight.

'Any boy without a public school education started life at an incalculable disadvantage,' David Niven wrote, so I am not sure if I have been educated or not. The dame school at Trowbridge was followed by our coming to Friern Barnet, and I became a pupil of Friern Barnet Grammar School. It was a Church of England grammar school; it was small and housed in a drab Victorian school building opposite the church and surrounded by an asphalt playground. Every Wednesday morning the whole school crossed the road and we participated in a church service. Prayers were held every morning and collects were learned. The Bishop of London was the Visitor. The rector of the church opposite, the Rev. E. Gage-Hall, addressed the school once a week. I wrote an Odd Ode about it (possibly one of my first), a parodic, in which Dotheboys Hall became Greengage Hall, but the rest I cannot remember. The cane was much used. Mr Million was the senior master and a great disciplinarian. One certainly knew where one was with him and he was also a very good amateur conjuror in great demand for all charity concerts locally, and this made him popular; possibly enhanced because he also looked exactly like Schnozzle Durante.

The headmaster rarely taught anything to our form, he used to read *The Times* a lot, with his legs wide apart in front of the fire. He had a habit of raising the paper above his head and stooping with his head between his legs and spitting into the fire. This was all done in one quick, surprising manoeuvre, finishing with the hissing of the protesting embers. He had a bullet head, which was shaved like a convict's. The French master, I am sure, was out of his mind. He would thresh about with his cane, his face red, his neck bulging with veins and his eyes popping out of his head. There was a constant working-up into this terrifying spectacle and as he addressed you, rather loudly and quickly in French, glaring the while right into your face, I personally became immediately tongue-tied and Francophobic. The English master used to inquire of us, 'Was you talking?' If only I had reported this to my father earlier! I was taken away at once and resumed my schooling, indeed, finished it as well, at Woodhouse School, Finchley, which was a co-educational grammar school where teaching was orderly, sensible and academic. It was also a new school and the main building was a late Georgian house in a spacious park with walled kitchen gardens. Our form room at one time was the old drawing room with beautiful convex french windows on to the vast lawns, specimen trees and shrubberies. And how I groaned, young boy that I was, when some of the trees and shrubs were bulldozed out to provide space for football and hockey and cricket. But here, among the ancient walls, I had a school garden of my own which won me the gardening prize.

Being a new school we needed all kinds of equipment which an older foundation would have acquired through the years. A library fund was started, and I went to the headmaster and told him I would produce a concert in aid of library funds. How did I know, I wonder, that I could do this, never having even been in an amateur concert of any kind? And how did I also know that I was going to be the leading performer? We are back to *Iolanthe* at Trowbridge! It was all a great success and the school magazine proclaimed the advent of a new comedian. These shows then became a regular affair. We did several, and in each one I did a little more and got a little more certain of getting the laughs. Imagine my joy when four of the original cast were rounded up by Eamonn Andrews for *This is Your Life* fifty years afterwards. To me, not having seen them since, they looked still like the same small boys – but with white hair!

I failed miserably academically because running shows and the debating and literary societies, and all my other *extra curricula* activities, left me very little time for study. On my last day at school I was giving, with the aid of a funny straw hat (left over from one of the concerts), a very laughable impression of the senior mistress. Was it as funny as my form mates were making out? Only because, behind me standing in the doorway, was the subject of my impersonation! 'Fletcher,' she said in a voice of thunder, 'you have fooled enough in this school.' I was hurt. I must have been. I have remembered it for nearly fifty years.

At the end of the Second World War all State schools were given a sum of money to celebrate the Victory. It was the unanimous desire of Woodhouse School to be entertained by Betty and me for their celebration. We were perhaps at our most famous then, with a whole lot of successful radio series and stage shows just completed. 'I cannot accept money for this,' I said. 'It must be put towards a War Memorial for the school.' So we went, much flattered, to do the show. The whole school was assembled. The staff were in the front row. I mounted the platform, from which I had done so many happy concerts only fifteen years earlier, to be greeted with an enormous roar of applause. I eventually quelled them and said I was afraid that there would be no show that afternoon. Groans of dismay from the children and blank hostile glances from the staff or quizzical looks from some of them. 'You see,' I went on, explaining the situation, 'on my last day here, Shuvver [the nickname by which the whole school knew the senior mistress] told me I had fooled enough in this school – and unless she is kind enough to tell me I may fool some more I'm afraid there can be no show.' She nodded her permission. We got on with the performance.

I never went to university. Who was it who said, 'After university it's a straight run through to the grave'?

2 Early Stages

'The youth who daily farther from the east,
Must travel, still is Nature's priest.
And by the vision splendid
Is on his way attended.'

– Wordsworth

I left school in 1930 at the age of just seventeen, and although dearly wanting to make the stage my profession, could not bring myself to announce such an outrageous suggestion to my father. I had already upset my father by failing matriculation three times in French (it was necessary in those days to pass in all of several subjects), and he was a little inclined to think in a somewhat old-fashioned way that I was what was known as 'a hopeless ne'er-do-well'.

I think it might be here mentioned that possibly one of the reasons why I failed matriculation with such relentless monotony might have been attributed to the fact that I was away from school for a considerable length of time due to a very severe mastoid operation which leaves me, I understand, with a very thin covering to my brain, and possibly accounts for my being a comedian. This operation, although a nuisance at the time and terribly painful during its six long weeks of daily dressings, had a fateful influence on my career in that it made me Grade III and, in consequence, not called up when war began in 1939, and enabled me to continue my job throughout the war as a comedian.

It was always my secret fear throughout the war that some young service chap of similar age (I was twenty-six) should interrupt my performance while I was topping the bill at some crowded variety theatre and ask why I was not in the forces. I had always intended to think up some rather splendid witty reply to be ready for the occasion, but I could never think of one, until to my horror, at a packed second house at Chiswick Empire, a delightfully drunk and slightly confused young sailor reeled to the orchestra rail and, with arm raised pointing at me rather like a maritime Kitchener, yelled: 'Why aren't you in the forces?' I found myself replying, 'If you come to the stage door I will show you my operation.' This got a splendid laugh and a round of applause, and the sailor, when he came to the stage door, did not see my operation but went away happily with a little more beer inside him.

It would only have exacerbated matters to have told my father of my theatrical ambitions. Indeed, it would have seemed an outlandish Bohemian dream to a Town Clerk brought up by Methodist grocers in a small provincial town. How then was I to set about such a career? I felt the only thing to do was to get to London, it being the centre of the entertainments industry. So I announced that I would go to London and get a job. There were over two million people unemployed in 1930, and back much to my father's surprise I came with two jobs. Both were jobs as office boys; one was with a solicitor in Holborn, the other with Louis Bambergers, the timber firm. I accepted the latter and was with them for six weeks, after which my uncle got me a job with the Scottish Union and National Insurance Company in Walbrook opposite the Mansion House. My uncle was the Borough Treasurer at Watford, and on behalf of the corporation had a large insurance connection with the Scottish Union. I had no sooner taken up my position with them when some sort of contretemps arose between my uncle and the insurance company and he took away his corporation's considerable business from them. Their original enthusiasm for my services cooled.

However, I *was* in London, and very soon I found myself in the Foreign Department where one of my jobs was the translation of French policies. Enough to turn anyone funny. I was very happy with the Scottish Union: I ran the annual office dance, and an unofficial office magazine in which I wrote highly libellous Odd Odes about the heads of departments and management generally. Leslie Wood, my fellow office boy who did the illustrations, has now been the secretary of my theatrical production company in his spare time for over thirty years.

While with the Scottish Union I went as an evening drama student to the Guildhall School of Music. When I left three years later it had been renamed the Guildhall School of Music and Drama (coincidental, I am sure). My first tutor was Frank Ridley, an old Shakespearian actor who had toured with Frank Benson. Handsome, with white hair and blue eyes, slim and smart, he must, I suppose, have been in his late sixties. He was a man of enormous charm and style, and to me, a raw clumsy oaf of an insurance clerk, he seemed God-like. The lessons only lasted for half an hour and cost two guineas a term for twelve.

I asked Frank Ridley how I could best impress my parents with the fact that I could perhaps be a successful actor. He said I could pass the various examinations that the Guildhall held each year and eventually become a licentiate for elocution, or I could enter for an elocution competition. He added that the competitions for the London Musical Festival were about to be held. This festival before the war was a vast affair, rather like a metropolitan Eisteddfod. There was every conceivable variety of competition, ranging from brass bands and orchestras and all kinds of solo instrumentalists to humble tenors and sopranos and, of course, elocutionists. Each section was divided into primary, intermediate, final and gold medal classes. The entrance fee was half a guinea, a large sum for a very junior insurance clerk. (I earned, when I first went to the Scottish Union, £50 a year, not £52 you notice, which would have been a magnificent pound a week; it was a niggardly nineteen and something. A

Scottish Insurance Company, remember. It may account for the fact that when I sign the register at an hotel I never put ditto marks in the nationality column after the word 'British'. I always write 'English'.) I entered the competition and informed Mr Ridley.

'What have you entered for, my boy? The primary or the intermediate?'

'The gold medal, sir,' I said.

I have seldom seen a man so angry. However, he tried especially hard on my account to safeguard his reputation and I tried especially hard to save the half-guinea and I won the gold medal. The runner-up was a Mr Bamberger, who was the son of the principal of the timber firm for whom I had 'office boyed' earlier on. I dashed home to tell my parents as quickly as possible. I was so pleased and proud and thrilled. They were out. When they came home, my mother said, 'Oh, yes.' She had expected me to win and was not in the least impressed that I had done so.

The doyenne of drama teachers at the Guildhall was Kate Rourke, whose pupil I then also became. She was a West End star in Edwardian and Victorian times, playing at one time as Irving's leading lady. She had theatrical magic. Not only was she a great teacher but, aged over eighty as she must have been, she could, were she playing Juliet to my Romeo, not only sound like a young girl, but, ugly old lady as she was in the harsh stage working light of the little Guildhall Theatre, manage in her magical way to resemble a young girl.

While I was a pupil of hers she asked me to play the Voice of God in *Everyman* – the morality play – for some Catholic charity at the Albert Hall. This I did for her daughter Zoë Rourke-Cree. It necessitated my climbing a very high ladder behind some flimsy impressionistic scenery, and then, without the aid of a microphone, booming God-like from my precarious perch. God did not seem to mind – he didn't knock me off the ladder, then, or when I did it for them again at the Rudolf Steiner Hall. As a reward for these appearances I was invited to Kate's to dinner in a Regency house where she lived in Marylebone. A vast portico dwarfed my shy figure and I was let in by her old maid who had been Kate's dresser in the days of her stardom in the theatre. The table was elegant with old silver and linen napery. There was a tall epergne of silver trumpets full of maiden-hair fern and carnations. The maid served a delicious meal. There was a whole quality of life in this house with its beautiful pictures and ornaments, Aubousson carpet, period furniture and heavily draped Regency windows. It was perhaps my first glimpse of a life-style that I thereupon decided to emulate and enjoy.

I appeared as Antonio in *The Merchant of Venice* at the school which was produced by Robert Atkins (producer at the Old Vic at that time, and also of the Open Air Shakespeare in Regent's Park). At the end of one of the performances of *The Merchant* I was sent for by the principal, Sir Landon Ronald, and told that as I had such a resonant speaking voice I must have singing lessons too. These I had with my mother kindly paying for them, but I was not very interested in singing. I had no musical knowledge and, as any who have suffered my singing will know, am tone deaf.

Nice One Cyril

I won the school elocution prize, shared the Rudyard Kipling prize, and became a Licentiate of the Guildhall School of Music and Drama for elocution with merit.

In order to pay for two lots of drama lessons at the Guildhall and to pay for fares and other expenses, my tiny insurance stipend was stretched to the nth degree. I decided to write myself an act and to perform it at club socials and dinners and the dinners and annual gatherings of my friends' football, cricket and indeed lacrosse clubs as a comedian. As Charles Lamb would say, 'I had a tincture of the absurd in my composition.' These shows began to snowball and I earned many an odd guinea and half-guinea this way while I was at the Guildhall. I wrote a lot of the material during lunch-hours at the Scottish Union, consuming sandwiches in the privacy of a strongroom in the bowels of the earth known as 'the Back Safe'. This was discovered later to be in the nearest possible proximity to the Temple of Mithras, the Roman remains found after the war when they were excavating the foundations of the new buildings which rose over a bombed and ruined Walbrook.

I used to get a lot of pleasure out of asking for time off, to go on several occasions across the road to the Mansion House (I did not tell them why), once with a Roman toga in my little attaché case, to perform as prize pupil in the Annual Guildhall Concert in the Egyptian Hall before the Lord Mayor and Corporation and Music Committee. I even did a funny as well as a serious piece at a Mansion House banquet, but that, of course, was not during office hours.

It is amusing how fate will arrange everything once she has set you on course. The man I sat next to, and my immediate boss in the Foreign Department of the Scottish Union, had an aunt who was one of the founder members of the Concert Artistes Association, which was and is a society of concert artistes gathered together to administer a benevolent fund for their less fortunate fellows. They had in those days premises over Leicester Square tube station (they have premises of their own today next to Moss Brothers), with bars and a concert hall where they held shows every Monday night; and also one Sunday in every month they would hold a concert for booking agents at the Hotel Cecil in the Strand. It was obvious to me that to join this club and perform my sports-club act might be a great help towards getting more after-dinner engagements, and this, with the aid of Mr Chesson's aunt, Miss Winifred Mansfield, I did. I have been a member now for forty-three years, I was president for several years and now have the honour of being one of their patrons. Any success I may have had has come directly from being a member of the Concert Artistes Association.

It was in 1955 that I was elected President of the Concert Artistes Association and I was very proud that my friends and fellow artistes had been kind enough to honour me in this way. It's certainly one of the nicest things to have happened to me in forty-three years in the business. They made a bit of a habit of it actually, as I was again president in 1956, 1957 and then for a two-yearly stint 1963/1964. The first year our Annual Dinner was televised, we had a magnificent star line-up of speakers consisting of Elsie and Doris Waters, Terry Thomas and Kenneth Adam, the director of BBC TV, and it helped to publicize the Benevolent Fund. Then, to help the Benevolent Fund we decided to have a sort of Command Performance – all of concert artistes, as opposed to variety artistes, and again we had a splendid programme. The date was 13 February 1956, and Her Majesty Queen Elizabeth the Queen Mother most graciously came to the concert at the Scala Theatre. Oh, what a thrilling day this was. As president I had to receive Her Majesty, make presentations to her, entertain her in the interval and produce the show and appear in it.

For weeks, then days, then hours, one is filled with apprehension; not necessarily that one will let down the Concert Artistes Association, but that this dearly loved and distinguished person shall, as well as fulfilling her duty, also thoroughly enjoy herself. (How many dreary mayors and how many uninspired performances must, year in and year out, fill Her Majesty's working hours!) Every little detail was attended to, even down to the particular vintage and label of the champagne (which, incidentally, she didn't drink, and I like to think she did not need to!). One of my duties was to present the committee, each, of course, by name. 1 cannot in this instance plead senility, it was but twenty-two years ago. Most of the committee I had known all my semi-professional and professional life – had I not been a member for twenty-three years? All went well until I neared the end of the line. I suppose I presented fourteen or so in all. As we neared the last chap – most lovable, and such a worthy and conscientious committee member – I knew I had forgotten his name. I willed him to realize this. He didn't. There was the slightest of pauses as I realized I would have to invent a name. He suddenly became Mr Cuthbert Cropp and he has never spoken to me since. (Cuthbert Cropp, by the way, is a character in an Odd Ode: 'This is the tale of Cuthbert Cropp/Whose hair was getting thin on top.' Why I chose to pick his name out of the air I'll never know – this committee member was positively hirsute!) Then to present Betty – I did remember her name – and my daughter Jill presented a bouquet perfectly. Then on to the royal box. We took our momentary leaves to present and appear in the show.

Here I was presented with a dilemma. Through the years I had appeared many times with Betty in my summer shows, in a West End show *Keep Going*, and on TV in a revue sketch by Desmond Davis called *Violetta*. The theme of the sketch is that we feel that the importance of opera as an art form lies not in the music but in the words. So here is an opera without music. Then four characters, Violetta, the Nurse, the Hero and the Villain, play a scene only with words. It's hilarious, and through the years we have added a lot of visual business. My sword one night caught in the slat of the seat while I was wooing the heroine. The seat then followed me round the stage. One night a pillar constituting part of the set fell down. I picked it up and re-erected it at the same time as a feather and chain from my hat caught in the top of the pillar. The hat left my head and was at the pinnacle of the pillar and out of reach by the time the pillar was standing. All of these laughter-provoking routines were 'left in', and performed every time we did the sketch. The whole thing was such a riot of fun, and the original idea so sophisticated and amusing that I bought the copyright of it from the author years and years ago. One night, in frivolous mood, as we performed this sketch in the summer show, I decided to be a fat decrepit tenor who played the hero instead of, as I was then, a thin decrepit tenor. I made myself a lovely little pot-belly out of newspaper. This not only dried up the cast, but it made the audience laugh even louder than usual. The next night I used even more newspaper, and during the duel it fell out in front of the audience. More yells from cast, Cyril and audience. This piece of business was then 'kept in' until we were able to time it to get the biggest laugh possible. The dilemma which exercised my mind was: should I let my stomach of newspaper fall out in front of the Queen Mother or not? Would the audience consider it vulgar and not laugh, or worse still, would the Queen Mother consider it vulgar and not laugh? I find that with me fate has a way of deciding these things. I decided not to let the newspaper fall out.

The sketch was going splendidly – when quite by accident it happened. The looks of real horror on our faces made the audience think it a very real mistake, and, as always, as when the man falls on the banana skin, they yelled with delight. When the whole show had come to a triumphant conclusion – how very proud I was of my fellow concert artistes and their wonderful assembled talents: both the famous and the unknown who helped to make this memorable occasion in the history of the association – I went to escort Her Majesty safely to her car. She told us how much she had enjoyed the show – she mentioned several highlights in it and said to Betty, 'It was such fun when your husband's tummy fell out.' You see how unnecessarily I had worried. How unnecessary was our worry about the reception and entertainment of Her Majesty; she, with her radiance and charm, made Betty and me feel at home and seemed to insist that we should enjoy this, one of the most important days of our lives.

The following year HRH Princess Margaret and Lord Snowdon were kind enough to honour our next Royal Concert. Again all went well and the show's artistic standard was impeccable. Her Royal Highness was in great form and was very happy and made the whole evening enjoyable. Indeed, she was enjoying it all so much and talking about the first half of the show so much in the interval that I was most worried about getting the curtain up on the second half in time to complete the show at the appointed hour. I do not know whether the public knows, but for charity shows the artistes, from chorus to celebrated stars, all give their services free, *gratis* and for nothing; not so the musicians who accompany the show in the orchestra pit. The Musicians' Union insists on their being paid. If they play over a certain length of time they have to be paid at an overtime rate. I was well aware that if the show over-ran – I had carefully timed every act and every scene – we should have to pay overtime to the musicians and the Concert Artistes Association Benevolent Fund would be the poorer by quite a large sum. It was a large and expensive orchestra.

I went into the ante-chamber where Her Royal Highness was being entertained, and in my diffident way mentioned in passing that the second half was about to begin. I did this twice to no avail. I could visualize Betty having to cut out a whole lot of the second half of the show and reshape it and, worst of all, explain to the artistes concerned how their services were no longer required for the Royal Show. All looked very black indeed. Jimmy Edwards was in the second part of the show, and I had an inspiration. He knew the Royal Family well; played polo with some of them; would he have a go at trying to get the royal party back to their box? You bet he would. In his wonderfully extrovert way and yet deferentially, so as not to cause offence, 'Ma'am!' he cried at the top of his voice, 'Overtime and beginners! We are about to begin the second half!' 'How enjoyable!' she said and went into her box like a lamb. Panic over. Big success. Lots of money for the Benevolent Fund.

After doing a performance at one of the Concert Artistes Association's Monday nights, a Mrs T. Arthur Russell, whose husband was a concert promoter, asked me if she might book my act for a Sunday performance at the Prince of Wales Theatre where her husband ran shows more or less in opposition to the National Sunday League concerts at the London Palladium. The fee, for me, was enormous: two guineas. The audience was a delightfully receptive one – as Sunday audiences so often are – and they rewarded me by calling for an encore. As I did my encore, Mr Greatrex Newman, owner of the famous summer show, the *Fol-de-Rols*, came into the theatre, and he was a great man for discovering new talent. He telephoned me the following day to ask if he could see the whole of my performance somewhere. (You will realize how excited I was when I tell you that the following great stars had all been *Fol-de-Rols*: Elsie and Doris Waters, the Western Brothers, Leonard Henry, Jack Warner, Arthur Askey, Dickie Murdoch, Eric Barker and Robert Harbin; more recent ones included David Nixon, Norman Wisdom and Leslie Crowther.) I had to own up that I had not got an immediate booking that he could be present at; so he booked me for a show for wounded soldiers in the hospital at Colindale. My act went quite nicely, but not as well as at the Prince of Wales. Mr Newman asked me to his opulent flat, which was over Fortnum & Masons in Piccadilly, and I told him that I was an insurance clerk. 'All this,' he said, pointing rather grandly to the Persian rugs, the Chinese lacquer cabinets and the Copenhagen porcelain, 'I have got from entertainment. You could do the same.' So I asked for a rather larger salary than I had at first envisaged – £10 – a week – in response to his kind offer for me to be comedy entertainer in the *Fol-de-Rols* at the White Rock Pavilion, Hastings, that summer. He said he would pay the sum of £7 a week, £8 a week in August.

Having been awarded my licentiate, I had applied for an advertised post to teach elocution to divinity students of Spurgeon's College. I was one of two applicants short-listed for the job. An Elder asked me at the interview whether I thought I was sufficiently competent to keep divinity students (many of whom would be older than me) in proper order. I replied that, being divinity students, they would doubtless be well-behaved and therefore easy to control. It was this that got me the job, which was part-time and to be in the evenings.

Fate was frightfully busy on my behalf that week in March 1936. The very same week I was summoned to the London manager's office of the Scottish Union and National Insurance Company. The London manager was a man of considerable presence and personality, and a much better actor than I will ever be. He was a sallow, saturnine man; not unlike the gipsy who had terrified me in Watford High Street, except that he had very even teeth and not a trace of an earring. He had once, after returning from a long tour of the company's South American agencies, asked me to buy and send out to some southern señorita's address several copies of the most romantic melodies of the day. He waved me laconically to a chair, swung his own chair dramatically round to face me and said, 'We would like you to be our junior representative in Rangoon.'

This surprised me; was my work so unsatisfactory? I would now surprise him. 'Thank you for your confidence in me,' I said, 'but I was coming to see you at the end of the week to resign.'

'Oh,' he said rather deprecatingly, 'and what sort of job had you in mind?'

At this time I was a rather thin, diffident, shy, gangling and bespectacled young man; something between Mr Pooter and Mr Polly. 'I am going to be a comedian,' I said. To say he was considerably disconcerted by my answer is a grave understatement.

He was a generous man, however, and when I finally took my leave at the end of the month he said, quite sure that I was doomed to instant failure, 'Should you, er – um, find that the world of the theatre is, perhaps, a harder one than you anticipate, we would be happy to welcome you back.' Some of my more timid colleagues were worried in a kindly way for me. Was it right for me to give up a regular salary and a pension? The three most concerned for me in this way died in harness before they themselves ever received their pension, and I do not think I am being unkind if I say they possibly died from sheer boredom.

So, at the age of twenty-two I became in 1936 a professional comedian.

We rehearsed the *Fol-de-Rols* in a pub called the Goat and Compasses in Euston Road. There was a lot of highly polished red linoleum and brass fittings. Rather stupidly, I arrived five minutes late with the idea that I did not want them to think me too eager. I was wearing a dark grey suit, a bowler hat and clean yellow wash-leather gloves and I held a tightly rolled umbrella. In short: my clerk's outfit for the City. The assembled cast thought I was Greatrex Newman's secretary, or, at best, a rather young baritone. They just could not believe I was a comic.

I could not dance and I could not sing; and I had no aptitude for either. I could do a strong comedy single act lasting, at most, a quarter of an hour in which I featured what I called 'Odd Odes', and I could play a part in a straight play, be it farce or Shakespeare, but the producer, George Royle, decided to start rehearsals with me performing a song-and-dance number called 'Always Keep a Shine on Your Shoes'. The producer decided very early on in rehearsals that I was one of Mr Greatrex Newman's mistakes.

We opened at Her Majesty's Theatre, Carlisle, and we were there for about a month, and then we came to the Winter Gardens, Eastbourne, for a fortnight, and then we opened at the White Rock Pavilion, Hastings, for a season ending in September. It was a long and most enjoyable engagement. Apart from the agony of rehearsals and the hell of being a 'slow study' (as someone in the theatre is called who takes a long time to learn his lines), I was very happy indeed and could not believe that, at the end of the week, I was actually being paid for enjoying myself so much. As well as my own act, which was well placed in the programme (second spot after the interval), I did any compèring necessary, featured in the big ensembles and performed small, strong cameo character parts in the sketches. Mr Edwin Adeler, famous for his Adeler and Sutton's Pierrots, was at that time manager of Her Majesty's Theatre, Carlisle, and he was very kind indeed. He not only encouraged me by saying how well my single spots were going, but he also booked me to play at the theatre for two weeks in variety in October when we had finished our run. It was a great beginning: I had resigned from my insurance company for a twenty-week contract, and here was the future already getting booked ahead. What happened, however, was that the theatre was sold, Mr Adeler lost his job and all his contracts were cancelled.

I stayed in 'digs' for the first and second from last time at Carlisle. They were very crowded: the pianist, the dancing Volonoff Twins and the soprano were all staying there, and the lavatory was in a little shed at the end of the garden; readers of *The Specialist* will know exactly what I am describing!

In the cast of the *Fol-de-Rols* my second summer was Bill Stevens, one of C. B. Cochran's character actors, together with his wife, Anne Bolt (who had been at the Guildhall with me, had played Nerissa in *The Merchant of Venice* and was the daughter of one of the professors there, Madame Ginette, a member of the famous circus family). Bill Stevens had worked a great deal in London and New York with big managements and was a very good performer. Like most good performers, he had a lot of touring provincial experience behind him, and he also had a book of addresses of theatrical landladies marked with stars, asterisks and commendations such as no good food guide would ever dare to print.

He would often accuse me of not being a good 'pro'. This was a little unkind because, compared with his long experience, it was true, except that I was certainly a fully employed member of the theatrical profession. 'You always stay in hotels,' he said, 'and never in digs.' This was also true, and referred back to my very first weeks at Carlisle. I decided from then on that I would stay at small hotels, where perhaps I would pay a little more but have some privacy and comfort.

Bill kept on about this, and the result was that I said, 'All right, when we play Torquay I will stay at one of your precious addresses.' He looked up his list of Torquay digs. One was many-starred and highly recommended. The terms were exactly the same as those I intended to pay at a small hotel that I knew of which was on the front.

We travelled to Torquay from Scarborough in the early summer weeks before we finally settled into our resident summer season at Hastings. We were to be in Torquay for about a month. The journey was a long one, and we arrived late in the afternoon with a view to getting to the theatre to set things out for our opening show. We went to the digs first.

Nice One Cyril

I have been to Torquay innumerable times since. Indeed, I presented my own summer show there for three whole summers. But I have never been able to find this particular part of the town, which shows that it was certainly obscure. This queen of watering places must, I suppose, have a murky corner here and there, and we certainly had arrived in one.

All the houses were pretty dilapidated and run down. On our side of the road there was one long dreary terrace. We stopped at a house which was obviously empty, its front door hanging open with a tuft of grass growing half in, half out, of the front doorstep, no curtains at the windows and a jungle garden. Next to it, in slightly better repair in that it had curtains, a lawn of sorts and two hinges on its front door, was our 'highly recommended' address! The door was opened not by a cherubic Devonian landlady, but a tiny little Tynesider in a flat-'at, no collar and bedroom slippers. He gave us a grudging welcome. My heart sank and I began to think of my nice little hotel.

'We are full up in this house, hinny,' he said. 'Your rooms are in the annexe next door.'

We went down the path of the passably habitable house and up the path of the derelict one next door. We stumbled up the bare boards of the stairs. Wallpaper was hanging in damp festoons in places, and we were shown what he called 'it' on the mezzanine floor where a handful of newspaper was stuffed behind the down pipe against the peeling mouldy distemper. 'No Fletcher has ever used newspaper,' I said. Up, then, to a little landing with two rooms side by side; one for me and the other for Bill and Anne. Mine was a small bare-boarded room with a bed, a chamber pot, no other furniture at all and, as aforesaid, no curtains. I began to get a little giggly. 'Where do I hang my clothes, hinny?' I said. 'In the pot?'

Off we went to the theatre. As it was a Monday night, it was a tiring performance. One has to get used to a theatre, and one has to get all one's clothes and properties assembled and checked before the show. There is always a certain amount of anxiety on Mondays, so that by the time we got back to the digs we were pretty weary and hungry and ready for one of the splendid meals so highly recommended in 'The Bill Stevens' Digs Book'. It consisted of a minute portion of tinned salmon and lettuce, with thick brown tea out of an enamelled tin teapot – the sort of tea on which mice can skate round the cup. I kept saying to myself that I would either have it out with Bill later or have a good laugh in the morning, but I knew that the rest of my stay would be at my nice little hotel on the front.

I was very soon asleep. I was awakened as the Town Hall clock struck two. I was very wide awake, sitting bolt-upright as one sometimes does, and I looked round the bare room brightly lit by the moon through the curtainless window. I heard footsteps on the uncarpeted floor of the hall passage. They came up the stairs. I was staring fixedly at the door handle by now, knowing that it would turn and the door open. The steps came across the landing, the handle turned, the door opened and in walked what is most quickly described as Field-Marshal von Hindenburg in a nightshirt. His hair was crew-cut, he had the same sort of moustache as the German Field-Marshal and erstwhile President, sturdy legs, barrel chest and thick with grey hair, and he advanced towards the bed. I was almost speechless with horror and did not quite know the best and most polite procedure under the circumstances. He began to get into the rather sparse iron bedstead. I said, 'Can't you see that I am in this bed?'

In deep sepulchral tones he answered, 'You're John, aren't you?' and realizing in a flash the inadequacy of my first name, the name which, with Claude or Cuthbert, is used for all the silly-ass characters in the dirty postcards at seaside resorts, I said, feebly, 'No, as a matter of fact, I am Cyril.'

I was by now fending him off and he was trying quite happily and with little malice to get into the bed.

The dénouement of any true story is often lacking both in punch and probability. I had a brainwave.

'What number house do you want?' I said.

'Eight,' he said.

'This one is number six,' I replied.

He got up from the bed, turned, went out of the room, down the stairs and out of my life forever. In the morning no one knew anything about my visitor but I knew he was not a dream because Bill and Anne heard our little exchange through the wall.

I paid the Tynesider a token sum in settlement and moved to my hotel. Bill refused to pay anything and went to another of his addresses. He was sued by the Tynesider. He had to pay the full rent with considerable costs as well.

Robert Harbin, the great magician, died the day before I was writing this. When I joined the *Fol-de-Rols* in 1936 he was in the same company. Indeed, he was in two companies at the same time: he would do his act in the first half of the Eastbourne programme and then join us at Hastings to do his act in our second half. Some of his journeys were a little dramatic, but he never missed a performance.

Robert's pretty and vivacious wife, Dolly, whom he adored, and who was some years later to be terribly disfigured in a fire, was appearing with him as the inevitable conjuror's assistant. In her tights and sequins she would make the whole act more decorative and glamorous as she undid handcuffs, caught doves and was daintily levitated or sawn in half. In one illusion, to a dramatic fanfare and roll on the drums, she would leap out of a cabinet which the audience had known, positively and without doubt, to be empty. It was very well done – Robert was a great inventor – and the audience used to be most impressed and appreciative. One night the Eastbourne comedienne Gladys Merridew (and once again as I write this, I remember curiously that about ten years ago she died horrifically in a fire) claimed that Bob and Dolly's cairn terrier Dickens, of whom they were inordinately fond, had bitten her. I think it was eventually agreed that she had. This unsettled Dolly, who had a cairn-like temperament. Robert was on the stage and he had shown the empty cabinet to the audience. There was a flourish of trumpets and a roll on the drums. But no Dolly. She was very busily explaining in minute detail to the Hastings comedienne in her dressing room how and when Dickens was supposed to have bitten the East-bourne comedienne in hers. Robert was left nonplussed and alone on the stage – but such was his love for Dolly that he forgave her at once – but she never ever forgave herself.

Robert was one of the kindest and most generous men I have ever known. At this time in the winter season he was one of the busiest entertainers in the concert and after-dinner entertainment scene, and would frequently do three and four private shows a night. The London hotels are all near to each other; and in those days every Masonic ladies' night would have at least three enter-tainers at a function, and these would be booked by the lodge organist. There were also countless small agents who booked acts for these shows, some of them being artistes themselves. Being so busy and in so much demand, and also being a methodical businessman, Robert had very nearly a thousand of the bookers' names and addresses in a card index. Every year he would design a new brochure for himself and send one to each booker. He knew of my ambitions; he knew I had burned my insurance boats and that the empty days of my winter diary were a worry to me; so one Sunday he took me to his house in Mill Hill, and there we sat copying out all his addresses – the whole of his private show connection which he had built up over the years – and then he designed a brochure for me, and it was dispatched to all the addresses: the result being that I had a very busy time in the concert and after-dinner entertainment circuit that winter, and because of this splendid amount of work, was able to improve my act at every show (work is the only way of improving a comedian's act – he has to play all the time to an audience), and I never looked back. There is no one I have met in the world of entertainment other than Robert Harbin who would have made such a generous gesture to another artiste.

I was able to repay his kindness in a very small way. When he finished with ENSA at the end of the war and things were a little quiet for even so great an illusionist as Robert to get started again, I was able to give him his very first job immediately on his return – the next day, as it were, in the first summer show I presented – as guest and star. I am sorry I shall not see the slow smile again or hear the deeply warm voice say, 'Hello, my boy, and how are *you*?'

While still on the subject of generosity, Max Miller had the reputation of being a mean man. This was made much of in *Max Miller, The Cheeky Chappie*, a book by John M. East, greatly to my annoyance. During the war when Betty and I were playing prior to London in her revue *Keep Going*, we toured for four weeks, one of them at the Theatre Royal, Nottingham. This was immediately next door to Nottingham Empire . . . a lovely Victorian variety house with a very warm and appreciative Midlands audience. Max Miller was top of the bill at this theatre. His show was twice nightly and ours was once nightly; such was wartime theatre business that we were both playing to capacity houses. By careful timing Max was able, so near were the stage doors, to see the whole of our show between his variety appearance. We had an anaemic sketch which either needed the transfusion of comic lines or comic business or being deleted from the show and replaced by another. Night after night Max would suggest new lines, a new tag, new funny business, and out of his own vast repertoire of sketches (he even sent home for some) he bombarded us with material – all free; all to help another comedian to get laughs. Is that mean?

Billy Bennett – 'Almost a Gentleman' was his billing – specialized in zany monologues. He would wear a very dilapidated evening dress, red and white navvy's handkerchief hanging from a pocket, and a cummerbund, his hair parted with an exaggerated quiff and on his feet enormous brown boots. He was Queen Mary's favourite comedian. We frequently appeared together on variety bills at a time when I was a great novelty and getting all the attention and also frequently enhancing my fame by broadcast after broadcast. For each broadcast I needed new material; new Odd Odes. Billy Bennett, this great master of the monologue, would say on a Monday as we started a new week together at a different variety theatre, 'Cyril – have you got any Odes you are having trouble with and with which I can help you?' All his years of expertise were mine for the asking. The great variety stars were truly generous people.

But, as always, there are exceptions which prove the rule. For younger readers I had better describe Nellie Wallace, that very funny lady of long ago. Her face was a cross between the Duke of Wellington and Ken Dodd. She had the Duke of Wellington's nose and Ken Dodd's teeth, and was very funny with her hands. She was certainly one of the great music-hall stars of all time. Off stage she was a dear woman and we enjoyed her company, and on stage she still, although at a great age, had her public. For both reasons I was keen to include her in a pantomime which was presented to reopen the theatre at Stoke Newington. It was *Dick Whittington*. She was the Cook and I was Idle Jack, and we were playing a shop scene which I had played many times before and knew exactly where the laughs were. On the first few performances I didn't get a particular laugh, which was a sure-fire one and very necessary in its particular place in the routine. I eventually found out that Nellie was cleverly killing it with some funny movements of her hands. Very gently I explained to her how necessary it was to get this laugh, how she was killing it and asking her if she would please wait for the laugh. She could then get a further one herself with her funny hand business, and instead of getting no laughs at all we would get two, one for me and one for her. 'Yes, yes, Cyril, how silly of me,' said the great old lady, and proceeded for the next three performances to kill the laugh in exactly the same way that she had previously done. Knowing that it was usually the old music-hall comedian's desire to kill everybody else's laughs and preserve their own, and that it was ingrained in her after perhaps fifty or sixty years in the theatre, I was in a little bit of a quandary as to how I might stop her naughtiness. My youthful ardour and the same instinctive desire to have as many laughs for myself as possible came to my rescue. At the next performance, before I knew what I had done, she having killed the laugh with even more aplomb, I slapped her across the face with a property kipper. She was obviously slightly hurt, both morally and physically, and decided that it wasn't worth it. She played the sketch perfectly from then on, allowing me to get my laugh and then getting her own. She died the year afterwards, aged seventy-eight, and I am still ashamed at having slapped, however, lightly such an elderly lady across the kisser with a property kipper.

But I must take you back from the halls to the gentler world of concert party. After two years at Hastings with the *Fol-de-Rols* and a second most successful winter season with radio, TV (yes, already!) and cabaret, I was booked again for the next summer at Llandudno. This was 1938, the year of Munich. (The next time I played Llandudno in 1940 France fell to Adolf Hitler, and the time I appeared there ten years later in 1950 the Korean War started. I really dare not play there again!) The show was a happy one, business was good and we once again did a broadcast from the show. I was short of material as usual and was persuaded to recite 'Dreaming of Thee' – a poem by Edgar Wallace, written when he was the Kipling *manqué* of South Africa. I rearranged it a bit and did it in an extraordinary voice – a cockney caricature. It was sub-titled 'A Lovesick Tommy's Dream of Home' and I used to do it in a green spotlight and wearing a soldier's hat. The constant refrain at the end of each verse, 'I'm dreaming oh my darling love of thee', got yells of delight. A lot of this I thought was due to the way I looked, lovelorn in the green spotlight. Unsuitable for radio, I thought. How wrong I was. It made me, and later when we returned to London after a repeat performance on BBC's *Music Hall*, I became a household name like Guinness or Harpic. The morning after the second broadcast I was on a bus and the conductor was saying 'Dreaming of thee' to every passenger with a passable imitation of my funny voice as he gave them their tickets, so I guessed that perhaps I was made! It was a wonderful thing to happen to an unknown artiste who had been a professional comedian for only three years. But, at the same time, I was very lacking in the experience needed to exploit the situation.

My fourth year with the *Fol-de-Rols* was at Hastings again. War broke out at the end of the season, and my next and last happy summer with them was at Llandudno. For my last three seasons I had no written contract with Greatrex Newman: such was my personal regard for him that a handshake sufficed.

3   Betty

> 'As this wild rose, no more than a whim of the dust,
> Achieved her excellence without intent,
> So man, the casual sport of time and lust,
> Plans wealth and war, and loves by accident.'
> – Humbert Wolfe

My wife is beautiful. She is beautiful in her thoughts and in her mind and in her loyalty. As a young woman, she was breathtakingly beautiful: people, women as well as men, would turn to look at her in the streets. Motherhood made her more beautiful still. Even when she was ill – and twice death has been very near to her – she had a shadowy beauty, and my tenderness and love for her made me see new beauty and serenity showing in her very desire to stay alive for me. Savage Landor wrote: 'Whereas for the creation of some women Nature reserves the May morning hours, when with light and dew she woos the primrose from the turf and the life from the moss-roses.' So it is with Betty.

I am incomplete without her. Just her presence in a room or in the house with me gives me a warm glow of satisfaction. If she is not at 'home' with me, I am in a 'house'. It does not matter that I am surrounded by her things and by her paintings, her embroideries and her décor; I am honestly in a slight degree of misery without her. This has always been so. This is not an experience which has grown through the years; this has been so since that magical day when we met at the Colston Hall, Bristol, and why we saw each other only six times before we were engaged and another six times before we were married.

Betty's version of this momentous day is as follows:

'One day in 1940 I was working on a programme which Ronnie Waldman was directing when he said to me, "I'd like you to come and sing for us at the big Home Guard Concert at the Colston Hall." At the time we had all the big stars working with us at the BBC in Bristol so I said to Ronnie, "Come off it – you've got Vera Lynn, Anne Shelton, Dorothy Carless – they would do it so much better than I." "Yes, I know," he said, "but they're all busy so we'll have to have you" – which was a charming invitation I couldn't refuse, so I went along to the Colston Hall. I was a little nervous, but in the event it wouldn't have mattered if I'd sung them the railway timetable, since the hall was packed from floor to ceiling with chaps who were going to give their full attention to any pretty girl (not very modest, am I?) – and with Sir Adrian Boult to accompany me I naturally went rather well! When I came off stage Ronnie said, "You look as if you could do with a drink." Now, I don't drink, though on that occasion I should have liked to say yes. However, a glass of orange juice would have been bliss so I said, "Yes." He kindly took me by the arm and led me straight downstairs to the gentleman's lavatory by mistake – and there we stood for a moment, looking rather silly – and then I said, "I don't think this can be quite right, can it?" and he said, "No," and kindly took me by the other arm and going out of the door I fell over Cyril. I don't remember actually doing so, but he says I trod on his best corn.'

We broadcast in a *Henry Hall Guest Night* the week after our wedding, which was at St Martin-in-the-Fields. There were a lot of showbusiness personalities present, and instead of TV cameras, it being wartime, the cinema newsreels were there. The reception was at the Trocadero, the only hotel or restaurant which would do a wedding reception on a Sunday, and it was just when sugar rationing had been brought in. There in the centre of a magnificent wedding breakfast table was a mountainous wedding cake of three most beautifully decorated tiers. Sugar rationing indeed! The head waiter at the appropriate moment came forward with due ceremony to offer us the knife to cut the cake, but before we were allowed to do so – hands poised locked together over the handle of the knife – with a well-rehearsed gesture he siezed the 'icing' on the middle tier of the cake and swept off like a conjuror the white plaster façade (for that is all it was). Underneath, hidden by the plaster and silver mock icing of the bottom layer, was a cake, quite bald, looking for all the world like a lost Christmas pudding. The newsreels even had shots of this dramatic Lucullan moment.

It was a hilarious wedding; half the guests from showbusiness and the other half from both our families; oil not mixing with water. My sister was matron of honour, and my life-long friend, Allan Perry, was my best man. Richard Hearne (not yet Mr Pastry, but a West End star with Leslie Henson and his 'gang' of talented comedians) read out the telegrams with the aid of Bruce Belfrage (the BBC announcer whose fame was enhanced by being the one who was reading the news when a bomb actually dropped on Broadcasting House). They invented more spurious and libellous messages than the genuine ones to our delight and the dismay of the relatives.

The Reverend Eric Loveday was the vicar of St Martin-in-the-Fields during the war. He died shortly afterwards while touring Australia. He was hardly middle-aged at his death, and this good man had obviously worn himself out in his devotion to God and man. A simple example of his generosity comes immediately to mind: we naturally wanted our daughter Jill to be christened at St Martin-in-the-Fields and by Eric Loveday. There was a lot of bombing in London at the time, raids by ordinary planes as well as V1s and V2s. 'No,' he said. 'Not with all this bombing. Have her christened at Welwyn and I'll come out there.' So on a Sunday, which was the only day that actors and their fraternity could manage and which was the busiest day of the week for him, sweet

Eric Loveday came all twenty-five miles out to Old Welwyn Parish Church to christen Jilly and dashed all the way back again for the next service at St Martin's.

We had a short rehearsal of our wedding with him beforehand. 'At one point,' he said, 'I shall say when you are kneeling, stand up and follow me; this is when I want you to come nearer to the altar. The reason I shall say stand up and follow me is because at my very first wedding, I was naturally very nervous, especially as it was a grand naval affair. The bride and groom were nervous, as they usually are, possibly more so because of me. "Follow me," I said at this same juncture when they were kneeling there. And instead of getting up they followed me on their knees, with the naval lieutenant's sword clanking on the stone-flagged floor and the bride's gown in a sorry state from the twelve or so yards it had traversed!'

Eric Loveday was a dear man and much-loved Christian. We think of him warmly whenever we go to St Martin-in-the-Fields. Every year on our wedding anniversary, Betty and I go to St Martin's, and at the exact time of one o'clock Betty takes off her wedding ring and gives it to me, and I give it back to her, putting it on her finger to renew our vows for another year. Then, wreathed in silly sentimental smiles and humming the 'Wedding March' quietly under our breath, we rather pompously march arm in arm down the aisle and out into the sunshine to see what fate has in store for us as we face the world for another year. Together.

Once or twice if we have been on tour we have been 'married' in some other church, and although we enjoy it very much it has not quite the same magic as when we celebrate the occasion again and again at St Martin-in-the-Fields.

Although as a young man I had always had an ambition for theatrical stardom and therefore knew exactly where I was going, I could never visualize my future wife or my future married life. I was very much an individual citadel and the thought of sharing my oneness was slightly disagreeable. Solitude I had always enjoyed. I could, and can, always find plenty to do on my own. I am a great reader and walker, gardener and potterer; indeed, I was about to contradict myself and say I am often happy on my own. Before marriage, I was happy on my own. Since marriage, on my own I can be happy but with an ache.

When every day is precious and so full and enjoyable, a day apart is almost a day lost. But as a Sussex farmer said to me once, 'There's plenty of time. There's years and years not broken into yet.'

It is supposed that most theatrical marriages are failures. I do not really think that this is true. We just always hear if a stage marriage breaks up because it is news, but not news when one goes happily on through the years as ours has done. There are, of course, very many happily married couples in the theatrical profession. There are Michael Denison and Dulcie Gray, John Mills and his wife Hayley Bell, and Michael Denison and Dulcie Gray. . . !

One of the reasons for our happy marriage is that we play a particular game. I will tell you about it, but it is one of those games where you have to be married to be able to play it. You have to be staying at a hotel; this is easy if, like us, you are itinerant jesters. You sign in at the reception desk. You go upstairs to your bedroom. Then either one or the other of you goes out on an errand. I might want a newspaper or Betty some hair grips. Then the one left behind hides in a wardrobe or under the bed. There are not many imaginative places where one can hide in a hotel bedroom. The one on the errand comes back and searches for the hidden one, discovers him and releases him with a kiss. Oh, you sneering sophisticated reader, it is a splendid game; played with enthusiasm.

I would like to tell you now of a particular time we played this game at Reading during the last war with the most alarming consequences. We signed in at the hotel on a winter's afternoon and we went up to our bedroom. I had got my hair grips, so Betty went out for her paper. I hid under the bed. I must explain that the large double bed took up most of the space in the room, and as you entered, the bed was on the left. There was a wardrobe immediately at the end of the bed, and facing the other side of the bed, as it were in the opposite position to the door, was a dressing table.

I had no sooner got under the bed than a chambermaid came into the room. This did not greatly worry me; it is one of the hazards of the game. Betty had once been in a wardrobe when a chambermaid had tried to hang a coat in it, and although the chambermaid very nearly poked her eye out with the hanger, gallantly she stood doggo behind the hanging clothes.

I am lying under the furthest side of the bed from the door and the chambermaid comes in, walks right round the bed and sits immediately on top of the part of the bed I am under. She reads the newspaper. She tries on some of Betty's more improbable hats. I think she is going to be there forever, and I am just debating whether to get out from under the bed and say, 'Isn't it extraordinary how these beds get on top of one?' when she leaves the room.

That is really the whole point of the story; she did *not* leave the room. She went round the bed to the side by the door; and got under the bed. I was under the bed with a chambermaid, in Reading, during the war. I shut my eyes at once, they being the brightest part of my anatomy, and lay quietly by her side. It was very quiet indeed under the bed, side by side, with the chambermaid. It was so quiet I began to think that I had imagined her getting under the bed with me and that she was not there at all. I opened one eye for a quick look. I could see her form – rather a splendid form, as I remember – silhouetted against the winter's afternoon. She was there all right. Another long vigil began and things were again unbelievably quiet. I tried not to breathe to see if I could hear her breathing. I could not hear her breathing, and in my panic I opened both eyes and had a really good look. She was not breathing. I was under the bed with a dead chambermaid, in Reading, during the war.

At that moment Betty came back. I didn't want her to have the shock of looking for me and finding a corpse, so I got out from under the bed and shouted to her, 'There is a dead chambermaid under the bed.' Betty didn't turn a hair. 'Oh, yes,' she said. Comedians' wives have a built-in something.

We were, of course, very worried. Theatre folk, especially if they are top of the bill, as we were at the local theatre, know how headlines are made. We could see the local papers – 'Cyril Fletcher found under bed with dead chambermaid'. This we felt was not exactly my image, especially as I had just completed a week of the morning record programme, *Housewives' Choice*, and these headlines would surely ensue if we rang the police. If we rang for the manager the same thing would happen. I said, 'I know, we will ring for the chambermaid.'

We rang for the chambermaid. She came in, a neat tidy little person, and I said, 'We have some very serious news to tell you. You had better sit down.' She sat down. 'There is a dead chambermaid under the bed,' I said.

'Yes, that's right,' she replied. 'I put her there.'

Well, it seems that commercial hotels hold displays of the wares of commercial travellers in hotel rooms, rather like trade exhibitions in miniature. Every Monday a certain commercial traveller would take the room next to ours and prepare his wares for his showing on the next day. He travelled in all sorts of uniforms; commissionaires' uniforms, chauffeurs' uniforms, all kinds of servants' uniforms, overalls, hotel uniforms, chambermaids' uniforms, and he would dress a model (the sort you see in a draper's window) in a chambermaid's uniform and leave it standing outside the two rooms, his and ours, in the corridor. Our chambermaid being a tidy little person would take the model chambermaid every Monday and shove it under the bed of the room adjacent to that of the commercial traveller. (So it was not a dead chambermaid after all.)

I am stating a showbusiness axiom when I say that comedians' wives have a 'built-in something'. It consists of the 'ability of complete ignore'. (This is used if perchance the comedian should choose to have an imaginary conversation with somebody presumably trapped inside one of Her Majesty's letter boxes in a busy street.) Another virtue is to have a ready laugh for the most improbable and obscure joke, or to feed in the necessary line off which the husband can (with impeccable timing) get his usual laugh. This needs stamina too if the marriage is a long one, and an ability to suppress the look of, 'Not that old one again!' For the wife to have a merry and spontaneously sounding laugh is a must. On the other hand, if any laughable experience should happen to me when Betty is not there, possibly on the stage or some adventure when I am travelling from show to show – perhaps some hilarious adventure with the public – then I cannot wait to get home and tell Betty. The greatest joy and pleasure out of any funny experience is the telling of it and the sharing of it with Betty afterwards.

Betty has all this. But above all there is her unswerving loyalty to our partnership. Her resolve that everything should be a success. Once she was about to go into the London Clinic because she was severely ill and needed specialist attention. (It was *after* this illness that I discovered medical insurance provided by BUPA!) Knowing that her absence from the summer show would surely cause financial loss at the box office and the cost of a replacement as well, she was searching her mind for economies and ways of helping financially. Ill as she was, with a sewing machine on her bed she made a set of chorus costumes which she sold by phone to another management and then went off to the London Clinic.

Nice One Cyril

When one is in the entertainment business one is a freelance unit of employment and the hazards of unemployment are ever present, and the losing of popularity and of box-office drawing power if one is a star. You add to these hazards enormously if you become management yourself and present your own shows, as Betty and I did for twenty-five years. Today one only has to look to see how many actor/managers there are! Is there one left? So, together, we have braved many storms and I'm happy to say scaled many modest heights. We talk sometimes of our successes and our failures and we laugh a lot and talk of the might-have-beens. Betty, after one of these reviews, said, 'Say what they like – we have always "piddled" our own canoe!'

In the words of Winston Churchill, 'I got married and lived happily ever after.'

4   Variety

'Music hall songs provide the dull with wit, just as proverbs
provide them with wisdom.' – Somerset Maugham

Variety came from the shows provided in taverns and clubs and became popular
entertainment in late Victorian and Edwardian times, graduating to variety
theatres, many of them being especially built around that time to house in a
new theatre of opulent gilt and plush and plaster the new entertainment for the
middle class and the working man, usually with grandiose names – Coliseum –
Palace – Hippodrome – Grand and so forth.

The Grand Theatre, Croydon, was a beautiful example of the Edwardian
theatre, all gilt and red plush and white plasterwork. The plasterwork really
was most elaborate, with white cupids (putti) rampant round the dress circle
and joining hands across the front of the first tier of boxes. When playing Dame
there I was able, because I am exactly six feet tall and wore very high heels, to
lean on the side of the box and chat confidentially to my audience. I would in
the course of the chat tickle and fondle the cupids' feet. One joyous afternoon a
piece of cupid's foot came away in my hand. This was a good laugh to start with,
and then to build it up I ate some of it. This caused screams of mirth and possible
constipation – very old plaster is not too edible, but mindful of the old adage
'anything for a laugh' I went on with it. From then on I had the local confec-
tioner make me a cupid's foot out of meringue which was fixed to the plaster
cupid, and I ate it with relish twice daily to peals of joyous laughter from the
children.

Knowing the squalor of the lower-class dwellings, the back-to-back, quickly
built terraces of working-class houses built for the Industrial Revolution, the
music halls not only provided entertainment, but they provided a warm and
glowing paradise for the recreation of the masses. The managers were popular
local personalities and the stars were beloved performers who often met their
public face to face in the brightly lighted bars of the theatres or the taverns in
the town. The stars were usually simple people of the same class who had the
magic of the top-line performer, and there were often several well-known names
on each bill. They toured from hall to hall and from provincial town to provincial town; once their act became well known and popular they never changed
it; indeed, their public would not have allowed them to change a word or a note

of music. Sometimes the same routine would last a lifetime. An established star would be booked ahead every single week for many years and would know ahead not only the town they would be in on a particular week, but the size and position of the names printed on the bill, and, most important of all, the salary they would be getting for several years. The halls were prosperous, the stars were prosperous and the agents and impresarios were in clover. These were the days remembered by George Robey, Harry Lauder, Nellie Wallace, Harry Tate, Harry Champion, G. H. Elliot and many more who were still names on the bill when I joined them in variety in the 1930s.

But by the 1930s how this scene had changed: the cinema was the first blow the music hall had to suffer. Every town had several cinemas; to begin with, the modest flea-pit for the silent movie and later the opulent picture palaces and finally, with a new style of architecture all their own, the Odeons and Gaumonts. Here was warmth and glamour, and in the days immediately following the First World War at a tiny cost one could see the shadows on the silver screen of world-famous stars continuously supported by imaginative publicity pumped out by multi-million pound companies. When the talking picture came in the late 1920s, it seemed that the death knell of the halls had been finally struck. Then came radio. A further blow surely to the halls, which catered for those families who had a weekly date with them. Oddly enough, radio helped the halls; fascinating and tantalizing voices entertained the public – indeed, entertained an even larger public than had frequented the halls. One must agree that the audience did not have to pay to hear their radio variety programmes and they did not have to go out in all sorts of weather to their local theatre; but they could not see those nebulous stars whose voices they knew and loved and whose jokes and personalities they suddenly seemed to know as well as their neighbours. What did they look like in the flesh? Could they meet and savour the personalities of their idols? Yes, they could, because the music-hall bookers began to realize the drawing power of the radio stars. Each star would bring in his own public and new audiences were drawn to be entertained and to enjoy themselves in the old music halls. Again several stars would top a bill; Elsie and Doris Waters went round supported by such acts as the Two Leslies and Norman Long and Clapham and Dwyer. And together with such purely radio names were cleverly mixed the hard diamond core of old variety bills like Harry Tate, Nellie Wallace, Wee Georgie Wood, the Houston Sisters, Max Miller, Lucan and McShane, and very many others.

This 'shot in the arm' of radio names to variety was well established by the time I first played these theatres. The principal circuit was the General Theatres Corporation, with head office above the London Hippodrome – run by George Black, who had started as a cinema- and theatre-owner in the north-east, a rough, tough northerner with an instinctive flair for showmanship. He was the originator of the Crazy Gang at the London Palladium, and with this great theatre heading his list for prestige shows and variety bills he also had that smaller popular variety house, the Holborn Empire, as his other London shop window. Finsbury Park Empire was the next London house of General Theatres

Corporation importance, especially after the Holborn Empire was bombed early in the war. Others in the chain were the Hippodrome, Birmingham; the Empire, Nottingham; the Palace; Manchester; the Empire, Newcastle; the Empires at Edinburgh and Glasgow and other big houses throughout the length and breadth of the country. George Black's right-hand man was Val Parnell, similarly rough and tough, who was also a charming bully, and Cissie Williams, a wily spinster who was in charge of bookings – possibly five hundred artistes every single week. Geography was not her strong point. Thus she would book you one week in Edinburgh, the next in Swansea and the week after in Glasgow – necessitating travelling by sleeper at the weekends. There was never any chance of gainsaying this – you just grumbled and got on the train!

Glasgow Empire was an especial hazard for an English comedian. 'There they would sit in the front row eating thistles,' as Jimmy Wheeler used to say.

The second important circuit was the Stoll. It was owned by Sir Oswald Stoll who did a great deal for variety, bringing it from its rough beginnings to its artistic hey-day, with variety bills at his principal London theatre, the Coliseum; when a week's presentation might contain a sketch with Sybil Thorndike and Lewis Casson, the Diaghilev Ballet, and the whole bill topped with the Houston Sisters (Renée and Billie). His halls included the Chiswick Empire; Shepherd's Bush Empire (now the BBC TV theatre); the Hippodrome, Bristol; the Ardwick Hippodrome, Manchester; and many, many others. One could, when I was playing variety during the war, play for twelve weeks or so, all number one dates, in London alone. Today in London there is variety at the London Palladium alone, and then only for short, intermittent seasons. Where has the glorious enchantment of variety and music hall gone? And where is now the cradle for the stardom that the halls so liberally supplied?

After my first season at the seaside with the *Fol-de-Rols* I came back to London and, thanks to the generosity of Robert Harbin, began to build up an extensive connection of single-concert dates in the London hotels. Sometimes there were several in the same evening. The winter of 1938–9 was a very busy one indeed, and at only two guineas or three guineas a performance I was often earning over £50 a week. It was the autumn of 1938 that George Black was in hospital and heard my performance of 'Dreaming of Thee' on the radio. This appealed to him, as it had done to the general public. Also at the same time, to reinforce his opinion of me, I had appeared at a charity show at Holborn Empire, and Bertie Adams, the manager, had rung up George Black and told him of the 'new comedian' who had gone well at this performance. Cissie Williams was alerted and it was mooted that I should tour the General Theatres Corporation theatres at a splendid salary for a newcomer of £40 per week; out of this salary would come my fares and my hotel expenses and the agent's booking commission. I was living at home with no expenses for £50 a week and was able to do frequent broadcasts to further enhance my drawing power by making my name and my Odd Odes famous with the listening public. George Black and Cissie Williams could not believe their ears when their offer was refused. I even had to show my diary to the agent to prove the truth of my argument. It was at this time that Charles Tucker, an American, who also managed Larry Adler, Leslie Hutchinson (Hutch, that most stylish of coloured singers) and Max Wall (he was later also to manage Julie Andrews), became my agent, and he was keen for me to go on to the halls so that he could make money out of me. He used to book the Trocadero Cabaret and he asked me to audition for him. There he sat one Monday afternoon after the acts booked for that week had rehearsed with the orchestra; next to him was a glamorous lady who only spoke French. I went through my routine; there was complete silence from the two of them. 'I liked the way you did it, but I didn't care for your material,' said Charles Tucker in his American drawl. 'Have you any other material?' 'Plenty,' I said. 'I write my own!' Actually I had performed to Tucker the best 90 per cent of my material, and as each joke was received in dead silence I had dashed hopefully on to the next. 'All right,' he said. 'An act has fallen out of tonight's bill – I would like you to try out this other material tonight and for the rest of the week.' The Trocadero had two cabarets each night, one a night spot, somewhat like 'Talk of the Town' is today, with a glamorous cabaret production presented by Charles B. Cochran, the greatest impresario in the world at the time. (Mr Ziegfeld might have considered this an overstatement, but whereas Charles B. Cochran presented shows all over the world, and in London and New York, Mr Ziegfeld did not operate in London!) The other cabaret was a miniature variety bill of four or five acts, compèred by Maurice, a French head waiter, the top of the bill being a big star who would 'double' at some near-by music hall such as Finsbury Park Empire, or the Holborn Empire, Chiswick perhaps, or Shepherd's Bush. Max Miller, then at the peak of his stardom, frequently topped the cabaret bill at the Trocadero. This show was in a smallish room upstairs, at the civilized time of ten o'clock at night. The audience was there for the meal and the show; they had not come on from a theatre, the evening was their night out. They were a middle-class audience, not a sophisticated socialite one, and were a delight to play to. I did exactly the same act that night as I had performed at the audition. The audience laughed a lot. Afterwards Charles Tucker said, 'I liked your new material very much indeed. I'd like to be your exclusive agent'; and so he became.

I was to play the Trocadero many, many times. Maurice fell ill shortly after my first appearance there and I took over as compère for several weeks running. It was a happy venue for me and my wedding reception took place there in May 1941. Later, when the Trocadero had its fiftieth anniversary, I was to compère a distinguished all-star bill and make my entrance coming out of a real iced cake, which was ten feet tall.

My first variety date for George Black was at the Portsmouth Hippodrome, with Ambrose and his Band featuring Evelyn Dahl, Sam Brown, Max Bacon and a newcomer recording phenomenon, Vera Lynn – a slip of a girl from the East End of London who was to become 'Sweetheart of the Forces', a big star, a wartime legend, and then Dame Vera Lynn; and to still remain one of the sweetest people in showbusiness today. Here is a performer who has never changed, except that she becomes more professional every day. In those days she was all of seventeen, and how the chaps at Portsmouth adored her. They quite liked me too.

The Holborn Empire, I have explained, was almost as important as the Palladium. With proper productions and stage shows at the Palladium, the Holborn Empire was certainly the No. 1 variety date in the country. This, thanks to George Black, was my next variety date. They were such a warm, friendly audience. The house was not small, but it was intimate to play to. You were near to the audience, and a whole lot of that audience knew of me and had heard me on the radio, both BBC and Radio Luxembourg, and they met me half-way. It was an enjoyable début for me in West End variety.

Then George Black decided to take over the Adelphi Theatre. He was to present a show which he left in the – to be – capable hands of his son Alf Black. (Some years after the war Alf Black and his brother George were to become impresarios in their own right and a great credit to their father George.)

The show was called *Let's All Go Down the Strand* and featured Charlie Whittle, the old-time music-hall star whose song this was and which gave the title to the show. Charlie Whittle was brought out of retirement especially. The tops of the bill were Duggie Wakefield and his Gang (Duggie was brother-in-law of Gracie Fields, and a weird, turned-up-nosed, gormless Lancashire comedian with a gang of three clever and acrobatic stooges who had worked out several successful visual and slapstick routines through many years of music-hall touring revues), and Jimmy James, the comedian's comedian, who was an original. It is difficult, nay impossible, to describe his zany humour, the dry way in which he delivered it and the droll comic essence of his wit. Jimmy James was a music-hall star for very many years. Not a lot of his routines were changed, but they were always acceptable to both the public and his fellow artistes. The third top of the bill was Cyril Fletcher, who at the age of twenty-five had achieved his impossible dream of being a star in the West End of London by the time he was twenty-five. When I set out to do it, it was my ambition because John Gielgud was a star in the West End at twenty-five and my original ambition was to be a straight dramatic name! What a different destiny fate reserved for me.

The sad thing was that my contract was for six weeks and the show folded after two. I was one of the two acts retained to be in a variety bill topped by Max Miller and Florence Desmond, the brilliant and satirical impressionist. This was when my long friendship with Max Miller began. He was kind enough to watch my act. 'If you told this story first, son, and then that one last you'd find it would go better. Eh? Eh? Well, try it, boy, try it!' I did and he was right. For the placing of a gag and for the timing of a joke he had and has no equal. Ken Dodd might be the equal among today's comedians, but his knowledge and skill comes from endless and scientific trial and error; Max's was from a natural comic instinct.

As well as my act I had to stooge as a straight man to the worldly and experienced Duggie Wakefield in a well-known act, and I'm sure I was the only professional comedian alive who had not seen it. This was for an important first comedy spot in the show. He went through it a couple of times and decided this was enough. After the run-through Cissie Williams decided it was not nearly enough, and this rather quaint middle-aged cockney lady came to my dressing room and, making a most realistic impression of Duggie Wakefield's gormless comic character, went through the act with me time and time again. She had seen it so many times on bills she had booked she knew the act word for word and action for action as well as he did, and as fresh as hemlock she insisted in her acidulous way that he should rehearse incessantly with me too.

War broke out and theatres were closed, but soon were open again and playing to capacity business. George Black decided he would use me again, this time to play the lead in a tour of *Black and Blue*, a show of his which he had presented for a most successful season at the Hippodrome starring Vic Oliver, Frances Day and Max Wall. It was smart and sophisticated in its mounting and décor and it had a mixture of broad music hall with it. It was decided that I should play most of the Vic Oliver parts and the Max Wall parts rolled into one, and that Renée Houston should play the Frances Day parts. Maurice Colleano and family, that great circus mélange, would also strengthen the bill. We opened at the Empire, Nottingham, and did enormous business. I had several good sketches where I had strong character comedy roles: a lecherous Victorian husband on honeymoon with a completely innocent and ignorant bride, and a cockney attendant at an art gallery indicating the finer points of nude pictures (played by actual nudes behind thick gauze and artistically lighted) were two of the best. Renée's act with Billie had split up because of Billie's ill-health and she had formed a partnership and later marriage with American film star Donald Stewart. My fear was that Renée would want all the best parts in the sketches and scenes for Donald, and this she could well have engineered with her great experience in the profession and my newcomer's ignorance; however, this lovely artiste, very beautiful as she was then in approaching middle age, inventively clever and changing the script brilliantly every night, realized how important this show was for my variety career with George Black and used her vast store of experience to help me in every way. It was a joy to be in a show with her and to perform in items with her. I watched her skilful act every night and learned a lot from her impeccable timing. In her autobiography, *Don't Fence Me In* (Pan Books, 1974), she generously says:

> The great thing about that show was Cyril Fletcher. He was absolutely marvellous. The trouble with him was that he didn't know just how good he was. For while he had been great on radio, the kind of revue we were doing was new to him, and he was a little shy of putting in the kind of ad-lib that he was capable of.
>
> When we were on stage, he used to mutter little asides to me that dried me up.
>
> 'Go on, say it out loud,' I'd mutter back. But he wouldn't.
>
> So I got into the habit of stopping the proceedings and going down to tell the audience what Cyril had just said to me. Of course, they loved it.

After Nottingham came Sheffield, and then came Edinburgh and Glasgow.

I spent the New Year's Eve of 1939/40 in Edinburgh. I don't know whether it was a Hogmanay celebration, but I was told of the time when veterinary students, whose lodgings were in those Georgian houses high on the hill in old Edinburgh overlooking Princes Street, in their glorious frivolity took out one of the Georgian windows so that it was but an open frame, and with enormous quantities of thick elastic rather like a giant Roman assault catapult, ran, with the elastic stretched, to the back of the room. With the catapult loaded with old vegetables and rubbish from their dustbins, they let the elastic go and this terrifying slop launched itself on to unsuspecting, polite, charming – and possibly effete passers-by from Morningside – citizens of Edinburgh who were going to meet each other 'at MacVitie's for tea and a pie at five'. Covered in this ghastly mess they looked around them and could only imagine that it had come – as frogs do, so I am told – straight from the heavens; a sort of Frogmanay.

After we had played six weeks at the largest theatres with the show – I think that the Hippodrome, Birmingham, and the Palace, Manchester followed the Scottish dates – Renée and Donald and the Colleanos were needed for other shows and were removed and Judy Shirley played the Frances Day parts and the Cairoli Brothers were brought in. Judy was fun in the show, but her comedy was not as strong as Renée's – her singing compensating for this. The Cairolis held the Colleano spot, not so spectacularly as the Colleanos, who did every acrobatic trick possible as well as comedy. Charlie Cairoli as a young man was just as funny and lovable as he is now and certainly no act ever got more laughs. This happy show ran until the end of May, when I again joined the *Fol-de-Rols*.

At the end of the *Fols* season at Llandudno I played radio and variety intermittently. Doing the odd week here and there in a show called *Boys of the BBC* with Hutch, Billy Bennett and Oliver Wakefield. Again great success, and it was here that Billy Bennett was so helpful, not only with my radio material, but also with the shaping of my variety act.

Then came our marriage and, after a brief ten-day honeymoon at our home at Old Welwyn, we rehearsed for three days and opened with a new road show, *Dreaming of Thee*. Betty was starred in this too and it ran for about thirty weeks, playing to capacity in every large variety theatre in the land with twice-nightly houses.

When the curtain rose on *Dreaming of Thee* the principals were all sleeping in a monster bed and each got up to sing a verse in the opening chorus. At least the title of the show had something to do with me – there was one running at the time which rejoiced in the title of *Legs, Lace and Laughter*. The others in the bed were Nat Mills and Bobbie, a very strong variety comedy act who later made a name for themselves on radio with their catch phrase, 'Let's get on with it!' – and another double act destined to play at the Palladium many times in shows, variety and pantomime: Nat Jackley and his straight man Jack Clifford. Nat is a very strong visual comedian and at that time did as his speciality a guardsman drilling scene with very funny falls, leg movements and slapstick. He was an ideal variety performer, very funny to the most sophisticated while getting visual laughs from the dullest-witted in the audience.

Nice One Cyril

On looking back, one realizes the sense of the bookers. I was top of the bill with a talking act and radio reputation bringing in the fans who had heard me on the radio. The show was enhanced tremendously by the beautiful Betty, with her singing act of popular songs, and the audience's sentimental delight in our being in a show together immediately after our marriage. Then Nat Jackley and Nat Mills were visually funny, and there are several good speciality acts and a pretty chorus, plus very little scenery to travel around and a manager who 'doubled' as stage manager. Financially the show took a great deal of money. So did the manager, and he had to go to gaol for it. It was a first offence and he only got three months. When he came out he arrived at the show bright and breezy to wish us all well. He was so brash, that I was wicked enough to say, 'It's so nice to see you again after all that long "time".' We had a new manager, a girl, Jean Bell, who was to be employed by us many times and for some years afterwards in various capacities when we went into management on our own. When she was first with us she always wore trousers, which was unusual in those days, and she sank several pints of beer a night. She later adopted an orphan boy – a stage-hand whose parents were both killed by bombs during the week we were playing at a Midland town. Some years later she became a novice nun and then came back into the world and married happily. With her husband she now co-skippers a barge which takes corn and coal and goodness knows what (but no scenery) up and down the coast (and the Thames) to places like Ipswich. She had a particularly trying time at Ipswich once with one of our touring summer shows while we were at Torquay. Remembering this, she writes:

> While having lunch with Desmond Davis at the White Horse I was astonished to hear myself saying 'I'm finished, Desmond, I really am, d'you know anyone who can take over?' He said 'We all say it, duckie, cheer up, you'll feel better tomorrow,' and of course I did. I have been to Ipswich many times since then carrying 350 tons of wheat, and oh what a blessed relief to pause outside the White Horse for a quiet moment and reflect on strange prophecies. And on the benefits of Mother's Pride of course!

She also reminded me of the scratch stage staffs we used to exist with; so many of the regular technicians being in the forces. We would have to set up the stage with the scenery freshly unloaded from the lorry which had collected it from the train at the station that morning, while the company were busy with their band call. Some of the staff were working elsewhere during the day and would have no idea of the show until the first house that evening. 'A quick rapport with stage hands was a necessity' writes Jean – 'very necessary for the "Limes". [These were the following spot lights from the front of the house which needed all sorts of different coloured gelatines fitted into them from time to time.] They'd come in from the glue factory at the overture, you gave them the lighting plots and hissed encouragement at them and hope they would be sitting together since one would be colour blind and the other would not be able to read.'

There was one routine in *Dreaming of Thee* which closed the first half. Nat

Mills, Nat Jackley, Jack Clifford and I, dressed up as the then very popular Andrews Sisters, did a burlesque of their act. As I have already explained, the two Nats knew everything there was to know about visual comedy and funny movements. In rehearsal they exploited their expertise in this direction to the full. I was not at all funny in this way and it was obvious that they would get all the laughs. I did very little in rehearsal, but on our first night I very slowly took a large bun from my knickers and very slowly indeed and with a whitish dead-pan make-up on my face I ate the bun as deliberately and methodically and statically as it was possible to do. This way my sheer gormless immobility drew the attention of the whole house. It got yells. The two Nats thought they were doing very well indeed. The larger my laughs got the wilder became their gyrations. Slowly it dawned on them that it was that dreadful radio comic who was getting the laughs. It was then that I slowly wrapped up the remainder of my bun in a dainty handkerchief and stuffed it back up my drawers. It was a battle royal and we all enjoyed it.

The next road shows we appeared in were named after our radio series and contained characters from them. There were several: *Odes and Ends*, *Thanking Yew* and *Thanking Yew Tew*. This, with the interlude of two West End shows, *Magic Carpet* for Firth Shepherd and the other a show for which Betty wrote the words and music called *Keep Going* at the Palace Theatre, really completed our music-hall shows as such.

De Haven and Page, a comedy cross-talk act, were with us in *Odes and Ends*. Billy de Haven was the tall, elegant straight man and Dandy was short, Jewish (a Russian immigrant), very funny and very lovable. They had often been in touring versions of the Crazy Gang and were two of the nicest and most experienced artistes in the business. We had a pair of geese when we were at Welwyn named De Haven and Page – the tall one looking down on the fat, short one in exactly the same way Bill looked at Dandy. In a high wind and by mistake they once flew right over the house and squawked and honked in a very alarmed way until they landed. It was Dandy who laid the egg.

The real Dandy was the Landlord when we did the lodger sketch in *Odes and Ends*, and Betty was his wife. She was meant to be fat and padded her clothes out alarmingly, and her dear little thin neck protruding from all the padding gave her the look of a red-nosed tortoise. At any moment we expected her head to disappear into her shell-like padding. She used to spit with real venom on her flat-iron when ironing the lodger's combs and would often make me and Dandy laugh when she did outrageous things with our underwear. The scenery was never too firm or solid for this sketch as it had to be assembled quickly after a dance production number, and it was trick scenery designed to fall to pieces anyway. 'If it falls altogether and total disaster stares us in the face the joke to use,' said the knowledgeable Dandy, 'is for Cyril to say, "That's the worst of them council houses".' Every comic has used this old chestnut to cover up a wobbly flat. One night it did happen and half the scene fell over, disclosing a near nude chorus lady in the arms of a stage-hand. This was too much for Dandy and me – we roared with laughter and it was left for Betty to say, 'That's the worst of these council houses'. Which got a yell coming from the red-nosed, skinny-necked tortoise. Dandy and I became so helpless with laughter that Betty had to carry on the sketch without us.

It was De Haven and Page who advised me to finish a sketch with the word 'bloody'. They were Boy Scouts and I was my Aggie radio character – that nauseating child – disguised as a Girl Guide. We could not get a strong finish to this sketch the first week we were on tour with it and they trotted out their expedient of using this swear word. It will have extra comic impact, they said, coming from a Girl Guide. Even in variety in those days I was very worried about using 'bloody'; I was, after all, a radio comedian, and therefore a 'family' entertainer, and I was rather bothered by the idea. It seems absurd to be worried about such a thing today, but I was so put out at using the word that I said it in the middle of the sketch. It got a very big laugh. I turned to Bill and Dandy and said, '*Now* how do I finish it?'

In *Odes and Ends* we also had an act called 'Young Madrigal' who used to play the bagpipes, in a kilt, blindfolded on a unicycle. He fell terribly in love with a girl who posed in the nude covered with live doves. Their fathers were drinking pals, and one night they caroused too much and one father forgot to let out the doves. That was the night Young Madrigal fell off his bicycle.

In between the actual road shows, and also while we recorded the various radio series on Sundays, we played separate variety dates. Hundreds of them. One I remember at Chatham; there were two variety theatres in Chatham, one on either side of the street. We played them both and I forget which one this was; but always there were full houses and a large number of sailors and forces personnel in the audience. We had just finished in a road show when Betty's act was of a similar routine every night, and as she would be in sketches and production numbers throughout the show, her single act would not be as long as it would be in a variety bill. The band call was most unusually in the afternoon. I had been gardening at home at East Grinstead in the morning, we had motored over and I was wearing some rather shabby gardening clothes. Betty's act closed the first half of the bill, mine closed the second, and I decided that I would change into my evening dress during the interval. I thought I would stay on the side of the stage and make sure all was well with Betty's act: checking the lighting and making sure that the 'tabs' (a theatrical term, being short for tableau curtains) closed on the right bars of music at the end of a certain song. Also, with Betty wearing those enormous and costly crinoline gowns, it was a necessity to 'page' the tabs for her. This means that as the tabs begin to close a stage hand, holding the tabs in his left hand as he walks in with the tabs from stage left, meets but at an angle a stage hand coming towards him paging the curtains in his right hand from stage right. The left-hand stage hand goes slightly downstage and the right-hand stage hand goes slightly up stage, thus leaving a large space between the overlapping curtains for the artiste wearing a large costume to go through and acknowledge the plaudits of the audience. Unknown to me, Betty had changed her finishing song. She was going to have what is known as 'false' tabs on her usual finishing song (the one she had finished on for twenty weeks in the last road show), then the tabs were to open again and Betty had arranged to sing one more song. I, hearing the end of what I thought was to be her last number, saw to my horror no stage hands to 'page the tabs'. I signalled frantically to a chap to do one side – he didn't twig – while I rushed to page the other. The curtains no sooner closed than with a great flourish they opened again. The flourish swept the curtains from my hand, and there I was in front of a Chatham audience standing on the stage in my shabbiest gardening clothes next to Betty in a fabulous crinoline, beautiful and serene. I was now in the centre of the wide stage, so, of course, was Betty; I should have run to the side of the stage as quickly as possible. Somehow I was petrified with panic, and to my utter horror found myself on my hands and knees seeking sanctuary under Betty's crinoline. And there I stayed for the whole of the next number. Betty, before a packed theatre hooting with laughter, sang, of all songs, 'Bless this House'.

Clothes were rationed during the war and stage folk could get a supplementary issue of coupons – never enough for those wonderful crinolines which Bobby Roper (St John Roper, the famous stage costume designer, alas, now dead) created for Betty. Shoes were rationed too. One very dark night we were at Coventry Hippodrome, as it was then called. It was a Saturday and the end of the show. Lord Haw-Haw had forecast a second Coventry blitz, and it had already begun with warning searchlights and anti-aircraft guns. We finished the show and were loading the car in velvet darkness when I dropped one of Betty's shoes. It was imperative for me to find it, so I went down on my hands and knees in the dark so as to systematically cover as much ground as quickly as possible between the stage door and the car. What impeded me was a drunken man also on his hands and knees who was trying to find the stage door. We kept knocking into each other and apologizing with an exaggerated politeness. The shoe was triumphantly found and we left the city for the comparative safety of Warwick where we were staying at that blessed haven, the Wheatsheaf Inn, for the night.

Bobby Roper was a merry man, and after the war was to make the costumes for several of our summer shows. Once he was with us at Hastings for one of the openings. He was also designing the costumes for a new West End show starring Dame Sybil Thorndike, who was impersonating some dowdy spinster. 'Hastings old town,' said Bobby, 'will be ideal for me to get "her" sort of hat.' So Betty and I put him into the car and off we went. It is difficult to park a car at the seaside in the season. It was very difficult that afternoon. As I drove round and round while Betty and Bobby went from shop to shop I was not to know what was happening. Into each shop walked Bobby asking for those dowdy hats. 'I must see my wife in these,' he said to the assistants as he plonked them on to Betty's head. 'But Madam is too young for this sort of hat,' cried the assistants. 'I *like* these sort of hats for my wife,' said a masterly Bobby. The more hats they tried on the more exaggerated became their behaviour and the longer they took. I was getting quite annoyed as I brought the car down the main street yet again. They staggered out of a shop door, reeling, with tears of laughter streaming down their faces. Betty fell into the front seat of the car and Bobby into the back, where, in a silver-grey flannel suit, he sat with a crunch on to an enormous over-ripe melon which enveloped itself round his impeccably tailored bottom. We laughed all the more.

One of the saddest and most frightening weeks of variety I ever played was at New Cross Empire. It was in the thick of the doodle-bug time and Bert Montague had a touring revue booked there. Val Parnell thought the show needed a top-of-the-bill name added to it and I was asked if I would take it on. Not being in the forces, the least I could do, I felt, was to appear wherever I was asked, regardless of the conditions. I went, and Bert Montague also went to the theatre there every evening, and so, to his credit, did Val Parnell, visiting us on alternate evenings. Very few of the public did, but in the midst of appalling devastation we were not only keeping the flag of live entertainment flying, but we were endeavouring to show the public that one carried on life as normally as possible. In the middle of the week there was a terrible tragedy when a bomb exploded on Woolworth's and another on a cinema. The flying bomb on Woolworth's happened in the middle of the day when it was full of shoppers.

A very large part of the area was quite flattened, with an occasional building standing erect among the rubble – the theatre being one of them. As one drove into the show that week in high summer, there were so many pathetic little tableaux of small homes cut in half or knocked over, odd pieces of furniture askew here, there a bed hanging from a toppled top floor. One saw many little acts of neighbourly help and compassion. One saw, so often, the touching love and attention of a little old decrepit, shabby husband to his loved little old wife, whose whole domestic world was in ruins. You could see them determined all their lives not to be beaten by poverty, then not to be beaten by old age, and now not to be broken by this final calamity. One saw so often the sweet almost defeated smile of very old good people. There were little blossoms of divine love flowering in this desert of man's hateful inhumanity. The pity and the pride of small lives: the whole world is made up of small gallant lives.

What was so amazing was that the few who came to see us laughed. They were a warm, seemingly happy audience. When one was on the stage the act of performing allowed one to forget the bombs – certainly one would frequently hear one flying about – perhaps coming, perhaps going – it was the cutting out of the engine one did not enjoy. One's main preoccupation was in making sure that the audience did not see a shaking hand or a faltering smile.

It was at New Cross Empire earlier on in the war that I once shared the bill with Harry Tate. He was not at the band call on Monday morning. Ronnie Tate, his son, took the call for him and told us that his father had not been seen at all over the week-end. He presumed he was out with drinking pals on a bender! The manager of the theatre, a Mr Marner – a one-time manager of the Palladium – was pompous with a seedy evening dress, a monocle and an air of decayed grandeur. One might easily suppose he had had some feud with Harry through the years, such was his anticipatory delight at his not appearing that night. His deputy had been booked, the renowned Harry Champion (who would write and congratulate me on my wedding some weeks later and sign himself 'Yours respectfully' on wonderfully printed old-fashioned notepaper in the manner of a family butcher or grocer with copperplate printing. With no sense of theatrical history, I eventually threw it away.) All that was left for Marner to do, should Harry Tate eventually turn up at the theatre, was to sack him. Marner hovered around the stage door, and exactly at the half (all actors are requested in their contracts to appear at the stage door no later than half an hour before curtain-up), Tate arrived in a very happy and expansive mood. He was a large, fat, flamboyant man with a booming voice to match – a voice which dwelt sometimes on vowels and sometimes on consonants with the most telling and comic effects. Let me remind you that it was wartime, it was before the second front or even the North African landings. We were a tightly beleaguered island surrounded by our foe. 'Where have you been?' Marner thundered, enjoying himself immensely. Harry Tate, in his most booming voice and most beaming face, and with a great gesture to embrace the universe, said, 'I've been abroad!'

Another story which exemplifies the Harry Tate spontaneity of humour is told by Georgie Wood in his book, *Royalty, Religion and Rats*. Georgie Wood (only on his theatre billing did he use Wee Georgie Wood – he hated to be addressed by it) was perhaps the very first music-hall star I met. He was playing Hastings in variety when I was there my first season with the *Fol-de-Rols*. The Volonoff Twins, in the *Fol-de-Rols* with me, had just finished with the great little man a South African tour of his pantomime production from Leon Salberg's Alexandra Theatre, Birmingham. (Joan Volonoff was to marry Leon's son Derek, and Ardie was to marry Jack Stanford, the comedian, who was in several of our summer shows.) I have always admired Georgie Wood, a rare genius in his original acts, a very good talker and an infinite fund of music-hall lore; besides, he gave me my first good notice in *Cavalcade*, a monthly periodical he wrote for. But I digress – to Harry Tate. Just after the First World War, Tate asked Wood to take him to the House of Commons where he was, at that time, a frequent visitor.

Georgie writes:

> Tate took me to the House in his car with the registration plate T.8. He was a very great favourite of Lloyd George. We were given seats, in consequence in the Distinguished Strangers Gallery. During a momentary lull in a heated debate Harry's voice boomed through the chamber: 'They think it's all real.'
>
> We were quickly escorted out, and on reaching the lobby found, not an irate Lloyd George but a man convulsed with laughter. 'You aren't permitted to do such things, Mr Tate,' he said, 'but what perfect timing – as always.'

Timing, the essence of comedy, depends sometimes as much on the straight man as it does on the funny man.

When one of our comic giants, Sid Field, was being prepared for the West End, George Black decided he should have a new straight-man 'feed', Jerry Desmond. To my mind he was one of the very best in the business; the kind of feed to make a great comedian even greater. (Ernie Wise, although he too is a

c

comedian, because of the superb way he feeds Eric Morecambe, makes even this comedian funnier and funnier every time we see them together.) There is only one way for comedian and feed to rehearse, and that is in front of an audience, and for two weeks Sid Field and Jerry Desmond were booked into one of our road shows when playing Golders Green and Streatham Hill Theatre. Betty and I watched them night after night at every performance. Oh, what a lovable funny genius Sid Field was! What a shame that this great artiste should die so young! All that the younger generation knows of him are the clips out of his films – films where he was not performing to an audience and where the warmth which he engendered from an audience is missing. With his very confidential, sly way of seeming to address each member of an audience individually, and his letting each single member of the audience into the secret of his jokes, what a master of the television screen he would have been!

Some years afterwards I was playing variety in Southampton with my old friend Peter Cavanagh on the bill. He had helped me to write Odd Odes during the war, calling at the Shaftesbury Theatre in his battledress, his gas mask over one arm and a sheaf of Odd Odes under the other. We were recommended a hotel out in the country. 'You'll enjoy it out there,' they said. 'It's unusual.' It was so remote and isolated it was difficult to find. We eventually drove up miles of pot-holed drive through a neglected park with upturned trees and disgruntled-looking deer. The house was a replica of an enormous wooden Swiss chalet – with vast stable quarters in the rear with a huge decorative clock tower and belfry. I left Peter in the car and he saw me advance through a glass door into the hall. There was no glass in the door and I stepped delicately through the frame. A refined Scottish lady came into the hall. She had a Morningside accent with gossamer-thin vowels. She confirmed that this was where we were to be lodged for the naight.

'If ye'll ask Mr Cavanagh to cross the threshold I will ring for Eulialiah to show you to your rooms.'

She then opened a cupboard door and stepped down into it. Inside the cupboard was a large bell rope with a red and black plaited sally. She seized this and rose and fell about six feet at a time, and as she did so an enormous bell tolled out in the courtyard from the belfry. It was deafening and it brought a very buxom and be-bosomed Eulialiah from the stables; she had straw in her peroxided hair and she smelt strongly of horse manure. Eulialiah took us to the top of a wide staircase with Gothic windows and long arched corridors. Peter was directed down one of these and I was conducted down the other – miles, it seemed, from the comfort of company. It was cold and damp, and yew trees beat their dark branches against the dirt-stained glass of the windows of my room.

'If you are awakened by strange noises,' said Eulialiah, 'it will be my sister, she howls like a wolf in the night.'

She then showed me back to the dining room where thirty large and hideously hungry-looking stags' heads glowered down at us at every meal. Odd mangy moth-eaten patches of skin would drop off at intervals on to the cold linoleum, and once into Peter's porridge.

'What on earth is that?' I said to the Scotswoman when I returned to the hall. I was looking out on to a gravestone – a large gravestone – in the middle of the front lawn. It bore the legend JUMBO and there was a very large mound – almost a barrow.

'It's a grave,' she said in her best Morningside – and I was sure she was about to add: 'Just a wee elephant we were awfu' fond of'. But to my regret she didn't. It was the grave of a pet horse.

In the grounds they had been holding a fête and a vast area of brown hessian was stretched across the lawn. On one side of the hessian were three lavatory pans in a row, and on the other side (to please the economical Scots soul, I suppose) was a great archery target. One's mind goggled and giggled at the thought of a stray arrow hitting a sitting target of a different kind through the other side of the arras.

When we appeared at Birmingham, Dudley and Wolverhampton we would stay at a marvellous little pub called the Whittington Inn at Kinver. This was supposed to be the ancestral seat of the Whittington family, and something to do with Lady Jane Grey, but whether it was or not I don't know. In our day the host and hostess were great ones for sampling their wares. They were fabulous publicans. He, I think, was a retired tailor, and he had a sleeping partner who used only to visit the pub during week-ends. He was a dapper little man and thought he looked like Bobby Howes, but Betty, who had appeared in *For the Love of Mike* with Bobby Howes, assured me emphatically that he didn't. Having over-sampled their wares, these good people would go to bed at about two in the afternoon and come to again in time for the evening opening of the pub; but so enchanting was the place that many people would draw up and ask if they 'did teas'. When Betty and I stayed there, which we did several times, we didn't turn these people away, we 'did teas' for them for fun and left the money on the mantelpiece and then went off to the theatre.

One of the bedrooms was supposed to be haunted by Lady Jane herself, and we were therefore given the bedroom which was not. However, during the week, time and again, a very cold icy wind would whip the eiderdown off the bed, and we so disliked the atmosphere in this room that we asked could we please change over and sleep in the supposedly haunted bedroom. This we were allowed to do. We were happy in the haunted bedroom, which had no sign of malignant manifestations whatever.

Carousings would go on every night in the bar parlour. It was still wartime and licensing regulations were not observed quite so strictly as perhaps they should have been, and the carousings would continue until two or so in the morning. The host used to try and inveigle stars who stayed there to entertain the regulars each night, and we, rather disappointingly for them, used to hurry up after our meal and go straight to bed.

Now the sleeping partner was also a bit of a dipsomaniac, and he used to get very tight every Saturday night, so Saturday nights we used to go to bed even earlier, and this particular night, because we were going to Edinburgh the next day, we decided to go to bed especially early. At two in the morning we were awakened by a crash and bloodthirsty yells and shrieks. A voice yelled, 'Blood, blood, I am covered in blood.' It went on with such horrifying intensity that we decided to get up and investigate. I must also mention that there was an enormous bull-mastiff staying at the hotel. Nobody knew to whom it belonged. It just arrived one day, and because the hotel's kitchens had extra scraps and it could indulge its enormous appetite, the dog, being no fool, stayed on.

We didn't want to get involved in the fracas so decided to stay in the bedroom and watch through the crack in the door. It was a very thick medieval oak door, made of planks, and where the planks didn't fit very well one was able to look through on to the landing. It had one of those wooden latches, but no bolt. In our nightclothes Betty and I were, by now, on our hands and knees looking through the cracks in the door to see what on earth was happening. The blood-curdling yells were proceeding unabated from the haunted bedroom.

Up the stairs, falling and stumbling, trooped about twenty people who had been carousing in the bar for about the last four or five hours. They were preceded by the host's wife and the bull-mastiff, who both looked rather similar. With great melodramatic ham, almost like a Victorian Lady Macbeth, the hostess stopped at the stair-head where there was quite a large square landing and, looking into the room whence came the screams, yelled, 'Bloody hell, it's full of blood – can't let the dog into the room with all that blood. I know,' she cried, 'we'll put the dog in with the Fletchers.'

So she took the dog by its enormous collar and lugged it over to our bedroom door and started to open the latch. I shoved my finger in the wooden jamb of the latch, as there was no wedge of wood there to bolt it, while the dog panted in my face through the cracks. If you remember, I was on my hands and knees, and I was breathing back at the dog – and as the dog wuffed and puffed at me we were nose to nose, never mind eyeball to eyeball! The hostess gave up eventually and went into the haunted bedroom where the sleeping partner had seen his drunken face in the mirror (thinking perhaps it was the ghost in the haunted bedroom) and fallen forward and cut his throat on the broken mirror. It needed seventeen stitches.

Towards the end of the war I was booked as one of the tops of the bill at the Palladium. It was a rather odd bill. Lucan and McShane, with excerpts from their many 'Old Mother Riley and Her Daughter Kitty' road-show successes, took up the second half of the programme, and a rather quietly artistic bill with musical comedy star Binnie Hale and myself were in the first. Our part of the audience did not like Lucan and McShane, and Lucan and McShane, as a very good strong visual comedy duo who filled every single provincial music hall and cinema for years with their road show revues and films, drew in an audience who hated our half of the show. Oil did not mix with water. George Black therefore decided to mingle the two halves of the show. I was moved into the second half. This was in a way flattering, but for my act it was disaster. I had to follow a boisterous sketch of talk and visual comedy with not a note of music which went on for a hilarious twenty-five minutes. My act of twenty minutes' talking had been hilarious in the first half, but after such a rough and tumble as Arthur Lucan and Kitty McShane perpetrated for nearly half an hour, it was a little difficult to get a laugh out of suggesting some happening when the audience had seen it take place before their very eyes in a sketch a few moments earlier. For example, one of my most successful Odd Odes at that time described what happened when Cleopatra Drain had her bath in front of a kitchen stove, slipped on the soap and sat on the stove accidentally.

> *Cleopatra Drain*
> *Poor little Cleopatra Drain*
> *Will never seem the same again.*
> *One night some little time ago*
> *Whilst Ma was at a picture show,*
> *Thinking she might immerse herself*
> *She took a tin bath from the shelf*
> *And then, removing her attire*
> *She bathed before the kitchen fire.*
> *Her future might have held some hope*
> *Had she not trodden on the soap.*
> *Looking like nature in the raw*
> *She skidded on the kitchen floor.*
> *Then finished up this flight so strange*
> *By sitting on the kitchen range.*
> *The red-hot stove, I hate to say*
> *Was trade-marked in the usual way.*
> *Poor Cleo gazing in the glass*
> *Discovered what had come to pass*
> *For where she sat the poor girl saw*
> *Branded the word Excelsior.*
>
> *Well, war broke out and like a shot*
> *Her patriotism burned red hot,*
> *She went and joined the ATS*
> *Who asked her, would she please undress?*
> *The Commandant exclaimed, 'Come! Come!*
> *What is the word you have there, chum?*
> *A code word, unless I'm a chump*
> *That means an ammunition dump.*
> *We will have to blot it out, I guess*
> *And find another one unless*
> *You want to be shot as a spy*
> *But no one wants to see you die!'*
> *So they called in a local painter chap*
> *Who altered Cleopatra's map*
> *And substituted, what a farce,*
> *The bold words 'PLEASE KEEP OFF THE GRASS.'*

As luck would have it, the preceding sketch to my reciting this Odd Ode was a kitchen scene in which Kitty pushed Arthur on to the stove and his skirts caught fire and he dashed wildly round the stage with his bottom alight. It was not therefore a very happy season at the Palladium for me, but by changing things around and bits of new material here and there, as the weeks progressed I managed to get by.

One other variety bill I will always remember. It was after the war at Southampton Guildhall. We had a packed and most receptive house, and there was a fat, jolly man in the front row with a peculiarly individual, ribald laugh. The accepted comic procedure here is for the comedian to ask the laugher a whole lot of tried and true questions which are in every comic's repertoire, such as, 'Is that your own laugh? Or are you breaking it in for a friend?' Another might be, 'Are you sitting on a feather?' These remarks addressed to the funny individual laugher pinpoints the audience's attention to him (it's usually a 'her!') and then, when an especially good upsurge of joy comes from that quarter, just a look from the comedian will set the audience laughing once again. These merry members of an audience are a comedian's god-send. How we welcome a good extrovert laugher! Such a one there was at the end of the front row this particular night in Southampton. I played him as a fly-fisherman might play a salmon. I extracted every ounce of extra laughter out of the audience and out of the man. Suddenly there was a gurgle and a thud. St John's Ambulance men came down the aisle and carried him out on a stretcher. The audience was very quiet indeed for the rest of my act. I rang the hospital the next day. My laugher had died in the night. I was very sorry. I know it is the function of all comedians to make people die with laughter, but I wish he had not taken me so literally.

At the Princes Theatre (now the Shaftesbury) during the run of *Magic Carpet* I made a lady laugh so much that she gave birth then and there in the middle of an Odd Ode, to a boy child. He is called Cyril, of course! So I'm one in and one out!

During the rehearsals of a road show, or a variety bill, I forget which, I happened to overhear a conversation between George Black and Val Parnell, his right-hand man and lieutenant. 'I don't know what you see in Cyril Fletcher,' said Parnell. 'He isn't star material to me.'

George Black said in reply that he felt I was. He had gradually groomed me and used me successfully in variety shows and in road shows all over his General Theatre Corporation circuit. 'I think you are wrong,' he said to Val Parnell. I crept away into a darker corner of the theatre, thinking warmly to myself that George Black, thank God, was the boss, and Val Parnell the lieutenant. How grateful I was it was this way round. Sadly, in his prime, George Black died, and his place as the great impresario on the General Theatre Corporation circuit (and later in Commercial Television) was taken by Val Parnell. Bearing this in mind, and seeing how the growth of television must eventually kill the halls, Betty and I came to a decision. What will happen to showbusiness? What kind of theatre will last longest? we asked ourselves.

We came up with this answer: the family on holiday will always go and see the summer show or variety at the seaside; and the family at Christmas will always take the children to the pantomime. So we decided to launch out as actor/managers. We would present our own summer shows, and eventually our own pantomimes. As we predicted, variety did die; and no one feels it more sadly than we do. Variety was great individual entertainment. As a cradle for stardom it was unsurpassed; each artiste, given but a few minutes, frequently in a front cloth, had, with his own personality and his own material, to entertain an audience, take it by the scruff of its neck and insist that it enjoyed every precious minute that the act was on the stage. It was an exciting and exacting science, and the entertainment world is very much the poorer without its variety theatres and artistes.

5　Dogs

'The truth I do not stretch or shove
When I state the dog is full of love,
I've also proved by actual test
A wet dog is the lovingest.'
　　　　　　　－ Ogden Nash

If you hate dogs you must skip this chapter. Betty and I love dogs dearly; indeed, we have been members of the council of the Canine Defence League for many years. If this is a true autobiography, then dogs must feature largely in it, as they do and have done in my life.

Dogs have made my life richer and fuller. Even if one only gave them credit for getting us out for long country walks. Dogs give you more than that – they are loyal, companionable creatures with a great sense of enjoyment and fun. Man, when he first sought the companionship of the dog, and the help of the dog for hunting, not only helped himself to survive, he enlarged his capacity by caring for the animal kingdom.

I was seventeen. I had just left school and had worked for a month for the Scottish Union and National Insurance Company who (you will remember) paid me the magnificent sum of £50 a year. I had received a twelfth of this 'magnificent sum' and my father having paid for my first season ticket to London and my mother having paid for my first month's lunches, I was awash with untold wealth. I could spend 25s. (£1.25) on myself. It was a great moment.

I also knew on what I was going to squander this money. I also knew that it was not squandering; it was an investment. An investment of love. No, not an engagement ring – not for 25s., even in those days. But in a way, something similar. Something feminine and cuddly who would at times share my bed . . but we are racing too far ahead.

My great friend Allan had a dog. Indeed, they were a doggy family. His mother had had an endless line of pekes (as well as six children), his father had an Airedale, Allan had a most beautiful Irish setter – chestnut and sleek and shining gloriously in the sunshine – and I needed a similar companion.

All my life I had wanted a dog – my family had never owned one. Next door to us once lived a Mrs Caney, who was fat and jolly and white-haired and who had dirty hands and always looked delightfully untidy. She had several dog kennels in her garden and bred Sealyhams and West Highland terriers. All puppies, we know, are beautiful and were created by God when he needed some light-hearted entertainment, with lovable beauty thrown in at the same time. Sealyham puppies seemed to me, with their wide, white noses, minute stumpy tails and all-square pretended ferocity, the most joyous of God's creatures, and I wanted one. I had no idea of the cost. Actually, in those days – 1930 – you could get a passably attractive pedigree pet for two or three pounds.

Mrs Caney had moved out to Arkley, a matter of five miles or so from Friern Barnet. I walked. She had no Sealyhams for sale. She did have a litter of West Highlands, and how jolly they were, for three guineas each.

'No runt for 25s.?' said a sad-eyed Fletcher. I had considerable charm as a youth.

'No runt,' said Mrs Caney. I was leaving and she called me back. 'How about a Scottie?' she said. 'I could let you have a Scottie for 25s., but it would be a bitch.'

I didn't really want a Scottie. Out of politeness I said, 'May I see her?' She was tiny – a little, black, square-nosed rat. She was exactly the length of my outstretched palm, with her stringy tail extending up my wrist. I wanted her out of protectiveness more than anything. She needed care and love. She had, of course, the usual smell of puppies, which was a new, ambrosial smell to me. She wagged her little tail and looked quizzically at me with two shiny boot buttons. I put her in the collar of my coat, paid the 25s. most happily and walked her home that winter's afternoon with her looking up at me, or sleeping with her ears drooping and not cocked yet in the way of Scottie puppies.

I don't think I have ever had better value for 25s. in the whole of my life. So that is how Lady Macbeth first came into the family. We called her that because, as with all puppies, for two days it was a case of, 'Out, damned spot.' We called her Nipper, and later this became Tiggen – I don't know why.

For five years she belonged to an insurance clerk, and from 1936, as a comedian's dog, she appeared briefly in a circus number with the *Fol-de-Rols* at Hastings with a number plate on her rear with 1066 on it! She loved the seaside and for five years I did a summer season.

During the five years of working in the City I used to arrive home punctually at six o'clock. The six o'clock news in those days was always preceded by Henry Hall. My mother used to say that immediately on hearing the closing signature tune of Henry Hall's orchestra, the knowing little dog would get up, go to the front door and put her nose to the crack along the floor and start to blow through it, lying in wait for her master.

In 1940, when she was ten, she met, charmed and was charmed by my wife-to-be, Betty, who had a terrifying influence over dogs. They are always her devoted slaves in five minutes. Tiggen was our loving but somewhat inadequate bridesmaid in 1941 at St Martin-in-the-Fields and came with us on our honeymoon. She never married herself.

We used to take her on tour with us, and during the war there were variety theatres all over the country. We played the Palace Theatre, Plymouth, one week in the depths of winter and stayed outside, right in the country at Yelverton. The hotel was a large chalet type of building with the main bedrooms all along the front, each with a wooden balcony. The whole hotel seemed to be made of wood as I remember. We were asleep on the coldest night of the year. I don't think I have told you of the little dog's bladder trouble. In the middle of the night she wanted to go. The hotel was large, there was a fuel shortage and no central heating. It was very cold and the oddest thing about Tiggen was she would only 'go' on grass. (Once in Wolverhampton I had flu and a temperature of 103° and had to go out into inches of frost and walk round for at least half an hour with no grass in sight and no result, and eventually had to dangle her, with her harness, over the churchyard wall so that she could achieve her aim, if you get my meaning.)

I suggested to Betty that I would try Tiggen out on the balcony, but I hadn't a lot of faith in my idea. Overcoat over pyjamas, I stepped out on to the balcony into a frosty world with my little dog, who immediately went to the corner of the balcony and squatted at once. As she squatted, the fat little belly emptied itself of wind. Because it was a very still night and the hotel was in a valley and made of wood, the trumpeting of the small Scottie filled the night with an enormous sound. Betty, from the warmth of the bed, said as loudly as she dared, 'Shut up, Cyril.' To my delight the little dog obliged again, louder even than before. Louder than before from the bedroom came Betty with another stage whisper, 'Shut up, Cyril!' By this time I was crying with silent laughter and the dog, purely for fun, I'm sure, let forth an even larger trumpeting into the frosty night. A livid Betty was by now at the window as dog and master fell laughing into the bedroom while Betty said, 'Cyril – how could you? You must have awakened everyone in the hotel!' It was some minutes before our laughter allowed Tiggen and me to explain, and some hours before the three of us stopped giggling and went to sleep.

When Tiggen died at fifteen she was replaced by a somewhat sad little dog . . . almost the only Scottie I have ever known to be without character. This I think was because she was never very well. When she had pups she had to have a Caesarian operation and they all died. She was much overshadowed by Penny, a spaniel with an enormous character and sense of humour. She, too, had pups and I will never ever forget her great look of astonishment when the first one popped out, and then her disappointed look when she added only one other to it.

These pups were called respectively Tuppence and Halfpenny. Halfpenny we called Happy for short as she was one of the jolliest, most ingratiating creatures we have had the joy to own. This was in the days before hard-pad injections and it is a sad story. She caught it when she was two years old, she was ill for two days only and she died at the end of a long night and lay there with the morning sun shining on the exquisite gloss of her beautiful coat . . . just as beautiful as if she were but sleeping in the sun as a dog loves to do.

The next Scottie, Tiggen III, decided the moment I arrived at the breeder's kennels that I was the man for her, and I loved her and she me as much as with Tiggen I. She lived a merry twelve years, but had leukaemia for the last two years of her life and I had to make the awful decision of when it would be kinder to let her hunt for Elysian badgers instead of exploring the sett in our own Sussex fields as she was wont to do. I went with Betty and the dog – a very grey brindle by now, with a fine, delicate head and such soft, silky ears, and short, insistent chunky front legs which prodded you for attention when you were driving the car – to the vet's for that grim moment which we dog owners have to expect every so often. Betty took her in and held her in her arms. I, a fully grown man in his fifties, whose profession is laughter, walked up and down outside with tears coursing down my face.

After we were married (Betty, thank heaven, has the same dog mania that I have) the first Tiggen was joined by Tuppenny, our first spaniel (not to be confused with the Tuppence mentioned already), and George, a magnificent black and white pointer. Our first home was in Old Welwyn, Hertfordshire, where we had twenty-four acres and a thatched house, so there was plenty of room.

Tuppenny was as enchanting as most spaniels, and like all our dogs, except the Scotties, wound his emotions inextricably round Betty so that when our only child was born (I could only go through it the once) he became rather bad-tempered and very jealous, and had to be given to a loving friend where, I am happy to say, he settled perfectly. George was always a problem. He was a beautiful puppy and young dog, but was headstrong and disobedient – as we were away on tour with our road shows from time to time, the constant attention that a dog needs from one owner was lacking. So we decided to have him obedience trained because the sight of a retreating pointer's rear dashing off into the countryside is one of the most depressing sights I know. Once he killed a dozen Rhode Island Reds which had been enthusiastically adding to our egg ration. He rather artistically placed them in a row; a little like St John Ambulancemen do with the fainting ones at a demonstration. Another time he ran up and down inside a battery of laying hens belonging to a neighbour. The fantod those ladies got into during the horror of those ten minutes put them off their lay for weeks and started a premature moult. The sweet neighbour did not even suggest compensation.

So the delinquent was banished to Wales to a famous dog-trainer-cum-tamer for seventeen weeks at so much a week. When he came back he was accompanied by a demented railway guard whose van he had 'shared' on the journey and a note from the trainer to say that, in thirty years of dog handling, George had been the one dog to beat him. He was returning him unmastered, but he would lie down if you said 'Up'. Which he did. So George was kept in a large pen and was exercised on a clothes line, or in the wired tennis court, and was raced about as much as possible by us all – because we, too, were young in those days. Sometimes I would go and sit with him in his kennel if it rained . . . but he was the only dog, I feel, with whom we failed, and is a little bit on my conscience because he should have had more freedom and a merrier life. He lived to be ten, which is a fair age for a large dog.

Our first bulldog was Lucky Jenkins. Even as a puppy she had short, powerful legs, a deep, muscular chest, the tiniest and softest ears like unravelled Brussels sprouts made of velvet, a massive head, a funny bashed-in face with a little black, shiny, crusty nose. She had a wrinkled quizzical look. Snuffling, snoring, playful, obstinate, with a stiff, bent little tail which not only was wagged by her but which wagged the whole of her backside. She would, as it were, undulate sideways towards you, throwing her knowing head in the air like a pure-bred horse. She loved to accompany us to the coast in the summer.

At the seaside she would dash in off a short jetty quite out of her depth, and then surface beneath a terrified and unsuspecting swimmer like a hippopotamus, grinning ferociously – though she wouldn't hurt a fly.

In the garden she would walk through things, including all forms of fencing. In the house, similarly, she was sort of obedient . . . but if she made up her mind not to do anything you really could not make her. Like going to bed. Then you would have to carry her. All four stones of her.

Bulldogs don't live very long . . . as if any dogs do. But the joy of them is that their appearance and manner and personality are so similar that if you once have one then with its successors you almost have the same dog for ever, and so it proved with Lucky.

How many of you remember Oliver Wakefield, the stuttering comedian during the war? When radio censorship allowed nothing bawdy (halcyon days!) he made the whole nation whisper with shame when he said in a *Henry Hall Guest Night* that his next words would come from the bottom of his heart – and the heart of Henry Hall's bottom! He was a dear friend of mine and an usher at our wedding. Well, Oliver, the slim, handsome, elegant man-about-town and sophisticated star, had a bulldog called Squire. For some twenty weeks or so Oliver and I co-starred and toured in a road show called *Boys of the BBC*, and as Oliver lived a bachelor existence in Pont Street in the West End, Squire travelled with us too. He was red and white and was enormous. He was a great comedian (as I believe most bulldogs are), and he was very much in love with my Scottie bitch, who also travelled with us because she didn't like bombs.

It was difficult on tour with wartime food rationing to feed a dog the size of Squire. Constant scrounging went on from railway buffets, wayside inns, five-star hotels and soft-hearted old ladies. These gargantuan meals would be served in a chamber pot – and Squire could just get his head inside and that great lolling tongue would lick up every morsel. Oliver was a great Bohemian, and before he joined the RAF he decided to amass as much actual cash as possible. In those days the five-pound notes, ten-pound notes and hundred-pound notes were all large, thin, white affairs with elegant spidery copperplate writing on them. It seemed worthwhile owning a £100 note in those days. Oliver also had a large number of Savile Row suits and hand-made shoes and tailored shirts, and these were housed in three very expensive hand-tooled leather cases. In another similar case were stuffed hundreds of these white Bank of England notes – several thousand pounds' worth.

We were on tour – there was no petrol – wartime trains and wartime schedules and packed wartime stations and trains were our lot at the end of every week.

Oliver was terribly slack and casual with his luggage – it would be piled on a crowded platform. He would go off and leave it for half an hour or so to have a drink or to queue up for a spam sandwich. The four obviously very costly pieces of luggage were left unattended, including the one containing several thousand pounds in cash. Did I say unattended? No, Squire was there. Always, with discrimination, sitting on the one with the money in it. 'Stay!' Oliver would say, and if Winston Churchill (after all, another bulldog) or Field-Marshal Montgomery (Irish terrier?) had asked for the dog and the cases to be moved, Squire would never have allowed it. A dog you could trust. One day, I said to myself, I will own a Squire.

And I did. Lucky and Bumble. Not red and white, but orange and white. Dear, sweet girls. One following the other. Both died too young, as all bulldogs do. I like a dog to befriend me for a minimum of twelve to fifteen years. We had a twenty-two-year-old cat until recently. He and Bumble loved each other dearly. Bumble would suck the cat's ears in paroxysms of devotion.

Then we were owned by a beagle called Blossom who was partial to celery. She was, of course, a 'pack animal'. Beagles have not long been pets and have 'pack instincts' still. A pack sleeps in a heap, and the one at the bottom of the heap, while appreciating the warmth, will eventually need resuscitatory air and will then bite its way to the top. As Blossom slept on the bed (the only one of our dogs to do so), and regrettably sometimes in the bed, you can imagine that Betty and I had the most bitten bottoms in the business. This ancient instinct that was in her would make her rush to, and try to savage, the radio or the telly if she should hear a hunting horn giving some rustic background to a drama. She could hear her master's voice on the radio or see her master's handsome features on the television set and treat him with the 'utmost ignore'. (We have never had a dog fool enough to recognize me on television.)

There never was a merrier dog, so much of an up-and-doing dog, so much of a whatever-is-that-dog-a-doing-of dog.

So many beagle owners like me have felt that after the first six months, or even the first six weeks, of ownership, they would have to give in and find another owner. Beagle owners must have stamina. They must have infinite patience and a long purse. Because . . . Well, these are the reasons. There was never a more escape-capable dog, really more of a Houdini than a dog. No dog is less biddable. No dog is more destructive. No dog more disobedient. And no dog is more beautiful or more lovable.

My wife once said as we saw our dog disappearing over a Sussex hillside that God must have been particularly pleased and satisfied when he had finished creating his first beagle. The line of the dog is beautiful. The colour is beautiful and complements the landscape at all seasons. It runs so beautifully, its tail is so gay and so utterly expressive. The face is honest and the eyes are lustrous and knowing and wise and wicked.

Of the fourteen dogs we have owned, only one has had a particular adorable habit . . . Blossom the beagle when we arrived home would always immediately search for and find a present; and if she were particularly pleased to see us, would search round and find perhaps a shoe, a duster and a newspaper and bring all three in her capacious mouth and lay them at our devoted feet.

Destructive is not the word. We left her once in the theatre dressing room in a leather armchair. She was all of ten weeks old. Only an hour we left her while we were on the stage. When we returned the small red and white and black puppy was engulfed in a mound of red horsehair stuffing about five feet tall . . . there was no chair in sight.

In spite of the fact that Blossom the beagle was exercised only in our own gardens and fields and woods and the lanes around our home, she was poisoned in some mysterious way, and this very joyful dog ended sadly her over-exuberant life at the early age of seven.

If you lose a dog, a quick replacement is an absolute necessity. With the deaths of Bumble II, Tiggen III and Blossom all coming quite close to each other we decided on the replacement. Three puppies – all brown and white – and ranging in size from Samantha the English setter, via Jolly the cocker spaniel to Henry the smooth-haired Jack Russell terrier. All very much the same age and all gambolling happily together. Samantha and Jolly getting more beautiful every day and Henry getting brighter, cuter and more knowing.

Because of losing Blossom to some kind of poison she picked up, we decided to sheep-wire a six-acre field of ours – about three acres of garden we had already wired against rabbits – and only to exercise the new trio on our own land. When you have three dogs, they are very good at exercising each other, and at 8.30 every morning when I am home I take them out rain, shine, heatwave or blizzard for an hour in the fields. They then get a minimum of another hour after lunch and lots of time out as well when we are in the garden. We have a rookery at the end of our drive. The drive winds up an avenue of quite old trees, and near the gate there is this small rookery. If the rooks decide to build too near the house with their incessant noise and rubbish dropped from their nests, we always call in Jimmy Edwards, who lives fairly near, and he brings his shotgun with a view to shooting the nests out of the trees, not the birds themselves. Actually he only had to put his heavily moustachioed face round the door for the rooks, who are either over-intelligent, intuitive or psychic, to take to the wing and disappear! They then retreat to build at the end of the drive again, and it is a good excuse to entertain Jim, who is always amusing company. He is a remarkable character – and showbusiness is amazingly short of real characters. What comedian ever before has had his own string of polo ponies, playing with Royalty on occasion; has been a Master of Foxhounds; has stood for Parliament; flies his own aeroplanes; farms his own 1,000 acres of fertile Sussex land; and is an MA and ex-Rector of a University?

The rooks when resident at the end of the drive fly across several of our fields, but especially the dogs' field. They forage for miles and they come back frequently with crops full of grain seed. Some farmers use seed dressed with mercury. The rooks ate it and one fell dead in the field. Spaniels are bird dogs and greedy. Jolly must have eaten quite a bit before I was able to get the rest of the rook's corpse away from him, and even then I didn't know that it was a poisoned corpse. That night Jolly went slightly mad, and in spite of inspired treatment and sedation from brilliant local vets, eventually had to be put to sleep; doubly ironic when you think we only ever exercised this lively, beautiful little dog over our own fields. Our sorrow knew no bounds. Do these clever chemists and thoughtless farmers ever realize the extent of the damage to which the constant poisoning of our environment will eventually lead? All the time one hears of incidents, and all the time of side-effects, and side-effects leading off to side-effects. The balance of nature is all the time being over-weighted one way or the other with the indiscriminate use of artificial fertilizers and countless poisons; each invention seemingly more lethal than the last.

We will always miss Jolly, but we do have the great beauty of Samantha and the happy intelligence of Henry. Samantha, the English setter, is not only beautiful to look at, but she has a loving, generous nature. No wonder the breeders call English setters 'Nature's Gentlemen'. The tiny Henry, equally beautiful with his large, luminous brown eyes set in his tiny, eternally 'puppy-like' tan and white face, will go and take anything away from Sam – and Sam, Pluto-like, looks on, her tail gently wagging, not minding in the least even if he has robbed her of food. She is as noble as she looks.

Henry is a canine Mike Yarwood – one moment he looks like a miniature bull-terrier, another a beagle, another he is the trade mark for His Master's Voice, or he can be a whippet with his ears well laid back. Even the famous television mouse Toppo Gigio is not beyond his virtuosity.

So those are the present two companions who look after us, and are as amused at us as much as we are at them.

The world can be turned upside down and be solidly against you. Everyone can hate you, humanity can completely change its idea of you and its attitude towards you. But on your return home there is this small mute soul to welcome you lovingly. The face smiles, the eyes adore and never leave your face, and the tell-tale tail thumps out its message that here at least, no matter how humble, is love and devotion and an infinite pleasure in your very existence.

The dog loves you. You love the dog. And the world is a better and richer place because of it. As Horace Walpole said, 'The dear, good-natured, honest, sensible creatures. Christ! How can anyone hurt them?'

6   The West End

'Good luck always brings merit, but merit very seldom
brings good luck' – Somerset Maugham

Always the grass on the other side of the fence is greener. During the war years
we were being enormously successful in variety, filling variety theatres all over
the country and with never a week 'out'. No time off, I suppose, was the trouble.
We would dash home for a brief Sunday and off again the next Monday to some
far-distant provincial playhouse. Wartime trains were few and lethargic due
to the extra strain of travelling troops and transport of army supplies, and there
were disruptions because of random bombings so that the time we spent in our
new and precious home was minimal. How we envied the West End actor who
spent most of the day off at home and travelled to the theatre for evenings and
matinées. Also we reasoned that the West End star seemed to have a much longer
period of stardom than the variety/radio names, who burned brighter for a
shorter time. We were among the first of the new young variety names, and we
visualized a lifetime of work in the theatre ahead. Was there a long life of
stardom? We were keen to see into the future as much as possible and we came
to the conclusion that to have continuity in our careers, allied to our hankering
for homeloving bliss, we needed to become established in the West End musical
firmament; and we needed to do this while the momentum in our careers
remained.

I had appeared occasionally in the Savoy cabaret; because of the bombing
it had become a one-night-a-week performance and was in one of the basement
rooms; the audience were keen to be amused and met one half-way. The director
of entertainment for the Savoy Groups was Richard Collet, who was responsible
too for the Savoy Opera Company and the Savoy Theatre. Betty also was an
old friend of Carroll Gibbons of Savoy Orpheans' fame, and we decided to ask
their advice. Richard Collet was wonderfully friendly and helpful; he decided
our best course was to approach Firth Shepherd, who was presenting several
shows at West End playhouses at that time, including the Savoy Theatre. Firth
Shepherd had come to the fore as the manager of Leslie Henson and had presented most of his very successful West End shows. He then launched out as a
management on his own and imported several successful shows from America –
Arsenic and Old Lace, My Sister Eileen, The Women and many others. With

Leslie he had several wartime successes, such as *Shepherd's Pie* and *Fun and Games, Fine and Dandy* and *Up and Doing*.

Firth Shepherd decided to come and see us in variety; we were to play the Palace, Reading, an ideal small theatre with a joyously responsive audience. The night he came the audience was even better than usual and both our acts were seen to great advantage. He decided then and there that he would present us in our own West End show. Our manager, Ronnie Blackie (holding the fort while Charles Tucker was in America), was allied to the GTC and George Black and endeavoured to suppress such a sacrilegious suggestion; but our ambitions prevailed, and for a week or so we walked on air in the anticipatory glee of the fulfilment of our dreams.

The further we moved in time from Firth Shepherd's visit to the Palace, Reading, the less our chances became of starring in a West End Show. He was a man easily prevailed upon by his cronies. As easily as Mr Collet had 'sold' us to him, so his 'inner cabinet' of employees, financial backers and merely hangers-on would sway him from day to day this way and that. The great comedian and star of many of his earlier successes, Sydney Howard, was brought in; this to counter-balance the fact that I was not yet thirty, and these were not the days of the young comedian; it was also an insurance – not too much was to be left in the lap of novelty and inexperience. Other leading ladies were added to the cast according to the amount of money their *inamorati* had subscribed to the backing, and Robert Nesbit was engaged as Director/Producer. There was no more lavish or stylish a producer at that time in the West End, but his visual and artistic effects were most frequently allowed to swamp, or at least overshadow, the efforts of his comedians. Dancing and singing stars loved him, though even they were sometimes dwarfed by his superb spectacular scenic and lighting effects, but all comedians viewed him with suspicion. So it was to be; we both had to share and the impact we hoped for was blunted. At the dress rehearsal the show was more than half an hour too long. Not only did this throw balance and running-orders awry, but imagine the expense incurred for half an hour's worth of costly costumes, scenery, orchestrations, choreography and rehearsal time which were wastefully discarded. When the final results were cobbled together, much of lovely Astell was lost and even my single act of Odd Odes, for which presumably I had originally been booked, was done in front of the No. 1 running curtains with six inches of stage for me to stand on and the curtains on a windy night billowing and bellying around me.

My comedy was well contrasted with Sydney's. He was a comic genius. Once he realized that I was friendly and willing to share and did not want to hog it, he worked happily with me. He never gave me a funny line, or a funny suggestion, or developed funny business in my direction. He was elderly and he was worried by his wife's health (his beloved Diddy), and she was to die later in the run; so one cannot be critical of him. I think by then that his inventive days were over, and without a doubt he missed the support and the direction of his discoverer and mentor Leslie Henson. I learned a lot from Sydney, however, and I laughed a lot at him and with him. It was eventually a happy show.

One of the reasons for the show's happy atmosphere was the effervescent presence of Kim and Kay Kendall, whose dressing room was immediately adjacent to ours. Kay was sixteen and Kim eighteen. Kim, to my mind, was the more beautiful and Kay the more amusing. They came out to Welwyn to pick apples and we had very merry tea parties in the theatre after matinées. In the show I became a civil servant with Sydney and we town-planned the North Pole; and in another sketch we were weird shop assistant ladies who had a great deal of fun with separate display legs with stockings on and one of those overhead railways which sent the customers' money to the centre of a maze of mixed-up wires and shot the change back again. Sydney's face watching the return of the carriage containing the change seemingly through a labyrinthine mile of track will always bring a reminiscent smile. The show was a financial success and ran for about ten months until another spate of bombing put paid to several shows nearing their natural end.

In *Magic Carpet* we learned that it was difficult to trust implicitly in the word – or rather the promises – of managers, and we were keen this heartbreaking experience should not be repeated. We could only do this, we imagined, if, first, Betty wrote the words and the music of the show, and secondly, if we were the management, or at least part of the management. Playing in variety all over the country, including such venues as Glasgow, Edinburgh and Swansea, you will imagine it was difficult to get this 'impossible dream' properly launched. Here, again, in our youthful exuberance and keen desire to get the show started we compromised in certain directions. Obviously we would never get one of the big managements to do this for us: established West End stars were doing fabulous business in long runs and fortunes were being made. We eventually interested a small management, however: Jack Pemberton and Harry Dubens, who were having tremendous success with the Gingold/Kendall revues *Sweet and Low, Sweetest and Lowest*, etc. at the Ambassadors Theatre. They decided they would present it – provided we found half the backing.

The backing for a small West End musical in wartime was infinitesimal compared with the magnitude of the sum required today; at the same time, it must have been comparable, and the added risk of raids spoiling business, to say nothing of a bomb blitzing the show, made the hazards of quicksands seem like a safe harbour of refuge! However, we did find half the backing; Betty and I provided one-quarter, the solicitors of our personal company found a quarter, and Pemberton found 'angels' for the rest. Charles Hickman produced. Bobby Roper designed the costumes and Berkeley Sutcliffe the décor. Betty wrote the music and lyrics and devised the show. Van Phillips did the orchestrations and conducted the orchestra and a most excellent cast was engaged, with Phyllis Monkman starring as comedienne. There was also Avril Angers, an up and coming soubrette-cum-comedienne who was at that time beginning to make a name for herself on radio, and Billy Tasker, who had been in the *Fol-de-Rols* with me and had played many small parts as well as understudying and playing for all the leading musical-comedy stars in London. The comedy material was supplied by many writers, including Alan Melville and Hermione Gingold, Desmond Davis and Harold Purcell.

As with all theatrical ventures, at one moment it was all happening, at the next it was all off. The dickering went on for a long time from the end of *Magic Carpet*, when John Blore, Firth Shepherd's musical director, had been so enchanted by one of Betty's numbers, 'Memory Knocks at the Door' (since published by Chappell), that he personally made an orchestration of it and had his orchestra at the Princes Theatre play it to Firth Shepherd, until Jack Pemberton had agreed to do it. It took in all, I suppose, a matter of eight or nine months. Tours were taken up and cancelled and radio series kept waiting or prematurely advanced, and the personal plans of a young married couple were put in a very confused state of flux. By the time the management decided on production, Betty and I had also decided on production, and the result was that Jill had already been rehearsing her first appearance for three months by the time the first rehearsal of the new show began! Betty, mindful of the old adage the show must go on, mindful of the stop-go attitudes of management, besides being a superb trouper (I was afraid that word would get into this book at some point!) and a woman of resilience and great courage and ambition, said, 'Of course we will go on with the show!' And we did.

The first day of rehearsal came; it was the first day that the Germans launched the doodle-bug or buzz-bomb (V1) blitz over England. They rained incessantly on London while we rehearsed. The choreographer fainted. 'You have no idea, ducky, what I'm going through!' I had not, of course, but I knew what Betty was going through. We were rehearsing in the enormous old Stoll Theatre in Kingsway, which had started life as an opera house built by Sir Oswald Stoll. We all decided to take no notice of the bombs unless one came very near and sounded particularly ominous, and then we would, without fuss and not interrupting the rehearsal, move towards the outside walls of the building; then, should it be struck and the roof cave in, we would stand a better chance of survival if we were near a strong wall. We did this little silent operation many, many times. Each time we heard the thunderous noise off we would silently go to the side of the stage. It occurred to me suddenly that these excursions were occurring at very regular intervals. They were. The noises we were obeying parrot fashion were the sounds the trams made as they travelled through the tunnels under Kingsway. (This is now the underpass used by cars; every time I use it I am back at those rehearsals!)

Charles Hickman was a highly strung and nervous man. Beads of perspiration appeared on his forehead and upper lip when the alert sounded. He shook all over, but not for one moment would he let those wretched bombs intimidate him or deflect his attention from the production. We greatly admired his courage and control under the most awful conditions.

Because of the doodle-bugs all the London shows closed or moved on tour to the provinces, and it was only because I bludgeoned and screamed that we were able to get our management sufficiently alerted to book us four dates to tour the show: the Theatre Royal, Nottingham; the Prince of Wales, Cardiff; the Embassy Theatre, Peterborough; and the Kings Theatre, Southsea, which is where we opened. Once out of London we thought we would have some respite from the doodle-bugs, but, of course, Southsea was well within range of the French coast and we were still under fire. We thought we would stay outside Southsea and Portsmouth and be really clever and miss the bombs. We stayed at Fareham. Fools! We were not to know that Fareham was more of a target than Southsea.

The show, however, did well at Southsea. There was quite a lot wrong with it. Some of it was very good. We had written one most marvellous sketch, Betty's idea and largely concocted by Hermione Gingold. The V1s had sent London scurrying back for shelter down the Underground railways again to sleep in the two- and three-tier bunks erected along the platforms. Hundreds, possibly thousands, of people had made these bunks into their very homes – their own homes having disappeared in smoke from incendiary bombs or into thin air from explosives. In the sketch a tier of bunks had been made a home-from-home, and Phyllis Monkman and I, as two awful East End crones, were installed with curtains and Victorian pelmets with bobbles of red plush, family photos hanging round the family aspidistra, and the cage of the family canary. Billy Tasker was a dreadful little boy scoring the rudest bulls'-eyes with a catapult. Phyl and I sat on our bunks looking, as it were, at the place where the trains would run through, discussing our neighbours, their relatives, their relatives' activities, and Hitler and his activities and what we'd like to do to him with all the imaginative detail of the Cockney East End. Every time we led the chat up to a very rude and hilariously suggestive moment, the noise of an underground train was heard and drowned our obviously ribald repartee. We also played the Desmond Davis opera sketch which I mentioned earlier, and a whole lot of good comedy material. At Nottingham we played next to the Empire where Max Miller was turning them away, such was his drawing power, and helped us to fill our theatre. It was also here that he helped us to find another sketch which we badly needed.

The logical and sensible course of action would have been for us to stay on tour for several more weeks. In the four weeks we had already played we had roughly taken enough to defray our costs. An extended tour of a few more weeks would have given us enough in the kitty to brave badly bomb-affected business in London; and there was always the hope that the Second Front invasion would root out and annihilate the flying-bomb launching sites. It was really a matter of playing for time. However, we had only been able to book four weeks, the rest of the West End was on tour, and no more touring dates were to be had. On the other hand, we could have any London theatre we liked. It was very tempting, and alas Jack Pemberton was tempted. Although we had a good full orchestra with Van Phillips at the helm, we were an intimate show and a small theatre would have suited us best. Especially with bombing going on, it would be easier to fill a small one. But Jack Pemberton was too ambitious and chose the Palace Theatre. It was much too big for a show of our kind –

indeed, our scenery was not nearly large enough for the Palace, though with judicious 'masking' we were able to hide the smallness of the staging. There were two other shows in the West End when we opened: The Windmill, which never closed and which was accompanied solely by piano and drums, and Ralph Lynn in a farce which did not have the expense of a musical accompaniment. We had a cast of about twenty-five and an orchestra of sixteen. When we arrived in London from our triumphant tour we were to open in the middle of the week after the odd rehearsal or two. The bombs were still raining down. I had a 'first billing' clause in my contract which meant, in effect, that no one was to be billed above my name or be billed in bigger-sized print. There, outside the Palace Theatre on that vast frontage when we arrived, in letters several feet high, was the name Phyllis Monkman, with mine underneath. It had to be changed in accordance with my contract; the goodwill between comedian and comedienne, a vital ingredient in any comedy show, was hardly existent!

Our advance booking was negligible. The majority of our audience consisted of troops stationed in London, and the greater proportion of these were Americans. James Agate, the doyen and most formidable of the critics, said:

> *Keep Going*, the new revue at the Palace Theatre, is bright, quick-moving, reasonably entertaining, and competently and professionally acted. The programme tells us that it is devised, written, and composed by Miss Betty Astell. Does this suggest two Cowards in the field? No, but it points to a possible Coward and a quarter. While the lyrics are fair – perhaps 'bored' is not the rhyme Tennyson would have chosen for 'Maud' – the music is remarkably tuneful; the Tudor pastiche, accompanying words said to have been written by Anne Boleyn while awaiting execution, is extremely clever. My own view is that the stuff was probably composed by the bluff King himself!

Well, I can assure James Agate's shade that the bluff king had nothing to do with the composing at all. Betty did it on our piano and in our drawing room at Welwyn. Anyway, as James has now joined Hal in Heaven he no doubt will have been told.

There is a fire station opposite the side of the Palace Theatre, and we would sometimes hear the alert for the bombs go off before the wail of the air-raid siren. Then we would hear the nauseatingly loud throb of the bomb engine. This engine would then cut out and the bomb would drop and devastate. Somehow you felt safe if you could still hear the engine, and the louder it got, so long as it didn't stop its clamour at the crescendo, in a way the safer yet more vulnerable you felt; you knew it was in your area, was aiming at you, but yet might still pass over and land on some other unfortunate. It was a veritable Angel of Death, and something we must not talk to the young about today for fear of boring them; but this story I must tell.

The effective pastiche which had so pleased James Agate, of Henry VIII on Richmond Hill with his Court, showed us how they were making merry to keep the regal mind off the hour of execution of Anne Boleyn, who that day was in the Tower waiting for her sentence to be carried out. The Jester, played and danced most beautifully by Lulu Dukes (daughter of Ashley Dukes and Dame Marie Rambert), tried especially to divert the King; the Jester, secretly in love with Anne Boleyn, is also breaking his own heart at the same time. The music of Betty's for this dance was exactly right and the whole short scene most moving. We used the scene many times afterwards in our summer shows in various seaside resorts, and the supposedly less sophisticated audiences always were moved by it: some indication, I think, that this was a superb and magic moment of real 'theatre'. Then through a gauze, the woodland scene – of singular beauty by Berkeley Sutcliffe – would dissolve and you heard Anne Boleyn, played by Betty, singing a song (which Anne Boleyn is reputed to have written and composed, and which Betty set for the show), 'O Death rock me asleep' to a harp accompaniment, finishing on a still, small top note of touching sensibility. This, no matter how small the house, always went down very well indeed.

Betty on the night in question was about to begin her song. There was a warning, the song began and a bomb got nearer and nearer. It was a low-flying bomb and its noise was deafening. The still small voice of Betty continued without a quaver. I was to follow this number and was changing in my dressing room for my appearance. I hurriedly finished my change and dashed down the stairs and on to the stage standing behind the frail canvas scenery 'flat' which represented the thick stone walls of Anne Boleyn's cell in the Tower of London. In my mind, so loud was the engine of the bomb, I was sure that this was the one with our name on it and I wanted to be as near to Betty as possible so that we would 'go together'. The bomb got ever nearer and louder (according to the watchers outside, it was only a few feet above the roof of the theatre), but Betty sang her last top note with unwavering clarity. There was an ovation from the audience and Betty, dashing by for the next quick change of costume, caught sight of me out of the corner of her eye.

'Why are you standing there?' she cried over her shoulder. 'Did you think you could catch it?'

And off she went, this lovely wife of mine, carrying my daughter as well, to her dressing room. Later that night over dinner at Old Welwyn Betty's only thought was how amusing it was under the circumstances to be singing to harp accompaniment a song entitled 'O Death rock me asleep'.

There was one slightly amusing effect that the bombs had, and this was that as they came nearer, the members of the orchestra would retreat still playing under the stage, and playing more loudly as they went. The more static members of the orchestra, such as the pianist and the drummer, stayed behind like outposts of the Empire.

To pay a large orchestra and a fairly large cast, as well as the rent for a large theatre, we needed to recoup a great deal of money from the box office. On tour we had paid our costs and there was a little in the kitty. Once the original sum of backing was exhausted in London we had to close; and the sad thing is that, with a little managerial foresight, we could have gone on tour again and come back triumphantly to the West End once the bombs were finally silenced by the successful advances of the Second Front. No tour was booked and close we did.

The bombs killed the show, but not us. And to think the show was called *Keep Going*!

We had one other adventure with Harry Dubens. He persuaded us that he would like us to appear in a new and lavishly mounted pantomime he intended to present at the recently refurbished Stoke Newington Theatre. This was an old music hall in a somewhat dilapidated area which had been bombed and needed a great deal doing to it. He promised it should be all done in time for the pantomime. *Dick Whittington* it was to be, and again we had Bobby St John Roper costumes and a book by Marriot Edgar (half-brother of Edgar Wallace, writer of many Will Hay films and also of the 'Sam, Pick up Thee Mooskert' monologues featured by Stanley Holloway). He wrote a very good book. The costumes were excellent, Nina Walton did her usual excellent choreography, the casting was good. Jean Bell was stage manager, and until the first day of rehearsal Betty and I could not have been happier. There was not a lot of advance publicity, I remember, and obviously no one had worked on the neighbourhood to get party bookings. The front of the house was well done, the seats and decorations were like a new theatre, but once past the iron curtain, once past the pass door or through the proscenium arch, nothing was finished; indeed, there were enormous holes in the roof. It snowed during rehearsals, through the roof and on to the shivering company. There was no heating at all. There was no water. Only one lavatory – dry! We must have had a company of fifty, including musicians.

The builders had not completed in time. Have you *ever* known them to? Dancers rehearse with a minimum of clothing; we had the ancient Nellie Wallace in the cast, and we were ten days from opening. It really was a lovely show, and in spite of the arctic conditions (this was the winter of 1946–7), no matter how we cajoled or bullied Harry Dubens, we could get no further with the building of the stage. Retrospectively, my opinion is the builders had done as much as they were paid for, and as no more money was forthcoming neither was the work. One is sufficiently loyal to one's public. The first Christmas week was heavily booked, and we decided, come what may, to open the show on Boxing Day as required by contract. I was playing Idle Jack and could wear two pullovers and thick woollen socks under my Kate Greenaway-type panto/medieval costumes, but Betty for her single act wore a marvellous crinoline of net and lace and embroidery and satin and had completely bare shoulders. The snow and the wind fell about her. After four of these horrendous performances, she collapsed with a very high temperature, was rushed home and later rushed to East Grinstead Hospital. The specialist looking after her explained that it was exactly as if she had been found naked in a blizzard, and with extreme luck they might pull her through.

She was in an intensive-care unit with drip feeds and all the usual awful paraphernalia of extreme illness, and I was told to stand by and perhaps prepare myself for the worst. As the conditions of our work had been the sole cause of Betty's extreme illness, and as she was nearly dying, 1 had absolutely no compunction in missing the next two performances until she was pronounced out of danger. The Dubens family, father and two sons, were beside themselves with anger and announced to the audience that Betty and I were 'disposed' and there would be no performances that day. Betty was still very ill and remained in hospital for at least a month and was convalescing at home for many weeks afterwards. I returned to the theatre to be informed by Mr Dubens that I would not be paid because I had not played. Not even for the performances I *had* played. The fact that Betty had narrowly missed death because of their negligence and was still very ill indeed inflamed my reaction to this extraordinary behaviour. I was told this news in the morning. I had come up from Sussex in a small Ford van because I thought it was lighter and better equipped to deal with the snowy roads. With the aid of Jean Bell I went round to all the principal dressing rooms and collected all the main costumes in the pantomime and hung them in my van, drove the van two streets away, put Jean Bell in charge, and went back to the theatre. I summoned Mr Dubens, took him round the dressing rooms and showed him that there were no costumes and therefore the show could not begin. 'When you have paid me,' I said, 'I will have them brought back.' He paid me, and I brought back Jean Bell and the costumes. The show slid on to a miserable finish, and with a flapping tarpaulin of a roof I finished the pantomime. Nellie Wallace didn't even get a cold. It took Betty until about the end of March to recover. We had had our fill of West End managements.

7 Jill

'Like Cleopatra, with Imperial Rome
Prone at her feet, she moves in Majesty
Before their dazzled eyes, and then goes home.
To Kingston Hill and David and high tea.'
                    – Beachcomber (adapted)

My only child, Jill, was born on 8 January 1945. I wrote in my diary: 'Betty gives birth to Jill. Betty, the poor sweet darling, has a bad time and the daughter weighs 6¾lb. It is 3 weeks too early but so welcome. I am the happiest man alive.'

Jill was to have been born in a St John's Wood nursing home with a Harley Street specialist in attendance, but as she decided to rush things (come to think of it, she still is inclined to do things in a rush!), she was delivered by our local doctor at a nursing home in Welwyn. That morning I left home quite early to travel to Birmingham where I was destined to begin a month's variety performances at the Hippodrome, sharing top of the bill with Billy Cotton and his Band. I went by train from Euston, which stopped at Watford, and a very old friend of mine, Kenneth Hemingway, joined the train. He had been an insurance office boy with me and we had bored each other to death with our ambitious enthusiasms. I wanted to be an actor, he wanted to be a writer.

We naturally were delighted to see each other and had a great deal of personal news to discuss. These conversations I kept interrupting by saying that I must have food poisoning and would he excuse me, and again and again I kept going to the end of the corridor because of these excruciating stomach pains. But I just could not relieve myself of them. Please note that I knew nothing of Betty's activities whatsoever when I left home. As far as I was aware I was not to be a father for another three weeks. I was so glad Ken Hemingway was with me, otherwise I would have had no witness to this odd example of telepathic sympathy. When I arrived at the theatre in a snowstorm there was a telegram for me. There was a similar telegram for one of Billy Cotton's bandsmen to announce the arrival of his daughter, and we did two hilarious shows. I travelled home that night in the snow and was only able to be with Betty for an hour before I had to go back. This journey I then undertook, with a longer visit on the Sunday, of course, through deepening snow, every day for a fortnight. Betty was really

very ill, and although I had little enough strength myself at the end of the fortnight I was able to give her some during my short visits.

On 8 May 1945 – four months exactly after Jill's birth, I wrote at Welwyn:
'The war is over. I write this with the windows thrown open to a magic May
night – not a curtain drawn – London is making merry and we can see the bon-
fires – for all like London being blitzed . . . We listened tonight on the radio to
the cheering and the festivities and the celebrations but out here in the country
we have been quietly thankful . . .' Then I go on to write: 'Quite the most magical
little personality is Jill; so sweetly pretty, so pink and white with the brightest
blue eyes. Oh God, she does make Betty and me so happy. So very very happy
with a tender glow. I'll never forget her first smile – the sweetest, merriest
creasing!'

When Jill was six months old, we moved from Old Welwyn to East Grinstead.
What a glorious setting for an idyllic childhood this was. It had the most
beautiful gardens and a spellbinding view: a view to the south, taking in great
tracts of Ashdown Forest and broad fields and little Sussex farms – a view for
twenty miles or so of unspoilt English landscape. The garden had dells of
rhododendrons, thousands of bulbs, herbaceous borders, shrubberies, rose
gardens, sweeping lawns and tall stately cedars. There were rockeries naturally
fitted between tall banks of Sussex sandstone, two ponds, two summerhouses;
one of them tucked away in a rhododendron wood with its own miniature
cottage garden and wicket gate, old red Sussex tiles for a roof and mullioned
windows. Inside, taking up almost the whole of the space and facing the iron-
studded ancient oak door, was an inglenook fireplace, and in the winter we
would have huge log fires blazing in it, the flames reflected on real old willow-
pattern plates displayed on an Elizabethan Welsh dresser of oak. We used to
light this fire for cocktail parties on Sunday mornings, walking the guests through
the bulbs and rhododendrons to get to it. One little bit of the garden opposite
the cottage gate had a patch of bracken, and I never ceased to try and eradicate
it, and never ceased to delight in the golden-haired croziers as they rose almost
visibly from the peaty soil, so quickly did they grow.

My enthusiasm for this garden has taken me a long way from Jill, but I can
see her in the summer: aged perhaps two, stark naked but for a white linen
poke bonnet on her very blonde curls, sunning herself and racing Betty's jolly
spaniels across the lawns with our sedate second Scottie bringing up the rear.
It was a child's heaven.

When Jill was about two years old, she had one of her impossible days which
climaxed by her throwing a jar of marmalade at her mother. With food rationing,
this was unforgivable. 'This is the moment,' I said to her mother, 'when I shall
have to use corporal punishment for the first time.' I took my offending daughter
to her bedroom. I took down her drawers and I applied, so softly to her
bottom that she didn't murmur, a soft leather-soled bedroom slipper. I re-
adjusted the drawers, placed her upright again (she had been face downwards
over her Victorian father's knee!), took hold of her hand and led her downstairs.
Betty met us at the bottom of the stairs, and to rub the insult of the chastisement

and the message of the correction in she said to Jill, 'And are you not ashamed?' 'Yes,' said Jill, 'I'm very ashamed of him!'

When we left this for the water mill in Ashdown Forest, Jill was about six and I was most fearful that she might fall into the pond or, more dramatically into the weir, and be swept away and drowned. So I had it all fenced in with chestnut paling and she never, ever fell in; there were countless times, however, when she ran into the house and called to her mother, 'Daddy's in the pond again.' There was one moment when I had removed the fencing and levelled the banks and was driving, as I thought most expertly, the motor mower. It took me all too swiftly into the pond. They are heavy things, motor mowers in a pond, and the family were laughing too much to rescue me; had not my sister dragged me out I would be there yet!

Because of Betty being in the theatre with me, and many of the engagements being in the provinces, it was an absolute necessity to have a good nanny for Jill. I well remember that, no matter how long the journey, we would travel home every weekend to be with her. She had a Norland Nurse right from the beginning, and over eight years or so had five different ones. They were always leaving to get married. One of them produced a son who played rugger for England, and another went to Australia. Another is married to a court official at St James's Palace. There was a nervous elderly one who did not marry. She was very sweet and devoted to Jill. She spoke in little anxious squeaks like a mouse on fire. They all write to us still and were all such good friends to have in the house, unexpectedly so from their brochure, which advised 'Norland nurses are not expected to carry coals'!

By the time Jill went to school – she had a French governess who also was a jolly lady, who practised her English on us all, which is perhaps why Jill still cannot speak French – the first one we chose was a local PNEU School and it was excellent. It was a bit like my Miss Lansdowne's, only with a slightly larger staff. Jill loved it and learned with pleasure.

She grew out of this and went, as a day pupil, to a larger school in a distant part of Ashdown Forest. Alas, the teaching was less imaginative and it was from this time that she ceased to apply herself to any subject which did not appeal to her. On looking back and realizing how passionately fond of the theatre Jill is, we should have sent her to Elmhurst, where she would have had a full artistic and theatrical education, together with a normal school curriculum, as well as the company and friendship of many theatrical progeny. But we wanted her to have the chance of meeting more ordinary children, of more ordinary parents, to widen her horizon, and to become something honest, like a seamstress.

On the other hand, there were school performances through which we parents were expected to sit. (It's one of the hazards of being a parent.) There was a Nativity play at the second school in which Jill was just an 'extra'. The other 'extras' were all dressed as Arabs, in rather dowdy Arab clothes, but when they got to Jill they had run out of costumes. She was dressed as Puck. For the whole of the first scene the producer had insisted on poor Jill standing with her back to the audience and her face up-stage. This was just as well, because Jilly's expressively amusing face as Puck in the middle of the Arab urchins would have been too much for me. At long last the curtains were drawn for the interval. The stage for the first half had been an empty one – we were expected to imagine the scenery. Once the curtains were closed, however, a great bustle and activity ensued behind them. It was as if the chariots for *Ben Hur* were dashing around the tiny platform. There was a stomping, and stentorian instructions were given. Steps and ladders were thumped across the stage. The curtains bulged expectantly at times, as though what must be enormous pieces of scenery were being dragged on. 'We may have been a bit empty for the first half,' the activity seemed to foretell, 'but wait and see what a magnificent set we have for you in the second.' After what seemed half an hour of banging and crashing (in reality, it was twenty minutes), the curtains parted. Before our astonished and expectant gaze there was the same empty space surrounded by the same curtains – but pinned to the back curtain, and almost in the centre of it, was a cardboard star sparsely coated with glitter and measuring 6 by 6 inches.

This reminds me of the bishop who had sat through a complete *Midsummer Night's Dream*, played entirely by the girls of the school of which he was Chairman of Governors. He praised the girls' performance in his speech of thanks, saying, 'This, I think, is the first time I have ever seen a female Bottom.'

In about five productions Jill was only ever chosen to be a member of the chorus. Betty seemed almost to welcome this because she was so amused at my fury. I decided that a blow should be struck for our prodigy. The producer rather stupidly *almost* gave her a part. She was cast as the Princess's handmaiden. The costumes in this play were to be provided by the parents. The Princess on the night of the production was as adequately dressed and as regal as any busy mother could knock up for an end-of-term concert. Her lowly maid was, however dressed in the most magnificent costume, as worn by Betty in a pantomime finale as the Princess, costing, even in those days, well into three figures, to say nothing of almost every piece of stage jewellery Betty possessed.

One of Jill's happiest friends at this particular school was the granddaughter of the local squire. He was a legendary figure who, we were told, had made a fortune out of rubber or tin or oil in some distant land and, because of being 'in trade', had had to resign all his directorships to marry into 'the gentry'. One finds this difficult to believe even twenty-five years ago, but you may well imagine that a local comedian and his wife were *persona non grata* at the Big House. Noticing that Jill not only was a great friend of his favourite granddaughter, but seemed to speak without a local Sussex accent and to have nice manners, he was inclined, at last, to relent; he nodded to me in church some Sundays when he thought of it, and eventually asked me to have a drink one evening when fetching Jilly home from the grandchild's Christmas Party. It was a very grand party and had been a great success, particularly because of the professional conjuror from Harrods who was now packing away his props in the great hall as I entered with my host. The conjuror looked up as I came in; he was an old friend of mine who had done countless shows with me in my concert artiste days. ''Ullo, Cyril,' he beamed. ''Ow are yer?' I was even more delighted to see him than he was to see me; we had a lot to say to each other about old times. I am afraid I rudely forgot my stuck-up host in my enthusiasm for old friendships. The millionaire got rid of me as quickly as he could and we never met again.

Jill ran away from her second school one day and got a lift home, five miles across Ashdown Forest. Happily the headmistress rang to tell us of the tragedy, just as Jill skipped down the drive and I could see her from the window as we spoke. Happily, too, the car she waved down for the lift contained a kindly retired couple who were out for a drive over the forest and were only too pleased to deliver her safely to us.

I had opened a fête at Battle Abbey School the summer before and been delighted by the beautiful old buildings in their great gardens and by the happy atmosphere which seemed to exist between the pupils and staff – presided over by a charming youngish headmistress. They were kind and understanding, especially in her first few agonizing weeks as a boarder, but she was always looked forward avidly to Sunday when we fetched her home for the day – she called it being 'let out of prison'. She would bring several other girls with her, then, after a huge lunch, Betty would be left to entertain them while Jill spent a happy afternoon rummaging through her belongings, taking the dogs out and completely ignoring her friends as though they did not exist.

I think she was as happy there as she would have been at any school, but when she left the headmistress looked considerably older.

She left Battle Abbey when she was seventeen, and that same week joined our summer show, which was appearing at Sandown, Isle of Wight, the next day. We gradually edged her way into this scene and that. She was quite useful by the end of the summer. From then onwards she became very useful indeed. As we were actor-managers, she would help Betty and me in whatever chore needed doing at the time. She would help Betty with the wardrobe, she would help me in a get-in or a get-out with the scenery. She would be invaluable in the theatre while we were producing, first, as a dogsbody, and then with more responsible work. At the age of twenty we left her in sole charge of a pantomime at Harrogate where a new lighting board went up in flames on the opening Boxing Day performance, and she went on stage, shining a torch into her face, and entertained a restless house for half an hour until they could get started again.

Once, when a week before pantomime rehearsals we were told a very strong clown act was unable to appear and all children's specialities all over the country were booked for pantomime, it being so near to Christmas, she stepped in and said she would do a clown act, and so 'Clown Bolly' was created. A clown act that has been a most lucrative side-line for Jill ever since, be it in pantomime or for Harrods, like my old friend, as a children's entertainer.

She is truly dedicated to her work and does not mind the most menial task so long as it is in the theatre.

We played Ugly Sisters together at the Ashcroft Theatre, Croydon, some years ago, and Jill had wigs made exactly like mine. Her face had a red nose and other eccentricities accentuated in an exactly similar make-up to mine. She was a young, tiny, version of me. As we took our call in the finale a child in a piping voice yelled out, 'Oh look, they've both got the same face.' It was exactly what we had tried to achieve. Poor Jill! Her whole life is in the theatre. If a stage needs scrubbing she will happily do it. I have a vision of her in one of our panto-mimes when she played the Fairy – this, with us, needs a statuesque personality and an ability to speak verse well, and she is the possessor of a lovely speaking voice. As well as the Fairy she was also playing the Goose. There she was speaking verse, in a still, compelling, one might say Shakespearian voice, her ankles and feet hidden from the audience – and seen from the wings the yellow scaled legs and webbed feet of the Goose sticking out grotesquely from the classic white folds of her Grecian gown. She would then, as a Fairy, disappear in the way pantomime fairies do, and reappear in the wings in the prompt corner and admonish a flyman for being too far down on his short! (Note: Two ropes hold up scenery cloths on a steel barrel – the one nearest to the fly gallery is 'the short' and the furthest 'the long'. They must be equal.)

When Swanage built themselves an enchanting little theatre called the Mow-lem, Betty and I presented for them their first three summer shows with Peter Hudson as the comedian and Jill as the comedienne. She not only managed the show and played the female lead, but she created some very funny characters. Our idea was to use it as a vehicle for her, and she gained a lot of valuable experience out of it.

She has a strong comedy cabaret single act and she has two very effective after-luncheon or after-dinner speeches – one on 'Wigs' and one called ' "Louder and Funnier" said my Father'. She can stage manage anything from a small show to a large one. She has produced and created the lighting for several pantomimes and has even served a stint in a West End box office while doing cabaret shows in the evening.

As I write this, she is appearing at the Albery Theatre as the Undertaker's wife in a revival of *Oliver*. There is always a great deal of unemployment in the theatre – only about 20 per cent of us are in employment at any one time. And I am proud to say that Jill is always one of the 20 per cent.

8   Radio

'Whether in heaven ye wander fair
Or the green corners of the earth.
Or the blue* regions of the air
When the melodious winds have birth.'
                                        – William Blake

Early in 1936 I was auditioned twice by the BBC. One audition was for straight drama, and one as a comedian. Two letters followed, one from each department, heavily edged in black. The nation was in mourning for George V. The Drama Department were delighted: 'Your various accents are impeccable, your voice is admirably suited to a microphone, we will put you on our casting panel and you will be hearing from us at frequent intervals.' The Variety Department were sorry, but though they quite liked my performance they did not think a great deal of my material. They didn't actually say I was too tall for the microphone, but that was the only thing they left out. Now, I have never ever broadcast for the BBC Drama Department and I have been a frequent broadcaster for the Variety Department for forty-two years. And this is how it came about.

Radio in 1936 was as important to the public as television is today. It was the one way to a quick fame. The big names in those days, who were largely stars because of their radio appearances, were The Western Brothers, Elsie and Doris Waters, Leonard Henry, Stanelli, the Two Leslies, Tommy Handley (yet to achieve his ITMA fame), Claude Dampier, Ronald Frankau, Mabel Constandurus, Harry Hemsley and his imaginary family of children, Muriel George and Ernest Butcher, Stanley Holloway and Sandy Powell ('Can you hear me, Mother?'), Norman Long and John Tilley. Then there were the giant names like Gracie Fields and George Formby whose fame was further enhanced by radio, and then the strong music-hall names who were also a success of radio: the Houston Sisters, Wee Georgie Wood, Billy Bennett, Nellie Wallace, 'Hutch', Jimmy James, Harry Tate and Florrie Ford among them. Then there were names like Claude Hulbert and Enid Trevor, Jack Hulbert, Cicely Courtneidge, Jeanne de Casalis, Douglas Byng, Nelson Keys and Vic Oliver who were stars of the West End Theatre but who contributed very strongly to the success of radio

* Surely not in Sir John Reith's day!

variety. Television had begun, but it was little more than a toy, and because of the power of the sound side of the BBC it as yet had very little encouragement as a rival.

There was one very important variety show on Radio at this time: John Sharman's production of *Music Hall*. There were very good revue-type radio musicals, written sometimes by Eric Maschwitz and sometimes by John Watt, who was to succeed Eric as the Director of Variety. I think *Monday Night at Seven* (later to become *Monday Night at Eight*) had just begun or was about to begin. It was a variety magazine programme which had no audience, and lacked punch because of it, but still was a popular programme. There were outside broadcasts from various venues like concert parties, West End theatres, and cabarets and some from provincial cabarets (these produced by Leslie Bridgemont). *Band Wagon*, the first of the weekly series of radio shows, had not yet started. Even Workers did not start their Playtime until the war began.

That summer, Harry S. Pepper, who was to become a dear friend both professionally and off stage, decided to do a series of broadcasts from the summer shows round the coast. He started at Margate and worked his way round via Folkestone and Dover to Hastings, Eastbourne, Bognor, the Isle of Wight, Bournemouth, Torquay and then north up the west coast to Blackpool and back down from Ayr in Scotland via the east coast resorts of Scarborough, Bridlington, Yarmouth and so on.

These outside broadcasts were compèred by Davy Burnaby – 'Mr Concert Party' himself, who starred in *The Co-Optimists*, the most famous concert party of all, which ran for years in the West End. Each town like Margate would have two or three shows; one of them possibly alfresco, and it was from these shows that a well-balanced mixture of singers, instrumentalists and comedians was chosen to make a radio show. Greatrex Newman, that clever showman, had three shows round the coast – Hastings, Eastbourne and Sandown in the Isle of Wight – and he persuaded the BBC to produce an hour-long broadcast from all the *Fol-de-Rols*, the BBC engineers linking up the three far-flung resorts and, as a grand finale, a melodramatic comedy sketch with the hero in Hastings, the villain in Sandown and the heroine in Eastbourne, together with special audience reaction coming from each theatre. This was a clever gimmick for those days, and it also caught the imagination of the listening public. In consequence, the show had a very large listening figure. To appear on this show was to be noticed, and this was how, in 1936, I made my first contribution to radio. I don't think I impressed the public a lot with my first Odd Ode, but I was not only asked to do Empire broadcasts during that summer season. ('How did you manage that,' you may inquire, 'when you were playing every night on the stage at Hastings?' Well may you ask. There was no recording of programmes in those days. If you wanted to entertain the Empire, you had to get up and do it at the time the Empire was awake, and it was not difficult to reach London by car to broadcast at perhaps three or four in the morning. I remember compèring a star bill once with Nellie Wallace, Harry Champion, Harry Tate and

Ida and Cyril. This was my bridal attendant's costume.

My mother, Maude Mary Fletcher, née Ginger.

My father, George Trevellian Fletcher, in 1916.

1937. Were the early Odd Odes as innocent as I looked?

Left to right: Harry Hemsley, Tommy Handley, Elsie Day, Rupert Hazell and Cyril after a Music Hall broadcast in 1938.

Trying out jokes on a Scottish audience, 1938.

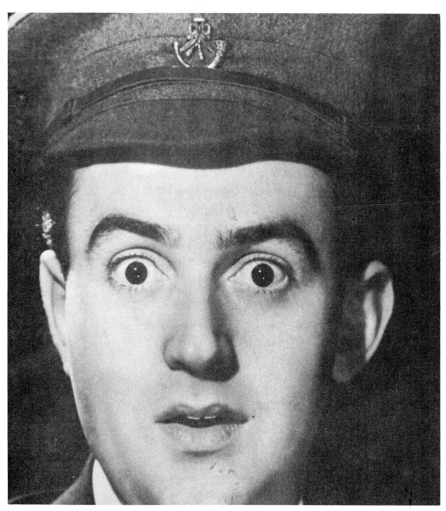

'Dreaming oh my darling love of thee' . . . (see over)

By now a television veteran — at Alexandra Palace in 1937 (Photograph BBC).

Me in my Fol-de-Rols uniform — Arthur Askey used to call them 'Greatrex Newman's perishing coachmen'.

Betty Astell — the girl I dreamed about.

Betty Astell as Nell Gwyn in *Thank You Mr Pepys,* Savoy Theatre, 1935.

Our marriage at St Martin-in-the-fields, 18 May 1941 and, below, our engagement picture.

When radio was the Number One medium I looked like *this*. Now that television is Number One I look like — ah well, *That's Life!*

Betty always looked beautiful.

Our first home at Old Welwyn which we shared with (left to right) Tuppenny, George and Nipper.

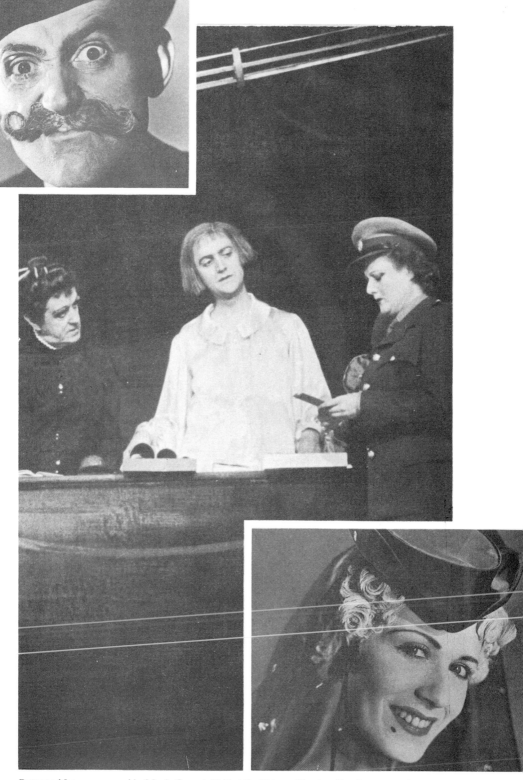

Betty and I as we appeard in *Magic Carpet*, 1943 at the Princes Theatre. On-stage scene shows me (centre) with Sydney Howard (left) and Betty Warren.

The Garden House, East Grinstead, and its view to the South to Ashdown Forest.

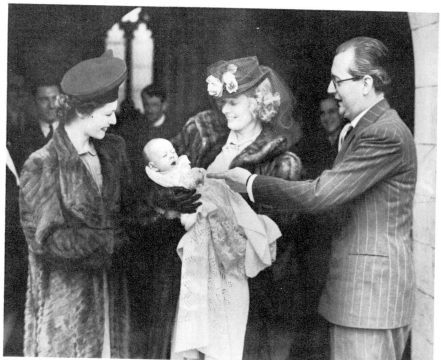

Jill was born on 8 January, 1945 and this picture shows her christening, with proud parents and her Godmother, Anna Neagle.

Xmas 1947. — The Garden House East Grinstead

Christmas Greetings from Cyril, Betty, & Jill.

Our Christmas card for 1947.

Motherhood — my favourite picture.

Portraits by Edward Seago.

Cyril and Betty in J. Arthur Rank's film *A Piece of Cake*, 1948.

Cyril as Mantalini in the Ealing Studios film of *Nicholas Nickleby*, 1947.

Pictures of our own 1960 production of *Summer Masquerade*. 1. The girl in the Crinoline Gown.
2. I only did it on the stage. 3. Being 'fed' by Ian Francis 4. Sitting it out with Betty Jumel.

Betty in Summer Masquerade at Scarborough.

Cyril and Betty surrounded by the cast of *Summer Masquerade* and, below, their home at the time — Newbridge Mill, Colemans Hatch, Sussex.

Pantomine. Photograph of me with Betty and with Peter Reeves in *Mother Goose,* and Betty, alone, as *the* Sleeping Beauty.

Edward Seago designed *Mother Goose* for us. Above shows the Hall of Gold and the photographs below are of Betty with Terence Dalaney and Mother Goose herself, an unlikely Lady!

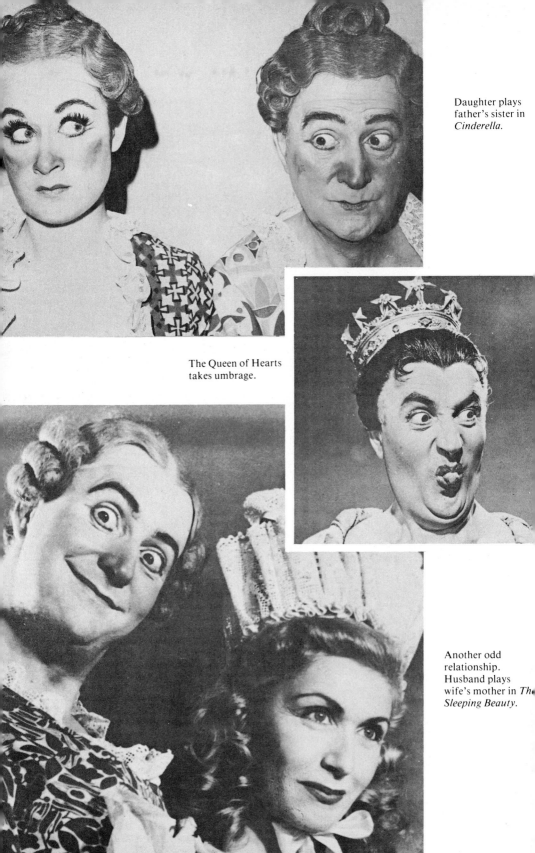

Daughter plays father's sister in *Cinderella*.

The Queen of Hearts takes umbrage.

Another odd relationship. Husband plays wife's mother in *The Sleeping Beauty*.

Jill welcomes Her Majesty the Queen Mother to the Concert Artistes' Benevolent Fund concert on 13 February 1956, watched by her proud father, the President.

Vic Oliver, Sir George Robey and Cyril at the last performance of John Sharman's BBC Music Hall.

The Dove House, High Hurstwood after our renovation, and inside, Betty with one of her many embroideries.

Our only daughter Jill (I could only go through it the once!) as she is today. The other photos show additional 'family' and our present home which we built as a replica of The Dove House.

Esther Rantzen, producer and presenter of BBC TV's *That's Life,* surrounded by her team, and nursing baby Emily.

The silly bees here are Cyril and Bob Price in ATV's programme *Gardening Today.*

Florrie Ford, and having to wake up each one in their dressing room as their turn came round.) But immediately on my return to town I did several broadcasts of various kinds, revues, musical comedies and cabaret-type variety shows. It was this winter that I did my first broadcast from the Royal Bath Hotel in cabaret for Leslie Bridgemont.

My second broadcast was memorable. It made history of a kind. It was called *Masculine Fame on Parade*. It was written by Joan Young and produced by the late Douglas Moodie. The abdication of King Edward VIII was imminent. The papers were full of Mrs Simpson and there were Mrs Simpson headlines on all the placards. I spoke a line giving an impression of that very funny comedian Claude Dampier, who had a character – to whom he often referred – Mrs Gibson. He used to leer at the end of the story, anecdote or whatever with a drawn-out and meaningful, 'Yerse . . . Mrs Gibson.' I did the anecdote and then John Rourke, as veteran and frequent broadcaster (nephew of Kate Rourke, my erstwhile Professor at the Guildhall) was to say, 'Yerse . . . Mrs Gibson.' With the headlines on his mind, to his great horror he found himself saying, 'Yerse . . . Mrs Simpson.' The show was immediately taken off the air – it was peak listening between eight and nine, and martial music from a brass band on a record was put on 'due to a lapse in taste in our advertised programme, etc.' All night the American newspapers rang me for my comment. I eventually sat at the bottom of the stairs in my parents' home (the phone was in the hall) until the early-morning newspaper's arrival and confirmed that this nightmare had actually happened. A full and formal apology was made on the Radio News, and John Rourke was suspended from broadcasting for six weeks. How different today when fun can be made of the Royal Family intentionally on radio and television and not, as this was, purely by accident.

The next spring we did a series of *Fol-de-Rol* broadcasts in each of which I did an Odd Ode. This series took over when the first series of *Band Wagon* was rested. At the same time from Radio Luxembourg, which was the principal pre-war commercial radio channel, I started a series of weekly broadcasts called *The Kolynos Variety of Smiles*, where I compèred a programme of variety and musical records with spots of my own slotted in. These I recorded in a Kilburn studio four at a time, and they were broadcast for over a year. All of this helped to make me known, but I still had not caught the public ear enough for them to be talking about me or for me to become a 'name'.

This was to happen in the summer of 1938 when I appeared in the usual BBC relay from the *Fol-de-Rols*. This time from Llandudno. A packed house roared with laughter at 'Dreaming of Thee'.

In London that autumn my diary was full of dates: mostly concert appearances and private cabarets; sometimes five a night. There were several more broadcasts and Ernest Longstaffe gave me another opportunity to do 'Dreaming of Thee' in *Palace of Varieties*. Douglas Young and Nan Kenway were to become a well-known radio duo at this time. They had been very helpful to me my first season as a concert artiste and they asked me to join their first series of radio programmes called *Trolley Bus* – it was not run on the old lines. These were done in the

D

afternoon so they did not have a very big audience, but they were the forerunner of Nan and Doug's famous radio series, *Howdy Folks*.

In 1939 commercial radio continued to use me. *Kolynos Variety of Smiles* was followed by *George Payne's Tea*:

> G.P. Tea-Time's On the Air.
> Cyril Fletcher's the compère.
> Cyril Fletcher that is me
> By courtesy of George Payne's Tea.

And the programme was a bit like that too! From Llandudno again at the end of 1940 *Fol-de-Rol* season I did a weekly 'Tommy's Letter Home' called *Dear Muvver*. I forget who wrote the scripts, so I cannot blame him! They were broadcast every Saturday night and were done in my dressing room at the Pier Pavilion without an audience, and they sounded flat, as all comedy does without its attendant laughter. The BBC Variety Department then decided to give me a comedy series with Henry Hall and his Orchestra, to be based on a series of scripts from America where a ventriloquist and his dummy were largely featured. (Could these have been Edgar Bergen scripts?)

It was by now wartime and shows must have been difficult to cast. For the ventriloquist they booked an ancient variety performer who had never broadcast before and who had never read a script before. Obviously his agent was good. I think this sort of thing happened a lot with the BBC in those days. An example of their naïve faith occurred when the new concert hall was built in the then new Broadcasting House. Every attention was given to its acoustics, its décor and its technical equipment. A most wonderful piano was built especially for the finest broadcasting concert hall in the world. The trouble was it was too large to get inside the doors of the hall! And yet both doors and piano had been measured; so it was decided to construct in feather-light balsa wood a replica of the piano case so that they would find, without damage to the fabulous original, the exact angle at which the piano could be eased through the door. At great expense, and with great attention to detail, the replica was constructed in a BBC workshop. When it was completed it was too big to get through the workshop door!

When an organization grows to the size of the BBC, so many things like this must happen. In the early days of TV I remember we were doing a programme while some Foreign Potentate was being shown over the studios as the actual transmission was taking place. 'If I pull that plug out,' said the BBC Mogul to the Foreign Potentate, 'the whole programme goes off the air!' As he said it he pulled out the plug to demonstrate and off the air we went.

We need not have worried too much about the booking of the inadequate ventriloquist, for I find, written in my diary at that time: 'The first two shows were blacked out because of raids and were never heard.' By the third show, Dick Pepper was brought in to write an original script and a great comedian, Charles Heslop, replaced the ventriloquist. The next three shows were heard all right, but three shows do not make a successful series.

After this there were several separate broadcasts – and I joined Nan and Doug in *Howdy Folks* for a series of six.

The BBC had moved its Variety Department from London to Bristol, so these last broadcasts of mine had been from there. Nan Kenway and Douglas Young were installed at Claverham, a village on the outskirts of Bristol, towards Weston-super-Mare, and they took me under their wing and found me a lovely cottage where my hosts were Mr and Mrs Corp. So I was living with the Corps next door to their daughter and son-in-law, whose name was Needham. He was an undertaker. It was from here that I performed in a Home Guard Charity Concert at the Colston Hall, Bristol, on 5 October. This was a grand affair; Henry Hall was conducting Adrian Boult's BBC Symphony Orchestra and Adrian Boult was conducting Henry Hall's Orchestra. Also on the bill was Jack Warner, Kenway and Young and a very beautiful singer, Betty Astell, and I've already described how it led to my first riding lesson! Bristol was often bombed and I was terribly worried about Betty, who was in the BBC Repertory Company. I remember calling for her once, ready to drive her out of Bristol to safety after her broadcast. The actual show was taking place in a bombed-out church. The BBC often ran out of studios, so often were they bombed. There was no electric light – they had candle stubs around the microphone and it was a macabre scene. The sirens had already sounded; a raid was imminent as they finished their lines in the play. I bundled Betty into my Sunbeam Talbot sports car coupé, which had a canvas roof, and we had one air-raid tin helmet between us. I wanted Betty to wear it: she me; so it travelled on her lap. I steered with one hand, the other over my head saying to the German planes droning above us, 'You cannot hit me. I'm a civilian,' as we drove southwards out of Bristol. Why the authorities did this I'll never know, but they would close some of the bridges south. You never knew which, so it was a lengthy race out of Bristol to the comparative quiet of Claverham. It was arranged, therefore, with the help of Nan and Doug, that they would live in my cottage at Claverham to chaperon us on the rare occasions when I was there – Betty being permanently with the Repertory Company, and me doing variety dates all over the country mixed in with my broadcasts.

It was thus that we managed to see each other six times before we were engaged and another six times before we were married.

I'll interrupt this saga of sound broadcasting now to tell you of Betty's first meeting with my mother. On the way from Bristol to London we first stayed the night with Betty's mother at Camberley in Surrey. She had a streaming cold and a very red nose – much redder than any comedian, but she made me very welcome. The weather for the next day was what is known as a silver thaw. It decides to thaw, wet is everywhere and then a heavy frost sets in. The world becomes an ice rink. Only love-sick fools were using the roads at all. I was driving very slowly indeed, and it took us a long time to reach my parents' home in Friern Barnet. Instead of being grateful that we had survived the hazards of the road, my mother was furious at the effect of our slow progress on her cooking and, flinging open the front door to two hoar-frosted travellers, proclaimed (indeed, these were the first words Betty ever heard her utter), 'You're late!'

My mother took me aside on this occasion. Into the kitchen would be more truthful. 'How d'you know this girl loves you?' she said. 'She may be acting. She is an actress.'

'And *her* mother is saying,' I replied, 'how d'you know this man loves you? He's a comedian. He may just be being funny!'

The next day we had a luncheon at an inn at Barnet where they did very passable meals. (One had to shop around with wartime rationing!) During the meal we had left my Scottie in my car. When we came out and I opened the car door, the little dog immediately ran, tail and rump wagging its warm welcome to Betty. 'Even the dog!' said my mother.

Immediately after our wedding our availability for broadcasting was spoiled by our twenty weeks' tour in the road show *Dreaming of Thee*. Also tired of being bombed so constantly at Bristol, the BBC Variety Department had migrated to Bangor in North Wales. In wartime, with no petrol for long journeys, this necessitated travel on heatless, foodless, wartime trains, often delayed by bombing: a most hazardous and time-consuming journey. Whereas we could often fit in a Sunday show at Bristol from a provincial town where we had played a week's variety or from London, the trek out through the mountains to Bangor took too long for one to get back to one's next town on the Monday in time for a band call at the theatre. What we did do was to try and take a week out and fit in as many broadcasts as possible during that week.

It was most important for stars whose *raison d'être* was radio to continue to broadcast, and in wartime radio was a wonderful comfort and companion as well as an entertainment. This fact was often difficult to din into the heads of greedy managements and agents. One was a draw in the theatre because of the radio, and for that reason they wanted your name on the top of their bill to fill their theatres. With every theatre in the land open and crying out for attractions, there was an unprecedented demand for the true drawing name. I remember we were once booked to appear at a cinema in the middle of Suffolk somewhere, a really small town, and that every single seat of a quite a large house was sold out twice nightly two weeks before we arrived. There was also the constant demand which one simply could not refuse for performing for the forces and the hospitals, and various wartime good causes. So there was a constant battle with agents and managements to make sure that one should broadcast enough.

Beatrice Lillie, one of the funniest of all comediennes, went to Bangor like the rest of us, and as she and her companion got into the train for her long arduous journey back to London a fan dashed forward and gave her the most enormous bunch of spring violets and primroses. Miss Lillie was most effusive in her thanks. She said, 'How kind of you. When I get home I shall so treasure your kind thought that I will press every single bloom separately between the pages of a book and keep them.' As the train drew out her companion said, 'When on earth will you find time to do all that flower pressing?' To which Beatrice Lillie replied, 'Oh, my dear, never.'

We next broadcast several comedy series with Dick Pepper writing the scripts and Harry Pepper producing them. They were usually for runs of thirteen or twenty-six weeks and were often on a Sunday peak spot between eight and nine in the evening. For several, we had that benevolent and benign comedian, Dave Burnaby, with us, and then we had that very clever music-hall star, Billy Russell, for some more. Betty used to sing every week (as 'The Girl in the Crinoline Gown', which was her billing on the halls) 'A Song to Remember'. I used to do Odd Odes every week, and I also became an extraordinary little-girl character (surely a forerunner of St Trinians) called Aggie. 'The Lodger' was resurrected. He had appeared for a couple of years throughout the early months of the war in *Monday Night at Eight*. (These were good funny scripts, but without an audience did not sound lively enough. We would record them in batches of three or so at a time in London, so it helped to keep our names in front of the public while touring.) I used also a Mummerset yokel character. This last was developed into a double act with Billy Russell playing the other part; they went under the names of Bob Under and Ben Tupp.

I cannot remember whether it was Stuart Hibberd who made the well-worn but gloriously funny clanger of announcing, 'The Band of the Royal Arse Hortillery', but it was certainly he, doodling one day when he was about to announce a programme Betty and I were in, who wrote this delightful Clerihew:

> The odd odes of Cyril Fletcher
> Are never lecher
> -ous. Otherwise Betty Astell
> Would give him hell.

Then came innumerable *Workers' Playtimes*, and I compèred the first series of *Mid-day Music Hall*. A new team of young comedy writers, Bob Monkhouse and Denis Goodwin, then arrived on the scene, and for Leslie Bridgemont; who had through the war years become the most successful of all comedy producers, we began a very successful but oddly fated series called *Mixed Doubles* in the late 1950s.

This was the first of the domestic series of comedy shows in which two families lived side by side. Betty and I were one family and Michael Denison and Dulcie Gray were the family next door. The scripts were excellent and the listening public liked it. It was during this series that Betty became very ill – indeed, we must thank Pat Hillyard, who was Director of Variety at that time for his kindness in postponing the beginning of the series so that Betty could take part. She again became very ill and indeed nearly died. Her place was taken by Ann Crawford, who played my 'sister' for another series, but she then became ill herself and later died. The series was still a success, and as such was a valuable property. So it was decided to bring it back, this time with David Nixon as my brother and his wife Paula Marshall as my sister-in-law. Again success. Now we were to record a special edition for Christmas, and we recorded to a most appreciative audience one lunchtime. David was appearing in pantomime in the north, and Paula with her car full of props drove off to appear with him.

Each was driving separately. She was involved in a car smash and killed. We decided not to do another series of *Mixed Doubles* on radio.

In 1950 I went to Germany to entertain the troops in a special BBC Forces programme. It was an all star-bill with Ted Ray, Monkhouse and Goodwin (who wrote the scripts), Diana Dors and Carole Carr, Geraldo and his Band and the Stargazers. Most of them went by air, but I was not allowed to fly at that time because of my mastoid ear and certain pressures. I went by boat. Diana Dors also came by boat – the plane had flown the previous day and I think she must have had film commitments. It was, they said, the roughest crossing since 1880. It was March and bitterly cold. No civilian boats had set out that evening, and this naval ship was venturing forth only because it was an old ice-breaker and would survive. Or so they told us afterwards. You will remember from earlier that I am a poor sailor. I was all right until I went to bed. I woke up to a douche of cold water. The porthole had caved in and an icy sea was lashing my bunk, me and the clothing in which I was to perform next day. I didn't care. I was going to die anyway, and the sooner and quicker the better. The ship was rising and falling twenty feet at a time all night. In the morning, as we disembarked, we were told that even the Admiral on board had been sick, the Captain of the ship certainly had; and every passenger; all except one, Diana Dors, who, with every blonde hair in perfect place, walked calmly down the gangplank in front of me. Brandy on the train quickly restored us and we embarked on a most enjoyable trip.

We performed at Hamburg and two other venues further east, and I remember one very funny incident after I saw what I thought was a particularly amusing and Germanic contraption in a jeweller's window. It was an instrument for the removal of hairs from nose-holes and ear-holes, and as I had no German whatsoever I had to indicate with gestures to the shop assistant exactly what it was that I needed out of the shop window. As I commenced this routine, Denis Goodwin came into the shop. Denis was an unbelievable giggler, especially when reading a script which he had written in front of a microphone; he seemed suddenly to enjoy anew his own comic invention, and, indeed, sometimes could not get any words out at all because of his suppressed laughter. Imagine this awful man, then, giggling at my elbow while I was endeavouring to explain to a fat, bald and, worse still, hairless German shop assistant what I wanted from his window. The more bewildered and angry became the German, the more confused and antic became my mime, and the more hysterical became Denis Goodwin. Eventually we ran out of the shop, pursued up the street by the fist-shaking Deutschlander. So I never owned one of these unbelievable instruments.

During the 1960s the BBC's peak variety show on a Saturday and repeated on a Sunday was *Variety Playhouse,* and it was compèred by Vic Oliver. In the summer it was replaced by *Holiday Playhouse* and I compèred this. It used to run for twenty-six weeks. It was recorded every Sunday and I did it over many years. Pat Hillyard, the Director of Variety for Sound Radio in those days, was like Eric Mashcwitz, a complete showman. He had very many radio successes during his long reign as Director, Pat, who had managed and produced for most of the West End managements before the war, was a frequent visitor to America, both New York and Hollywood. He brought many a New York stage success to London and *vice versa*. He is a personal friend of international stars such as Bob Hope and Danny Kaye, and though he is now retired, we continue our valued friendship with him and his ever-young wife Babs.

My last radio series as such has extended over very many years. It is, or was, one of the longest running radio shows ever: *Does the Team Think?* It ran for years and it was the Crazy Gang of the air. The team originally consisted of Ted Ray, Tommy Trinder and Jimmy Edwards, whose idea it was. We used to record thirteen at a time, and I used to be the other member of the team in eight of them – the other five being awarded to other assorted comedians. Then, for the latter years, Arthur Askey took over from Tommy.

Ted Ray was the kingpin and was very, very quick indeed. He had a computer mind which dredged up the exactly right old tried and true joke required for the immediate moment, and allied to this had a rapier-like wit and speed of delivery which enabled him to come out with original witticisms as well. Jim, on the other hand, was often Gilbert Harding-like in his simulated rudery to the questioners, and frequently the funniest of the quartet. Tommy Trinder has always thrived off the interrupter and the latecomer in the theatre and cabaret, and is the best ad-lib man in the business. For club work and cabaret he is a marvel, and though his gravel voice and cockney accent convey a general air of roughness (which made him a darling of the old variety theatres), his mind is often sophisticatedly comical and surprising in its originality. Arthur Askey one might describe in the same way as I described Ted Ray – not quite so quick, perhaps, but nearly so, and even more lovable with it. The joy of Arthur is that he is a tiny mercurial performer – always brightly on the simmer – and because of his years so knowledgeable in his technique. Arthur happily admits to being born at the turn of the century. That's not bad billing for him either. 'The Turn of the Century'. He doesn't look a day over forty-two!

So you can imagine how, with all this ebullient talent on the panel, Cyril could hardly get a word in edgeways. We used to record for an hour and the brilliant producer, Ted Taylor, would edit the tape until he had whittled it down to a very funny show and half an hour's rudery left on the cutting-room floor. I often have thought what a wonderfully funny long-playing record could have been made out of those miles of wasted tape. MacDonald Hobley, the first of the TV announcers at Alexandra Palace, was the question master and was very good indeed at it. If, for some reason, he could not manage a particular recording, we always noticed his absence and his masterful way with the often wayward comics. But Ted Taylor, so much younger than any of us on the team, was a very firm producer, and often read the riot act to the team, who frequently needed it. The whole show, as evidenced by its extraordinary longevity, was most popular. The mixture in every way seemed exactly right.

I was asked many years ago to open a fête in East Anglia. It was a Conservative, fête, and I do like to do things of this kind as well as possible, so I phoned the Conservative Central Office and got all the necessary gen to open a fête of this kind and I made, that sunny June afternoon, an impassioned plea on behalf of the Conservative Party. Now I must explain here a technical term which we comedians use called a 'running-gag'. Now a 'running-gag' means that you mention something early on in your dissertation, not necessarily funny in itself, but if repeated four or five times, by the fifth time it should be getting near hysteria. Those of you old enough to remember ITMA will remember a good example of a running-gag: 'Can I do yer now, sir?' The running-gag I chose on this occasion was that Harold Wilson was the worst Prime Minister since Lord North, and at a Conservative fête this went down very well indeed. Every time I said it there was a yell of delight. It went so well I felt quite sorry for Harold. After all, he was not there to reply. Harold Wilson didn't go to a lot of Conservative fêtes.

When it was all over I was taken by Lord Whoeveritwas into his spacious mansion in whose grounds the fête was taking place and he said, 'Fletcher, you must give it all up.' I said, 'Well, I've never done it before but I felt it all went rather well!' 'No,' he said, 'give up the comicking and take up politics.' I said, 'My Lord, you are being most unkind. There is a programme on the radio which has been broadcast for many years called *Does the Team Think?* in which I am one of four comedians and cannot get a word in edgeways. What chance would I have,' I said, 'with 600-odd comedians?' He then said, 'But you made a terrifying mistake!' I said, 'I expect I made several.' 'No,' he said. 'Sitting next to you on the platform was the only living descendant of Lord North!'

There is a sequel to this. I did my one-man show, *After Dinner with Cyril Fletcher*, at Dillington House at Ilminster in Somerset for the South-West Arts Association. Dillington House is a stately home which has been bought by the local authority and run as an arts centre. They have made a charming little theatre out of some Georgian stables, and it is a joy to play. In my show I have a routine about opening fêtes as one of the hazards of being a comedian. I tell this story about Lord North. When my show was over we were being royally entertained by John Pick, the Artistic Director, prior to staying the night there. 'D'you know,' he said 'that Dillington House is the family home of the Lord North family? 'And further,' he went on, 'you are sleeping tonight in Lord North's bedroom!' Needless to say I did not sleep. There were wee timorous beasties in the wainscot. Owls hooted, and the shutters went *bang, bang, bang* all night. It was the North wind!

When I was born, radio was in its infancy, almost its inception; and from this completely new and revolutionary medium of communication I was to lay the foundation of a whole career as an entertainer. I was a pioneer of radio comedy. If those of you who knew radio in the 1920s and 1930s will think back, you will realize that I was the very first person on radio to do 'funny voices'. Mabel Constanduros and Harry Hemsley had both performed whole families of voices; but these were very clever impersonations of real, credible people. Mine were the first ridiculous caricature voices. 'So common,' said my mother. 'We hoped you would be a straight actor.'

I wonder how many thousands, perhaps tens of thousands, of letters I have received, enjoyed and answered in my years of broadcasting. One poor soul wrote to me every single day for two years. Her husband used to write occasionally to apologize. Then, suddenly, one day he wrote and said all would be well. I would no longer be bothered by her daily letter as she now had a fixation for the new local vicar.

Auntie BBC is often caricatured and is much maligned by many, as any giant corporation must be. I have been pretty continuously employed by her, both for radio and television, for forty-one years at the time of writing and I have always found her fair and generous. And, what is more important, she has stamina! And Auntie BBC can be sentimental too. When I had completed my fortieth year as a broadcaster in 1976, for the Variety Department, Con Mahoney, the Director of Variety, was kind enough to invite me to share in a programme to celebrate the fact; and all my kind radio friends had their say about me. This sort of thing is very touching and it made not only a memorable milestone for me, but, in a way, is a double reward, because I was paid for all those broadcasts over forty years and really I should be thanking them.

9   Other Men's Shoes

Here in the country's heart
Where the grass is green,
Life is the same sweet life
As it e'er hath been.
            – Norman Gale, 'The Country Faith'

You will remember Shuvver – the senior mistress at Woodhouse School: now she is retired she devotes her time to working for St Joseph's at Chiswick – a hospital and home for incurable women patients run by Sisters of Mercy.

I was in East Grinstead some years ago; it was raining and I had gone into my favourite bookshop. I was suddenly aware that I was being stared at between a copy of *Salome Dear, Not in the Fridge*, by Arthur Marshall (who is also one of my favourite schoolmistresses) and *Haunted England* by Christina Hole. To my delight it was Shuvver. 'You have been sent,' she said. 'I may be dripping,' I said, 'but not sent.' It transpired that St Joseph's had been granted the time on radio for a charity appeal and she wanted me to do it for them. I tried to dissuade her as I realized the responsibility should I fail: to be granted a charity appeal by the BBC is a wonderful opportunity and I was worried lest this chance be muffed. She is a persuasive lady, and I agreed to go and see the hospital and see if I could manage what she wanted. It was a much easier task than I could have imagined. All I had to do in my appeal was to describe the loving devotion of the dedicated people who looked after the patients, and the quiet, happy, bravery of the patients themselves. This I did, and the resulting flood of money was the direct result: mites from old-age pensioners, large sums from the wealthy and a generous cheque from the late Dame Sybil Thorndike, bless her.

This appeal was heard by Miss Joanna Scott-Moncrieff, who produced the *Ten to Eight* programme on Radio 2 which used to be so much more aptly and poetically named *Lift Up Your Hearts*. Would I do one for Christmas week? she inquired. She had a very nice idea: it was for several well-known voices – Joyce Grenfell and Athene Seyler were two of them I remember – to give a list of their favourite things, sounds, scents. So I did one and greatly enjoyed doing it.

Then Joanna said would I do some more? This worried me a great deal. Who was I to preach, anyway? So I said, 'May I think about it?' Several weeks afterwards I hit upon the idea to use as a theme 'Other Men's Shoes'. It was a simple idea of getting listeners to imagine that they were in the shoes of special categories of people, not necessarily unfortunate people, and to understand their particular problems and outlooks. Then, having understood a little the problems or the angle of these people – the middle-aged, the unwanted, dreamers, worriers, were some of my titles – the listeners could treat these people, themselves in some cases, with a little more understanding.

We did the six and we were inundated with mail. This I found very worrying. Some wanted my help, others just copies of the script, and some just letters of appreciation. It was the 'help needed' ones which were worrying. Here, like the charity appeal, was a case when one could do a great deal of harm as well as possible good. I answered them all to the best of my ability. But they still worry me.

The reaction justified some more, and I did another six. They resulted in more mail – quite a fantastic amount which took more than the fee I received from the broadcast in postage and secretarial assistance to answer! This I didn't mind, but again I had the worry of giving advice which I'm sure is not a comedian's job and needs specialist handling. Also it brought a spate of invitations to preach in churches all over the country. This I really could not do. Not only did my professional commitments make it impossible, but the idea, to my mind, was too gimmicky and wrong. And don't laugh – you cannot believe the number of invitations to open church fêtes and bazaars!

Having told you about them, and in case ten to eight is a bit early in the morning for you, here is one of the talks from *Other Men's Shoes*.

1. *The Failures*

I want today to try and get into the shoes of the failures, although it is difficult enough to find out who has failed. You may fail at one thing, but succeed at another. There was the pop star who had enormous success, and because he had to keep up with this success and because he was travelling every minute he wasn't performing, he couldn't stand the strain and took to drugs. His success meant his failure. There was the chap who failed his exams twice and was so annoyed with himself that he reorganized his whole outlook, worked his whole life to a plan and a method, and became an enormous success because of his first failure.

I don't think you've failed if you've tried. You've failed if you've just sat down and allowed everything to go by you and over your head, and haven't tried to better yourself in any way – either materially or spiritually. But if you have made an effort, even if you haven't succeeded, you haven't failed; you've tried, and the chap who tries can always make a habit of it. Now there's a great joy in anticipating success, in anticipating the achievement of something that you've worked for, passing an examination, getting at long last a house for yourself, winning the local tennis tournament, winning a flower-show prize. I remember once I won a gold medal for elocution – many years ago – and I dashed home so pleased and so thrilled to tell my parents, and they were out. Now if you've had to struggle, the greater your success. If you've had a great struggle and only achieved a little, then your success is measured by the size of the battle, not the actual amount that you have achieved. So comparative failure can in reality be great success.

Some people achieve success by walking across a room. Some of you failures, you chaps who are sorry for yourselves because of what fate has done to you, get into the shoes of some ill person who finds a great success and sense of achievement in just managing to struggle across a room. And those who think that they're failures are more than likely enormous successes in other spheres – you may not think you have succeeded at the office; look at your wife's smile as she greets you when you come home. There's success – you love each other. What about the trusting hand and the voice that calls you mummy and daddy? The trust they have in you – that's success. And though you may feel that you haven't made a great name for yourself, or made a great deal of money, or contributed to the world's progress in any outstanding way, you may have given other people a great deal of happiness. You may have a large number of friends, you may be held in great regard and affection by your neighbours and your fellow work-people.

But then you are going to tell me to get into the shoes of the complete failure. I personally refuse to believe that he exists. There is surely never a complete failure. There must be some gleam, some facet of success. Time and again, you are going to tell me, this man has been struck in the face by fate. Time and again, no matter how hard he works, some calamity has put him back where he started. And I'm going to tell you that this man is a success. He's a success because he goes on trying. He is winning by the mere fact that he doesn't give in. Every failure will teach him something, so long as he doesn't falter, so long as he keeps going. He is winning and he'll eventually have his reward. Try and get into his shoes and help him. And some of his heroism will wash off on to you. It's the very strong ones who briskly go marching on, getting on with their lives, who don't realize sometimes what a terrible struggle it is for some people.

2. *Delights*

Some years ago I was asked by the BBC to broadcast a private collection of the things which give me pleasure. I had never assembled my particular delights before and I'm going to do so again, because they are part of that extraordinary rag-bag which is the mind of Cyril Fletcher, comedian and countryman, the saucer-like depths of which this book tries to explore.

All these particular things fill me with intense pleasure. I am filled with a warm glow by them – and even if I'm in an irritable frame of mind, the sight and sound of them will bring on a benevolent attitude to life once again – in the same way that some things give me exactly the opposite feeling: when David Frost pronounces 'edgercation'; also birds in cages, radio announcers who say 'strenth', hired suits at weddings, and zoos.

Here is a collection of some pleasurable things: the smell of a field of clover, of honeysuckle, the sound of water slap-slapping on the side of a boat when I am lying in it with the warm sun on my face. The first cuckoo . . . the dawn

chorus . . . and 'the music of the moon, sleeping in the plain eggs of the Nightingale' . . . June twilight.

> The twilight comes; the sun
>   Dips down and sets,
> The boys have done
>   Play at the nets.
>
> In a warm golden glow
>   The woods are steeped.
> The shadows grow;
>   The bat has cheeped.
>
> Sweet smells the new-mown hay;
>   The mowers pass
> Home, each his way,
>   Through the grass.
>
> The night-wind stirs the fern,
>   A night-jar spins;
> The windows burn
>   In the inns.
>
> Dusky it grows. The moon!
>   The dews descend.
> Love, can this beauty in our hearts end?

That was written by John Masefield. A great deal of his poetry gives me
immense pleasure. My daughter read it in the broadcast – her voice reading
poetry gives me pleasure.

The *Moonlight Sonata*, a child's laughter, and although she's no longer a
child, my daughter's laughter. The velvety sight, and touch, and smell of the
darkest possible red rose; they are almost black in the innermost recesses of the
petals, and the perfume is heavy and exotic.

The most pleasing sight of all – my wife's smile.

Shakespeare spoken well: the John of Gaunt speech in *Richard II* especially
pleases me because I love England. The distant sound of bells in the quiet
country.

I love the virtues of truth, beauty, tolerance, fairness, generosity, courage,
faithfulness and good taste; and although you may have all of these without
knowledge, add knowledge to these virtues and you have wisdom and, I would
imagine, a complete man.

There are two sayings which give me not only pleasure but a wonderful
feeling of well being. One from the Communion Service (and going to early

service on a summer's morning to some small and ancient village church is another pleasure). 'Come unto me all that travail and are heavy laden.' (I do hope they will not alter these words in the new version of the prayer book.) I have been a most fortunate person and my troubles have been few, but when Betty was very, very, ill some years ago, these words were a great positive comfort. Also, when I was a boy and went to the parish church at the end of our road in North London, the vicar was then old and much loved, and his blessing was the shortest possible and because of that the most effective. Whenever I hear it, I feel warm and happy and comfortable. 'The Peace of God which passeth all understanding be amongst you and remain with you always.'

10　TV

> With glazed, Cyclopean, exophthalmic stare,
> I cast my spell upon the family,
> Each member slumped in his accustomed chair
> Or lolling comatose on the settee.
> – Arthur Marshall, *Salome Dear, Not in the Fridge*

In 1976 I appeared in a BBC TV programme which celebrated forty years of television. Forty years ago was when a regular daily television service was started, and it is something we as a nation do not boast about enough. We were the first country in the world to have a regular television service, and I personally am very proud to have been one of the pioneers. As I was twenty-three at the time, and provided I am sufficiently careful when crossing the road, in a few years' time I shall be the only man alive who performed at the birth of television. I'm not sure that I hanker after this honour. The years disappear as quickly as the scenery once a TV play is over, and even when I think young I can't go below fifty!

Betty can go further back than this. She even appeared for Eustace Robb when he did experimental programmes from the basement of Broadcasting House earlier in the early 1930s. There is a plaque commemorating this in the basement of Broadcasting House now. No, not Betty's appearance: the early television programmes. This was when one wore white faces and navy lips – why bother to book beautiful Betty!

In 1936 there were two main studios at Alexandra Palace, a corridor alongside and a small studio for news. Miracles of organization went on with some shows, when, for instance, Eric Robinson might be conducting the orchestra in one studio with headphones and a monitor set while the opera singers he was accompanying were singing in the other studio. There were not a large number of technicians and one knew them all. I knew the make-up department when there was a staff of two. There were two lady announcers, Jasmine Bligh, who was fair and friendly, and Elizabeth Cowell, who was dark and reserved. Leslie Mitchell, the man announcer, was tall and handsome and had a booming voice and personality – he did everything; and even 'fed' comedians. There was a magazine programme called *Picture Page* with, at the switchboard, an unknown Joan Miller, who became the famous dramatic actress, and presided over by Joan Gilbert. Cecil Madden booked all the artistes and arranged the variety programmes. The programmes lasted for one hour every afternoon and were then repeated every evening. The afternoon programme was really a rehearsal, both for the artistes and for the technical crew.

There were approximately 10,000 viewers, all in the London area. Viewers would often ring us up and talk to us about the programme just finished, and one got to know some of them quite well. 'A wonderful programme tonight,' said one old girl to me on the phone. 'It's all in colour.' 'In colour,' I gasped – remember this was 1936. 'Yes, all in the most wonderful shades of red.' 'Switch off!' I cried. 'Your set's on fire!' And it was! We had a set at home. My father and I shared the cost of it. Reginald Smith, who had been a comedian in the Charlot revues in the West End, was one of the first variety producers. The big variety names were banned from television by George Black of the General Theatres Corporation, so the new medium had either to make its own stars – which it did quite quickly – or rely on the stars of the West End theatre. I compèred a series starring Nelson Keys, the great revue comedian, whose work, being neat and full of comic detail, was ideal for the small screen. This show was written by his son, John Paddy Carstairs; another series I compèred starred Douglas Byng, who was a very, very funny man and much loved by everyone, the leading and, as yet, unknown soubrette in this series being Valerie Hobson.

I did many single performances in variety shows of all kinds, usually reciting Odd Odes. If the bus which was used to ferry artistes from Broadcasting House out to the outlandish suburban reaches of Muswell Hill broke down or was delayed by fog, I was often called in at short notice to hold the fort. Indeed, the wardrobe department kept a special white evening-dress coat for me to wear on these occasions. Alexandra Park was only about two miles from my home in Friern Barnet; I was almost their resident comedian.

The first TV pantomime was *Aladdin*, actually written by Arthur Askey, but he could not star in it himself because he was appearing in pantomime in the theatre. Bill Stevens was Wishee Washee, Aladdin was played by Queenie Leonard, and I think the dame was a woman, because female impersonations were not allowed before the camera. Douglas Byng only wore wigs, furs, fans and furbelows over an immaculate dinner-jacket suit – but, to be perfectly fair, this was the way he appeared in cabaret. I played my first pantomime part ever in this production as the Emperor of Morocco. I still remember some of my immortal lines, which, for some reason best known to myself, I spoke with a broad North-country accent!

> I'm the Emperor of Morocco
> I'm nearly going bats.
> Because my gorgeous palace
> Is overrun with rats.
> I've had a very busy day
> Before I go to slumber
> I fain would see my damsels dance
> [*Claps hands to arouse harem*]
> Let's have a nifty rumba.

I also remember sharing a dressing room with an unknown young man called Danny Kaye, who was appearing in a cabaret show at Grosvenor House or the Dorchester Hotel (I'm not sure which), but he was complaining about the poor response he was getting from the late-night audiences in the West End. How differently they responded later.

The television service was suspended during the war, and Betty and I were very happy to be among some of the first artistes to return to it afterwards. There was a magazine type of *Monday Night at Eight* programme, devised and produced by Ronnie Waldman as a TV version of the radio show. In this Ronnie compèred 'Puzzle Corner', which was very popular. Because he had produced a 'Lodger' sketch in *Monday Night at Eight* on the radio for three years, it was resurrected for television.

On the halls, Betty and I had performed a most successful Lodger sketch in my road show, *Odes and Ends*. In it the Lodger, returning from the war, went to stay with 'Mr and Mrs H.' in their newly acquired prefab house. The Lodger was very similar in character to Michael Crawford's Frank Spencer. Everything he touched fell to pieces and he had a very similar apologetic cockney voice. I am not suggesting for a moment that Michael Crawford's fabulously funny character owes anything at all to my 'Lodger' – I don't suppose Crawford was born then – and there are a lot of these weird fumble-fisted thrust-upon types about in real life. Anyway, when the Lodger knocked at the prefab door it promptly fell inwards, he put his foot through the floorboards, water taps gushed gas and *vice versa*. When we did the sketch on the halls, every time the Lodger sneezed the sound of a lavatory flushing was heard off stage. It was amusing to see the effect on the audience. It was quite obvious from their reaction to the sound of the first sneeze that they thought, nudgingly, that some actor had used a lavatory in close proximity to the stage, and they were overhearing noises they were not meant to hear. The second time it happened they began to twig, and the third time brought a yell of delight. What also amused us was the fact that on the side of the stage a very solemn-faced assistant stage manager would be busy clanking a real cast-iron cistern handle before a microphone, and then emptying a garden syringe full of water into a bucket. This, when done three times solemnly and with a perfectly straight face by a serious and fully grown man, is extra-ordinarily funny. As a bit of 'business' it was considered somewhat vulgar in those days for the halls, and was certainly not allowed on television. Also in the sketch we perfected an old piece of pantomime business when a character – in this case me – as the Lodger leant on one end of a mantelpiece, which acted as a see-saw while a vase at the other end was shot across the room. We were only allowed one 'run through' with scenery and props in those days, which made the actual performance (which was live and not recorded as they are today) even more hazardous. When we did it in the run-through they had used a plaster vase instead of the requested papier-mâché one. Being so much heavier, it did not fly across the set to be caught by a supposedly surprised Mr H. It described a smaller arc and struck me weightily on the head and knocked me out for a moment. The staff on the set were kind enough not to laugh until I smiled a thin watery smile. There was not time to rehearse again with a new vase; so on the actual performance the new vase described a neat arc over my head but this time too near the wall. It struck, with considerable force, an unglazed picture which hung immediately above my head. It fell with a crash, my head coming neatly through the framed picture as a clown's head might come through a paper hoop. A month's rehearsing would never have created so neat and comical an effect.

As the comedy shows were not recorded, any change of costume had to be arranged while some other action was taking place before the camera. Similarly, there was very little time for an elaborate change of make-up. Every scene had to be, as it were, laid out ready on the TV stage and the cameras would move from miniature set to miniature set. The amount of space was at a premium in the studio and sometimes even when it was a show starring a comedian, a straight production dance number would take place in the front of the set, well seen by the studio audience, while a brilliantly funny cameo 'sketch' might have to be tucked away in some obscure corner where the studio audience could see only part of the action and so would lose interest. Then, without the audience reaction, the comedian and his 'funnies' would seem abjectly flat to the viewer, who would, of course, know nothing of the producer or the comedian's dilemma.

When our summer show, *Summer Masquerade*, had completed its third season at Torquay, we had four very strong stage programmes, each of about two hours in length, each lavishly costumed and with smallish scenery and all the comedy which had played successfully before an audience and all the music fully orchestrated for a section of the Torquay Municipal Orchestra which had accompanied the show in the theatre. Also, as our second comedian, we had Harry Secombe (whose first television appearances these were to be). Betty Jumel was our comedienne. Six programmes of an hour each were fashioned out of the four two-hour programmes and were televised for six consecutive Saturdays as the peak show. They were not designed for television, but they were a very cheap way in the days of small budgets for providing effective entertainment. Today, as television, they would be considered rubbish – but they were 'pioneering' rubbish, and there was a lot of good artistic material and music in them, and some of the comedy was extraordinarily successful in a medium for which it was not designed. One comedy sequence which had proved a hit in the theatre was a sketch where Betty and I were at a football match – I as a supporter of West Ham United. (It was prophetic of today's football hooliganism.) Briefly, I was explaining to my wife how a man behaved himself at a football match. There I would sit, quietly explaining the game. Suddenly I was on my feet, fired by the excitement of the action on the field, shouting the odds and creating a commotion – while Betty looked on amazed, dressed in an old raincoat and red beret and looking like any rather downtrodden cockney sparrow. She would ask daft questions and get yelled-out replies, until suddenly she too would get up and dash about shouting the odds. Finally I would run up and down with her head under my arm, her beret pulled over her eyes and her feet scarcely touching the ground. We did this sketch twice on TV during the course of a year or so. Every year the ATS held a reunion at the Albert Hall and balloted for a couple of stars to entertain them. One year, about this time, we were invited. Princess Elizabeth and Prince Philip were the Guests of Honour. Betty, wearing one of her gorgeous crinolines, sang, and I recited Odd Odes. I was appearing twice nightly that week at Finsbury Park Empire, so as soon as my act was over I had to dash back there from the Albert Hall for my appearance in the second house. Betty stayed and was presented. Her Royal Highness mentioned that we had not performed the football sketch. 'We have seen it twice on television,' she said.

'Yes, Ma'am', said Betty.

'The second time you did with all that running up and down, I don't think I have ever seen the King laugh so much.'

One does not realize that there are television sets in every home and that, quite unwittingly, I was a king's jester.

Shortly after Independent Television began we did a half-hour series of shows for Jack Hylton, who presented all the variety shows for Rediffusion, which had the weekend franchise at the time. Johnny Speight wrote some of the material for this, which was quaint and unusual.

For BBC we also did a television version of *Mixed Doubles* with Claude Hulbert and Enid Trevor as our neighbours, theatre contracts preventing Michael Denison and Dulcie Gray from appearing with us. There were other variety shows, including a one-man show of half an hour taken from my stage one-man show.

What's My Line?, possibly television's most popular panel game ever, ran for over ten series. With four panellists in a row, the end one was sometimes changed. It started with Jerry Desmond, then Bob Monkhouse, and then it made a star of David Nixon. I also took the end seat for three whole series. The panel, when I was on it, consisted of Isobel Barnett, Barbara Kelly and Gilbert Harding; with, of course, Eamonn Andrews in the chair. This programme took place on Sunday nights around about 7.30, usually for a run of twenty-six weeks, and it is said that many an Evensong service was hurried through so that the vicar's family could be home in time to view.

Today Eamonn is a good friend and we last met when he said those awe-inspiring words 'This is Your Life', and whilst on *What's My Line?*, I became the busiest Protestant comic performing for Catholic charities there has ever been – in fact, it was I more than Pope John who started this Ecumenical idea! Isobel is one of the most successful speakers on the panel of our lecture agency Associated Speakers (of which more later), and she is a dear friend. Barbara often books me to make personal appearances for her Prime Performers service. But the greatest personality and dearest friend of them all – and I'm sure the others would wholeheartedly and unanimously agree – was Gilbert Harding.

Gilbert was only fifty-three when he died. A delightful book of appreciation published a year after his death, *Gilbert Harding by his Friends*, is dedicated thus: 'To Gilbert Harding whose habit it was for half a century lavishly to bestow both his friendship and his scorn wherever he felt them to be deserved'. A sentence which aptly sums him up. He lived at Brighton, which isn't very far away from us. 'I'll come to lunch,' he would say on the phone, 'if Betty will make one of her flummeries.' And he would arrive, perhaps in the depths of winter on a cold frosty day, in an open tourer car, his face blue with cold but beaming with sheer delight at knowing that he was to be in the company of friends, cosily in the country, with good food and drink and 'conversation'. That was the joy of it. Gilbert did not converse. He held forth. He would talk wisely and long on religion. He would tell you in detail of his latest most embarrassing escapade – the more outrageous the funnier it would be. One of his favourite stories was that of a hostess who said, 'Do have another partridge; there is only saddle of lamb to follow!' He was a first-rate raconteur with a spectacular memory for fact and erudite detail. On form he was the greatest fun in the world. A lot of the time, though, he was a sad and lonely man. He was the supreme champion of the underdog and his great quality was his absolute honesty.

Eric Maschwitz, who had given me my first variety audition and who had turned me down, was, I think, the one who put me on to the panel of *What's My Line?* He was the Head of Variety for television at the time. He had seen me in cabaret before the war, and he saw me in cabaret at the Savoy a week or so before I was booked for *What's My Line?* He had also seen me in my summer show on the Isle of Wight where he had a summer cottage. The world of entertainment is the poorer because there are no longer any Eric Maschwitzes. He was a man of great charm and education and culture. He had style and wit. He wrote most successfully and was Director of Light Entertainment for radio and TV for periods of much fruitfulness. 'A Nightingale Sang in Berkeley Square' is a fitting memorial to his romantic charm. The success of his musical *Balalaika* is an example of his knowing, clever showmanship. He had a flair for living. I once had him as a guest in the Grillroom at the Savoy. Wine was ordered for him· It was 'corked'. I was too young and too ignorant to know this. The way he drew my attention to this without embarrassment, and with such humour and elegance, forever endeared him to me. He also owned a Yorkshire terrier dog who lived to be twenty years old, Cookie by name, and he carried him around on a hot-water bottle rather than leave him alone at home because the dog became distressed without his company. His house in the Isle of Wight (oh bohemian Maschwitz!) was on the side of a cliff, high up, and was dramatically slipping (because the foundations of the cliff were on blue clay) week by week, day by day, into the sea. Windows would fall out – a whole scullery would crash down the cliff – but serenely he would go to bed in this house and serenely he would sleep. I have this horror of heights and would only visit him fearfully in the summer daylight, but he would sleep there blissfully in the dark during a storm!

I wish I were able to put on to paper the flavour and atmosphere of early television. It was small and personal and we all knew each other. I think we all knew that we could earn a lot more elsewhere – in films, on the halls, in the theatre and even in sound broadcasting, the larger and more powerful sister in those days, but we felt we were in on something new and exciting. But only the most far-seeing could realize then its potential power and influence.

At the time of *What's My Line?* and also shortly after Betty and I had looked after HM the Queen Mother, when she graciously attended the concert for the Concert Artistes Association Benevolent Fund, I was invited by the Director-General to be among the BBC's guests when they entertained the Queen Mother to tea at the new TV Centre. I found myself one of the four at her tea-table. The conversation came round to Canada, and how Scottish comedians were so well liked there. 'The reason being that one of the chief exports of Scotland is her people', I said, and then added, 'For which, Ma'am, we English are especially grateful!' She turned on me her sweet beaming smile and my courtier's remark was most warmly rewarded.

One Easter, Francis Essex, a BBC variety producer at that time, decided to book Terry Thomas, Bob Monkhouse and me as the male stars, and Vanessa Lee, Jill Day and Una Stubbs as the female stars. It was an hour-long spectacular and Irving Davis was the choreographer and it was from this show that Betty and I persuaded him to be choreographer for our summer show, which he was with great distinction for some years.

As I discovered at my very first day's rehearsal in the *Fol-de-Rols* as far back as 1936 when I was young and athletic, I was no good in dance numbers. I could get by if well hidden in a general ensemble, and I always made sure that any of my twerp-sichorean efforts were well hidden. This did not satisfy Francis, who was determined that his six stars should all work in a fast and seemingly complicated dance routine to start off the show with zest. Bob was with Jill, Terry with Una Stubbs, and me with that gentle and lovely singer Vanessa Lee, who had found stardom in the Ivor Novello musicals and who was a very competent and stylish dancer. She was very patient with me and so helpful. I began to feel a little confident that in spite of the dance's complicated gyrations I would not let the show and Francis down. Vanessa had worked out a little scheme wherein I was to watch her feet very intently, and from their movement and beats I would be able to dance competently and almost with flair. So much for the well-laid schemes of mice, men, comics and sopranos. We did our last run-through without costumes. Then came the show, and to my horror Vanessa made her entrance looking ravishing in a white dress which came down to the floor and completely hid her feet. This is the reason why Francis Essex, who is now one of the bosses of ATV, no longer requires me to dance but to garden in front of the cameras; but more of that anon.

Another of my stage characterizations was used for a television series.

I had played the part of Lewis Carroll in a one-man show based on the writings of the creator of Alice, and it was devised and directed by Gyles Brandreth. Gyles and I first met in 1970 when I took part in a BBC radio parlour game devised and presented by him called *A Rhyme in Time*. Since then Gyles has become a most successful speaker and lecturer for my agency, Associated Speakers, and I have performed in various 'Son et Lumière' shows produced by Gyles with Sir John Gielgud, Sir Alec Guinness and Sir Michael Redgrave. An end to name dropping! Gyles also devised a twelve-part weekly TV show called *Lewis Carroll through the Looking Glass* in which I again impersonated Lewis

Carroll for Thames Television. They were delightful shows and were directed by Daphne Shadwell, whose laughing father Charles Shadwell was famous not only for his conducting of the BBC Variety Orchestra, but for his ready appreciation of the comedians' jokes which came over to the listening public because of his welcome proximity to the microphone.

Gyles and I have also had a considerable success, I'm happy to add, with a quiz book entitled *The Generation Quiz Book* in which I set the questions for the 'twenties, 'thirties and 'forties (not that I knew much about the 'twenties!', and Gyles looked after the 'fifties, 'sixties and 'seventies.

I was also the very first to broadcast on television *The Sunday Story*. I did several series of these, which were then taken over by my old friend and comical colleague David Kossoff. He wrote his scripts for himself, and they were so good that the religious side of his career has become quite an important one. We all mourn with this thoughtful and religious man the tragedy of his son's death.

One of the merriest guests we ever entertain at home is Malcolm Muggeridge and his quietly charming wife Kitty. As soon as he puts his foot over the threshold he makes us laugh and keeps us merry. One is inclined to forget, because of his present TV religious image, that he was once Editor of *Punch*. Malcolm is great company, and every minute that you are with him is worth while.

Another religious TV personality who lives locally is Lord Longford. I have opened his church fête for him and I have appeared on local brains' trusts with him. Indeed, on one of these occasions Betty called him a 'silly old man'. Arthur Askey apparently has also done the same. He must get used to it. This story, I think, proves that he's not. Lord Longford often goes to Lord's to watch the cricket. One day he arrived at his usual enclosure and the attendant said, 'We're full.' But as he was leaving, a woman asked for his autograph and the attendant, thinking he was somebody important, went across and said, 'We have room for you, sir, after all.'

This pleased Lord Longford, and as he sat there he realized there were a whole lot of other seats vacant nearer the front. He called the attendant over, pointing this out, and the attendant said, 'I'm sorry, they are reserved seats, but excuse me asking you, sir, are you Lord Lambton?' To which Lord Longford replied, 'No, I am not Lord Lambton, and I'm not Lord Lucan either!'

My most recent television appearances have been poles apart. Five years ago on ATV Birmingham I was asked to front and appear in a TV gardening series, *Gardening Today*, which started its sixth year in March 1978, and upon which I will enlarge in a later chapter; and *That's Life*, the lighthearted and seriously valuable BBC consumer programme produced and presented by Esther Rantzen, which has completed eighty-eight programmes in the last three years and which recommenced in the spring of 1978. This too I will enlarge upon in another chapter. I am, therefore, indebted to the small screen for many, many hours of work through the forty young years of its existence, to say nothing of the hours of laughter and years of valued friendships which I have made in television on both sides of the camera.

11   Actor Management

'Sit back and listen to me everyone,
Sit back in your seats and prepare
To hear an old story of magic and fun
And music to gladden the air.
Old is this story; older than me
And I was born before time,
It's as old as the sunshine, as old as the sea
Long before clocks learned to chime.'
     – From the prologue to Betty Astell's *Aladdin*

When the war was over in the late 1940s, the variety managements decided to import big American stars, and the names who had faithfully filled their theatres throughout the war were, in many, many cases, brushed aside. You will remember my overheard conversation between Val Parnell and George Black. After the war George Black died. This was a grievous blow to the variety and music-hall theatre; he was an unparalleled showman with a very sure finger on the public's pulse. It was a loss to me personally; I had lost my champion and the person who had given me many of my early opportunities. Not only were the American names coming in and replacing so many of the old 'tops of the bill', but television was beginning again, and it was obvious that if it should make the same progress it was already making in America, variety, and indeed the touring theatre generally, would suffer again rather as they had under the bludgeoning of the silent cinema and later the talkies. Simultaneously, a whole new batch of comedians and comedy writers, having 'found' themselves with great success entertaining their fellows in the forces, was beginning to make an impact.

Betty and I surveyed this scene as objectively as possible and said to ourselves that, if variety were to succumb, where would an outlet be of earning the same sort of money? Very few people had been able in the war to have seaside holidays; there had been little time for holidays anyway, and many of the coasts – the east and south particularly – had been forbidden areas. 'There is bound to be a boom in holidays,' we said, 'so there is bound to be a boom in seaside shows.' This, if successful, would take up half of our year, radio, television and cabaret the other half, and pantomime we felt might still be a success as everyone would want to take the kids to a show at Christmas.

Another well-considered reason for deciding to present our own shows was this way we would see more of our daughter Jilly. Playing variety all over the country, Betty would often yearn to be home to be with her, and so would I. To be in one place for twelve weeks or more would mean that we could take a house, have her nanny and a housekeeper with us, bring the dogs – in other words a home from home was set up, and, indeed, in the years we played Hastings and Eastbourne (seven years in all) we were able to live at home in Sussex fifteen miles or so away. What joy this was. Through the years we rented some extraordinary houses. On the Isle of Wight for three years we even hired an empty house and furnished it with odd pieces of junk we bought on the island, together with new furniture and antiques, some of which later became quite valuable. In a way it gave us a taste for the value of property and began to exercise Betty's flair for interior decoration, of which more anon.

We decided therefore to become actor managers and present our own summer shows. We would, however, begin in a small way to see if we could do it successfully first with the show built round some other comedian and then try with ourselves in our own show.

The summer of 1946 we were touring in *Odes and Ends*, but the White Rock Pavilion, scene of my first summer season, needed a summer show and we were fortunate in being able to persuade Charles Harrison, a very able summer show and pantomime comedian, to join our first venture. He had been a *Fol-de-Rol* comedian in his time, his work was meticulous and he was very reliable; he also had several good routines and sketches which he had worked many times, and he was known to the Hastings audiences. I also knew him well as an after-dinner entertainer. We booked a show of fifteen artistes. Charles Harrison and Colleen Clifford, comedian and comedienne, a baritone and soprano; Paul Rycroft who had been at the Guildhall with me as straight man and feed; John and Dolly Jackson, who were a husband and wife speciality dancing team; four dancers; a boy soprano who also played the xylophone, Jackie Trevor; with Jean Bell to be manager and stage manager, two pianists and a drummer. Nina Walton, who had been the choreographer with the *Fol-de-Rols* in 1936, happily joined us and eventually was our choreographer for about twenty-five shows in all, including our first Cambridge pantomime, and is still a dear friend. Bobby St John Roper designed and supplied the costumes. They were magnificent and created a standard of dressing and mounting for which our summer shows became justly renowned. Our wardrobe mistress was Gertie 'Malaprop' Holden, who had been a Tiller Girl but had been 'ravaged' by a dog which had bitten her cheek and eye and left her with a damaged duck. She had had fourteen operations committed on her by two sergeants from Harley Street. Her son was in the war as a rolly driver but his foot got too hot through being on the incinerator and he had to become a non-combadore. She complained of too much gaelic in her soup and the bad weather had nothing to do with you and your golf seams, it was caused by people's bad tempers condescending on the air. She had a very old sewing machine, always breaking down through mending delaborated dresses. She once described a costume as 'You know, missus' (she always called Betty missus) 'that one with the marrow bones round the edge' (meaning marabou feathers). The men wore bloaters on their heads in a seaside scene, and when we did the two gendarmes, we wore plockman's 'hemlets'.

Gertie was with us in all for ten years, and towards the end of her time with us we were again playing Hastings for the season, perhaps the summer of 1955. Hastings every year, in conjunction with the *News of the World*, holds a Town Crier Competition. Town criers come from all over England, and it is a fiercely contested competition. Usually the star in the summer show is raked in as one of the judges, and frequently as compère. The festivities are relayed over quite a wide area – the large front forecourt of the pier, around the White Rock Pavilion and throughout the White Rock Gardens behind the pavilion by means of microphones and an extensive Tannoy relaying system. It was from this that Gertie made her best Malapropism of all. And as this is a family show I don't really think I can tell you the story! Gertie, it seems, went to sleep in the gardens that afternoon. When we went into the theatre for the show she brought my clean evening-dress shirt round to my dressing room as usual. 'Did you see the Town Crier nonsense?' I inquired. 'No,' she said, 'I was asleep – then I woke with a start having heard your voice come ever so loud over the Tampax.' I had to keep a straight face.

In 1946 the show ran for fifteen weeks and we were asked by the council to present a show there the following year. That autumn most of the company, with Jean Bell in charge, went to Germany to entertain the troops for another twelve weeks or so. We were in management indeed.

The following summer we decided to present three summer shows, the Hastings one again, this time starring a well-known variety comedian, George Doonan. Charles Harrison and his company, virtually the same as before, toured Butlin's Holiday Camps, one night at Clacton, two nights at Skegness and two nights at Filey, returning to London on the Saturday with the Sunday off, the journeys and shows with a complete change of programme to commence the tour again the next Monday. There is a rather charming sequel to this engagement. Butlin's for the last six years have employed Betty to produce the finals of their Star-Trail Talent Contests each year at the London Palladium. Then at the Pavilion, Torquay, which was the only theatre in Torbay at that time, Betty and I appeared in our own summer show with six complete changes of programme, which means virtually the production of six completely different little revues with different costumes, scenery and orchestrations (we had an orchestra of fourteen) each week for six weeks and then they were repeated again, but in addition to this we also did a live broadcast every week for twelve weeks from the show with twelve completely different scripts. How we managed all this and remained alive and sane I do not know. The Butlin's show went off first and we then did a preliminary tour taking in Southsea and Reading so that we could get some of the rehearsal and production over before we arrived at Torquay. The Doonan Show then started about two weeks later. This show was a complete failure and never got off the ground because George Doonan was oddly uncooperative. He seemed to dislike the show, the cast, the material we supplied him with. Even the clothes, scenery and lighting were wrong in his opinion. He also slipped in a lot of blue material from his variety act, which is useless and unforgivable in a summer show, and he even frequently missed his entrances and left the stage empty. We lost money and also lost the goodwill of the Hastings Corporation, who did not book the show for a third year.

At Torquay we had Betty Jumel as our comedienne; she was to join our summer ventures many times through the years. She was a very professional, and very funny, lady; most meticulous in her work, always on time, always as neat as a new pin, both on and off the stage, and very diplomatic with the rest of the company. Betty Jumel did some splendid work in the profession, but never achieved a star position at the top of a bill. In many ways her work was too good for the halls and for summer shows and pantomime, and yet she never managed the West End, where I'm sure she would have been acclaimed. However, in the echelon she chose to work in she was never unemployed, earned very good money and obviously very happy in her work and private life. We had a company of eighteen; eight girl dancers, two men dancers, a baritone and a soprano. (Gordon Holden was our baritone; he was at the Guildhall School of Music and Drama with me. He would stay with us in the houses we took at each resort until the school holidays when his family would join him, and he was with us in successive shows for over fifteen years.) Bradley Harris was second comedian. I had known him all my professional and semi-professional life. (We had joined the Concert Artistes Association together the same month.) His work was quaint and original, one of his strongest acts being a one-man band in which he made every single noise of every single instrument, bringing in at the end a harmonium with its weird imaginary bellows worked by his feet. It brought the house down every time. On long journeys in the car these days, should I be with Betty and feel the slightest bit sleepy, I say to her, 'Do a Bradley,' and she goes off into a very funny caricature impression of Bradley's musical noises, and as she begins to work her feet with the imaginary bellows, I hoot with laughter and am wide awake again. Today, if there were a young Bradley Harris on TV, he would be a star overnight.

While with Robert Nesbit in *Magic Carpet* we had watched him light the show, and he was a master at it. Jean Bell had made us a model theatre in the loft of the garage quarters of our house at East Grinstead and we had quite a complicated lighting board on this with which we experimented and on which we were able to familiarize ourselves with various gelatine colours and their numbers. Our first show at Hastings had taught us a lot, and we always hired electrical equipment, eventually buying certain items and travelling them with the scenery, so that the lighting of the shows became quite a feature because the older summer entertainments had not bothered with lighting very much. The older shows were equipped with a lot of cut-out scenery and cloths, costly items, which in the expensive and shortage days after the war we found difficult to equal or excel, so that we depended on lighting effects a great deal. In a way we had found a new dimension for the summer show.

The writing, the composing of special music for the show, the direction, the dancing and, of course, the dressing of the show were largely Betty's departments. The scenery, the lighting and the comedy and the running orders and the business side of the billing, advertising, advance publicity and the contracts were largely mine. Auditions were mostly Betty's and the casting therefrom, but here again we would share our experience in the booking of the comedy artistes and specialities.

Auditions for us were usually unhappy times. Unhappy because the standard of talent was often poor and one had to turn so many people away. Betty was very good at this and would invent some kindly reason why a particular artiste was not engaged – she might say someone was too short or too tall, rather than say that their voice was poor or that they were utterly talentless, as so many of them were. One day when Betty had been dealing thus I arrived from an engagement elsewhere, and not knowing me as I barged through the queue outside, I heard two of them say, 'The silly old cow doesn't know what she wants.' So much for kindness. But her ire was sometimes roused as, for instance when one arrogant singer arrived for a pantomime audition. 'I am already booked for pantomime,' he announced grandly, 'but I understand you also present summer shows. I would be prepared to sing in that provided the theatre was the premier one in the resort, provided also that the leading lady [who would be Betty!] is sufficiently talented and blended well with my voice.' 'I'm sorry,' said Betty, 'I'm afraid we could not engage you for the summer show.' 'Why not?' he demanded. 'We would not be able to get your size head into our theatre,' said Betty.

It is most odd how these various departments fell into place and how each of us took them for granted. Indeed, our private life is very similar. We each have our own departments for the detailed work and we both join together for the main decisions. Later, when we presented two pantomimes at a time, Betty would cope with every department of the show I was not in, and half of the departments of the show I was in. Similarly Jill, when she joined the shows immediately after leaving school, took on little responsibilities, and as she grew older and more experienced, larger responsibilities. There is no more efficient or knowledgeable stage manager and stage director than my daughter today – we wondered sometimes latterly how on earth we had ever managed without her. She now produces pantomimes for other managements.

You can imagine that we were pretty stretched in 1947 with two touring shows, our own show, and a weekly radio show taking place live from the stage at Torquay. Ronnie Waldman produced these, and Dick Pepper (Harry S. Pepper's brother) wrote the scripts as he had done for *Hi Gang!* and many of our previous radio series. All the shows except Hastings, I'm happy to record, were successful, and we returned home to Sussex with a contract for next summer at Torquay.

Dick Pepper, whose father had presented *The White Coons* and other Edwardian concert parties, warned us that on the last night (this happened so many times to him and Harry at the end of their father's many shows), the chairman of the local entertainments committee would come forward and announce the return of the show next summer with the words, 'It is not good-bye, it is only ooo-revoo!' To Betty's and my delight, and that of Dick, whose purple face we could see in the front row, the chairman of the Torquay Entertainments Committee said these exact words with the exact pronunciation Dick had predicted.

That winter the original Hastings company, with Charles Harrison, toured Germany for the Combined Services Entertainment. This show came back together with its scenery made in Germany. We also owned the Torquay and Hastings scenery, and the costumes for all three shows.

The house at East Grinstead was a large one and we were able to make a large downstairs cloakroom into a theatrical wardrobe room with rails across to house the costumes. A lot of the scenery was stored in the garage and stable complex of the house, while the remainder was stored at a local furniture depository at East Grinstead. The manager here would tie some of the thirty-feet-long cloths to the roof of each floor. Sundry smaller pieces of scenery were stored here and there, higgledy-piggledy among his other clients' personal effects, sometimes with laughable results. But you can imagine the difficulty as, each year, I needed to get out various shows, each show having different scenery, when a lot of it was hidden away all over a very large warehouse. This became a twice-annual chore; it sometimes took more than a day to sort it out, employing costly labour. It was not until we moved to the Dove House at High Hurstwood in 1953, where I was able to build my own scenery and costume store, forty-five feet long by thirty feet wide by twenty feet high on two floors, that I was relieved of this worry. Through the years, mountains of new scenery and costumes accumulated; eventually, over a thousand costumes were stored and catalogued by Betty and stacks of difficult-to-move scenery flats and false prosceniums sworn at by me, with over a hundred cloths stretched their full length on racks – always the one you wanted being the one underneath the other ninety-nine. We always felt that there was nothing so tawdry or so valueless as old theatrical scenery and costumes – never, by the way, to be looked at in the open air with sunlight on them; the world of make-believe needs the dark mystery of a dim theatre. But when we decided not to be theatrical managers any more (the novelty having worn off over twenty-eight years) and to sell scenery, costumes and store, inflation, together with the cost of new properties and new shows, had caused values of even old stuff to reach astronomical heights, so that we sold with a certain amount of financial relish and 'gratis-faction', drying the sentimental tear before it had even decided to take shape.

Our third year at Torquay we had among a strong cast an unknown called Harry Secombe. He had not as yet acquired the stardom of the *Goon Show*. He had been on a variety bill with me at Grimsby (I only played the No. 1s!!) and I had greatly enjoyed his unusual act. This was his comedy shaving, finishing with a soprano and tenor duet with himself doing both characters, and I asked him if he would like to join us for the summer. He was keen to do it as he had a young family, and twelve weeks at the seaside was an attractive proposition. I explained to him that I wanted Betty to see his performance before we decided finally to book him, and it was arranged that Betty should see him at the Hippodrome, Eastbourne, where he was appearing – so oddly for Harry – in an all-male drag-show revue. In this show incidentally, and looking exactly like and equally as beautiful as Kim Kendall, was, aged about 20, an exotic performer called Danny La Rue. 'That one is going to be a star,' said Betty.

Now I must explain here that we had started to breed and show cocker spaniels with a small amount of success and one of our puppies had been bought by a couple at Brighton. 'We will take the puppy to Brighton,' I said, 'and then go on to Eastbourne and see Harry Secombe.' This we did. It was also the first puppy we had ever sold. He was beautiful and loving and I knew that parting with him was going to be difficult for Betty. The deal was made, the new owners approved of and we were about to go. As we said good-bye the puppy looked back at Betty in the way only a cocker spaniel can look back, and Betty, in the car on the way to Eastbourne, was in tears. As we sat in the circle of the Hippodrome watching Harry Secombe, Betty was still in tears; half for the disposed-of spaniel and half as tears of laughter at Harry. It says a lot for Harry's marvellous gift of comedy even in those early days for him to have exacted tears of laughter from Betty under these circumstances. Next day we bought the spaniel back and signed up Harry Secombe for the summer.

He was a joy to have in the show. He was so funny, so ebullient and so un-disciplined. On one occasion we were doing a sketch where Betty and Harry and I were drinking tea together. Things got so out of hand between Harry and Betty that Betty was eventually pouring tea out of the teapot over Harry's head and he was enjoying it enormously as if he were under a shower in the bathroom. One of the stage hands was a fisherman who used to peddle the most delicious prawns to the company. Harry would go on in a serious scene (a serious scene with Secombe!) with the odd prawn or two palmed so that the audience could not see, and as he danced the odd gavotte (he was slimmer then!) with Betty, she would find herself left holding a prawn, and this prawn would go round the whole of the company playing the scene quite unknown to the audience, who were possibly wondering why they all looked so happy up there on the stage!

Harry's whole concept of humour was original and a little before his time. The audience, not having yet been geared to the zany humour of the Goons, was a little unsure whether Harry was funny or not. A lot of them thought so. No one thought he was funnier than did Betty and I, who used to watch him with great delight from the wings. He never got enough applause for his funniest efforts, and knowing what a good tenor voice he had, we tried for some weeks to persuade him to finish on a serious song. 'No,' he said, 'I am a comedian.' 'You are a singer, too,' we told him, and eventually we prevailed. The result you know: one of Britain's greatest and most lovable stars.

For the third year at Torquay, Edward Seago, the eminent artist, who by then was a firm friend, painted a most beautiful design for a cockney Hampstead Heath first-half finale. It is a roundabout with 'Fletcher's Fair' painted around it, gloriously colourful and a most beautiful impressionist painting. The reproduction of this by the firm of Edward Delaney, the West End scenic painters, was masterly as well as costly, but worth it. A councillor member of the Entertainments Committee inquired: 'Why isn't the scenery properly painted and finished off?'

That winter when we came back to London we did the weekly peak show on BBC TV on Saturday nights. Six excerpts from the show – these must have been Harry's first television appearances.

We saw Sheila Hancock at Torquay in repertory some years later and engaged her as comedienne in our show on the Isle of Wight. She went straight to the West End that winter and became a star overnight in *Pieces of Eight*. John Boulter, the tenor on the *Black and White Minstrels* on television, started with us straight from the Royal College of Music. We gave his first professional engagement to John Noakes, the presenter of the children's magazine programme, *Blue Peter*. Anna Quayle was with us, and beginning with our singing chorus in pantomime have been such distinguished singers as Valerie Masterson and John Dobson.

In 1950 we went to Llandudno. The very large Pavilion there justified the booking of another star. Suzette Tarri, who had been a fellow concert artiste before the war, and a co-broadcaster during it, agreed to join us. Actually, she decided only to do her act with us in the show, in no way joining in the production numbers: just the opening, her act and joining in the finale. We again did six complete changes of programme, but this was easily found out of the three years of fifteen programmes we had already presented at Torquay.

We had a successful season and they asked me if I would return the following year. 'Yes,' I said, 'I will be happy to do so with Betty Jumel as my comedienne instead of Suzette Tarri.' It was our practice to change the comedienne for a second resident season. Quite a time went by and I could get no contract finalized with them, so I arranged with Will Hammer to present our show for him at the Theatre Royal at Bournemouth – a smallish, beautiful old theatre built in Edwardian times, near the centre of the town; but rather badly placed in a side-road. Jack Payne, the band leader of BBC fame, was Will Hammer's partner and was an old friend. We were to do two seasons at Bournemouth for them eventually and two seasons of pantomime at the Grand Theatre at Croydon, which Will also owned. Will Hammer (the founder of Hammer Films) was a stage-struck semi-pro who owned a chain of jewellery shops in the centre of almost every large town in the country. In his youth with a friend he had formed a double act called Hammer and Smith and it had been a disaster. Still enraptured with the theatrical business, he decided wisely on management, owned several theatres and summer-show pitches, and did a great deal of good as an owner of independent venues when the bigger circuits were making it difficult for smaller managements.

We always found him most fair and agreeable to work with, and our four shows for him were great successes. He died sadly and strangely. Although he was well over sixty he had been a keen cyclist in his youth and still cycled to keep fit. He lived far into the Surrey countryside and had a long driveway through a park up to his mansion. He used to stop his Rolls, his chauffeur would get a racing bicycle from the boot of the car and Will Hammer would cycle happily the remaining couple of miles or so home. Thus he kept fit for many years, One dark night he rode the bike into a pot-hole and fell off and broke his neck.

The Pier Company at Llandudno eventually told me that they would not be requiring my summer show for next summer as they had engaged a show from another management who had been able to procure the services of Betty Jumel. As soon as I knew I was going to Bournemouth for Will Hammer, I had put Betty Jumel under contract to appear with us there. To our amazement not only had the Pier Company widely advertised their new show with Betty Jumel on the bills, but they had also taken a whole page in the Llandudno Town Guide advertising Betty Jumel's forthcoming appearance. The Pier Company was a large responsible limited company who owned several large steamers which plied between Liverpool and Llandudno every summer. I rang up Betty Jumel and told her what was happening. 'I'll settle for a steamer,' she said. Actually we were not too hard on them. We just insisted on having all the advertising withdrawn, including the town guide!

Is it worth noting that on wet days it was possible to see members of the audience sitting in the dress circle of the Pavilion, Llandudno, with their umbrellas up? Perhaps they hired out the umbrellas!

I think I must tell you of a charity show which the two Bettys and I did when we were in the show at Torquay. It was a cabaret in one of the largest hotels. The two dancing boys did an act first, then my Betty sang followed by Betty Jumel and me doing one of her very funny routines where she is a wallflower of uncertain age and I am a dancer not likely ever to appear in *Come Dancing* – no matter how long they keep the programme on. There is a picture of us as these characters in this book. The dancers and my Betty have pleased the audience a great deal, Betty Jumel and I know that the routine we are about to do is very funny indeed and visually strong, admirably suited for cabaret in a large ball-room. We make our entrance. The audience laugh. We get settled into the routine. There is now not only dead silence, but a lot of movement and walking about. I was not wearing my glasses and was not sure what was happening.

'What's going on?' I inquired of Betty under my breath.

'They're all walking out,' she said back to me behind her hand. 'No! Correction!' she added. 'They are running out!'

'We can't be as bad as that,' I said.

Suddenly the lights went up and the whole audience had left. There were just a few over at one end of the room peering out of the window with their backs towards us. A car had caught fire in the car park and the audience had all left to move their cars. Victor, Betty's husband, was nowhere to be found, and I remembered we had left him charge of Betty Jumel's mink coat and my Betty's ermine one.

'Where's Victor?' I asked his wife. 'He's got the fur coats!'

'He's probably beating the fire out with them in the car park,' she replied.

Many years later, when Betty Jumel was well into her sixties, she appeared with us for a season at the Lyceum, Edinburgh. We did a hunting double in the show with Betty in full hunting pink, riding a pantomime horse with two stage hands inside; what is known most vulgarly in variety circles as the 'fart before the horse'. I do not know what happened in this instance, but one stage hand in the front fell forwards suddenly on one knee and this sent Betty right over the horse's head, headfirst herself on to her face. She broke her nose but insisted, streaming with blood and making all sorts of *ad lib* remarks about it, on finishing the sketch. She had the courage to do her own act after this the same evening: a Spanish number where a mantilla reinforced with heavy wire kept falling for funny effect over her face and nose. She had her nose set in the hospital the next day and did not miss a single performance.

'Does it look all right?' inquired *my* Betty of the injured nose, because although a funny lady, Betty Jumel was a pretty little woman.

'It will do for the rest of *my* days,' she said gamely.

Do you wonder we were fond of her?

Two seasons at Bournemouth were followed by four seasons at the White Rock Pavilion, Hastings. We loved it at Hastings, playing twice nightly to packed houses. One of my happiest memories was when Betty sang the aria from *Madam Butterfly*, 'One Fine Day', in her single spot and acknowledged her applause and went to her dressing room, quite a few yards away from the prompt side, and began hastily to change for her next number. I was to follow her on stage, but such was the volume and persistence of the applause she had to change back into her crinoline (her act in the show being always in the programme as 'The Girl in the Crinoline Gown') and come on stage again; a matter of several minutes, when, of course, the audience insisted on an encore. Betty's mother was in the audience that night, which made it especially pleasurable for all three of us. It may seem a small incident to recall in a provincial theatre at the seaside, but it was a magical theatrical moment: the house in an uproar insisting on Betty's return. Summer-show audiences do not often behave like this.

Some years ago I was presenting my summer show at Hastings, while living near Buxted. On my way home from the theatre rather late one night after the show, my car radiator began to leak and the water to boil. There was a pub immediately opposite where I stopped. They were just closing, but when I explained my predicament, the host – elderly, large and rubicund – said, 'We had better fill up a dozen bottles with water and then you can replenish your radiator as you need to.' I only had about twenty miles to go. The bottles were assorted: several pint beer bottles; one or two gin bottles; one or two whisky bottles – all in a crate. I only needed to use the one and then I was safely home and had my radiator attended to the next morning.

On my way into Hastings the next evening to do the show, I thought, 'As bottles are quite an expensive item, I'll return to the pub the crate of bottles that I haven't used.' They were, of course, still full of water. Elderly, Large and Rubicund was not there, so the barman just shoved the bottles under the counter for his attention later.

Well . . . you know how things get mislaid. Some months later, wanting to replenish his gin supply, Elderly, Large and Rubicund thought to himself, 'I must use up those bottles which have been under the counter for such a long time.' Having up-ended the bottle under the measuring device and poured out a double gin for one of his regular customers, he sat back to enjoy his friend's conversation.

'Yuck!' said his friend, 'there's no gin in this at all. It tastes horrible.'

'I'm sure it does!' said the landlord, the solution having come to him like a flash. 'What I have just served up to you is a glass of Cyril Fletcher's water.'

We were then offered the Essoldo Theatre, Brighton, for our next summer season. This coincided with my first season of *What's My Line?*, and knowing the fillip a series of TV shows gives to one's drawing power, we were sorely tempted to accept and we did. The Essoldo was being used as a cinema with an occasional stage show at odd intervals. It had been built in the late 1930s by Jack Buchanan as a very modern theatre, opened with a disastrous flop in which he starred and never really recovered. Brighton after the war found it difficult to support even its lovely old Theatre Royal – with prior to, or immediately after, West End productions, mostly of straight theatre. Not to mention the Brighton Hippodrome, where we had last performed with our road show *Odes and Ends* with excellent, indeed capacity, business for the General Theatres Corporation in the late 1940s. This theatre was still run by the same management as the London Palladium, and they decided to put in a Palladium bill for a summer show that summer to make sure of the early demise of the phoenix-like resurrection of the Essoldo. Frankie Vaughan topped the bill with Frankie Howerd, and they engaged the American and Viennese opera star Adele Leigh.

As well as Betty and me, we had Eric Delaney's Band (he at the top of his TV stardom at the time and a great drummer), and Craig Douglas, also at the zenith of his career as a pop star from the BBC TV pop-music show *6.5 Special*. I had used him to top my Sunday show presentations in the Isle of Wight when we were able to afford top-line names as we used both the Pavilion at Sandown and the theatre at Shanklin – one half of the bill opening at one theatre and then being transported to the next theatre for the second half and *vice versa*. He had packed them in for the most successful Sundays of all. What escaped my notice was that he started his professional life as a native milk roundsman on the Isle of Wight and was a great local favourite. We enlarged our show with extra dancers, and had a singing chorus as well as these expensive top-line star attractions. In this enormous theatre, twice nightly, we played to exacly the same sort of figures as we had done at Sandown for three years or Hastings the previous four. We had a salary list of an extra £1,000 per week, which in 1960 was a lot of money at the seaside. In short, with no guarantee from the theatre, Betty and I suffered a financial disaster.

Dear Gilbert Harding brought a big party to the first night and did his utmost with the local press and in every way as one of Brighton's local stars to help business for us. We could have put up the notice immediately and closed the show. We hated to do it, not only from our fellow artistes' point of view, but *Summer Masquerade* had been a very successful summer show for fourteen years and we wanted it to be a successful summer show for many years to come. We had to brazen it out. We decided to stay for a specified number of weeks and worked out the total loss we could possibly make if we played to completely empty houses; we then said to ourselves that anything we should take over this was profit of a kind! We did increase our business a little as the run went on and as Brighton got to know that there was yet another theatre to fill and that we were there. But we still lost a lot of money, and, of course, it was capital that we were losing. I am happy and rather proud to say that it was the only one of our actor/management productions (other than the Doonan Summer Show at Hastings which we were not in) to show a loss; and, counting summer shows and pantomimes, we presented in our twenty-five years of management over sixty shows. Sometimes, with a newly mounted show with costly scenery and costumes, our actual money profit was perilously small, but this would be recouped the following year.

Before we played the season at Brighton we toured with a few weeks at Great Yarmouth and Hastings. Our show was seen at Yarmouth by members of the Entertainments Committee of Eastbourne, who were on a Municipal Conference there, and invited us to Eastbourne. We were keen to go – they said go to the Hippodrome the first year and then the new Congress Theatre the next. For sixteen weeks we played, twice nightly, to virtually capacity business at the Hippodrome. Next year, as a reward, we were back at the Hippodrome. And, to rub in our success, for a third year too. The attraction for us was that we were as near home as we could be.

We decided to look at the Hippodrome before we started the season; we needed to see the backstage equipment, to see how many backcloths we could fly – whether it was too small for our false prosceniums, what lighting equipment there was. It was backstage we were interested in. We inadvertently walked in through the front of the house. It was an unbelievable dump; and a very in-inartistic dump at that, all in a very bad state of repair. In order to 'modernize' this charming little Edwardian playhouse with circle, boxes and upper circle, they had painted it with municipal oranges and blues; the awful decaying décor was a cross between an ancient Odeon and an ice-cream parlour in a dilapidated part of Margate front. We remonstrated with George Hill, the entertainments director.

'It's lovely, old boy – lots of bright lights.'

'For Eastbourne, which is a number one seaside resort,' I said, 'this theatre is an abysmal disgrace; it is not only decayed and dilapidated but the décor is hideously inartistic. Something must be done about it before we bring our beautiful show here.'

'It's very near your opening date,' said George, 'and the council have no money for inessentials, it is all going to the building of the Congress.'

'*We* will decorate it then,' said Betty, and George, not having worked with the Fletchers before, did not say her nay.

'Of course,' he said, thinking that was the end of the matter.

We immediately got into the car, went to some local builders' suppliers, chose some wallpaper. Betty bought curtain material for the boxes, and we had decorators in the theatre the next day. It all caused a great flurry from George's office.

'You cannot do this,' he said.

'We *are* doing it,' we said.

'It's the council's job,' he said 'to decorate this theatre.'

'Exactly,' we said, 'and why haven't they?'

All the time our men were putting up scaffolding, and Betty even got George Hill to hold her tape measure (rather perilously I thought) when measuring the top boxes near to the ceiling of the theatre. We personally had the proscenium arches and boxes painted and the two circles and the interior of the boxes papered, and Betty made very effective gold and white striped satin curtains with gold fringes and Georgian swags for the boxes. The difference from the municipal orange and blue distemper was a transformation. We shamed Mr Hill into getting the rest of the walls of the theatre done.

The next year the whole focus of attention, for both the Entertainments Committee and the town, was the Congress Theatre. We had shared the billing sites in the town equally with the Winter Gardens the previous year, and it was our arrangement to share them equally again. (I always check up on these things: so much goes towards the success of a show, especially the printing and publicity.) We found that we had a third and the Congress had two-thirds. This was most unfair. It stayed that way for the rest of the season. Several thousands of our hand bills (which we had paid for) were also missing. I had a van at that time. Day-glow painted bills advertising the show in enormous lettering were plastered over it, and a man was employed to drive it around the town hour by hour. It was also parked while he was resting sometimes on the front, and sometimes quite near to the Congress Theatre. The Town Clerk wrote to me and told me of some long-forgotten by-law that prohibited posters on vans driving around Eastbourne. I wrote back reminding him that there were several Carter Paterson vans much larger than mine driving round the town with posters on belonging to British Road Services. No reply. So I hired the advertising space on the Carter Paterson vans, all of them, which were constantly delivering luggage along the front and in the town for the rest of the summer.

I only include such an episode in this book to illustrate the difficulties of the small actor/manager. After our third record-breaking season with pantomime at a provincial theatre, the director came to us and said we were causing him a great deal of trouble by being so successful. 'Because of the box-office success of your pantomime each year,' he said, 'we are now running at an annual profit, and before we know where we are we shall lose our grant from the local authority, and our grant from the Arts Council!!' Such are the exigencies, the embarrassments and perplexities of the small management.

Betty's and my last two summer seasons were at Edinburgh, then Brighton (this time at the Dome), after which we presented a smaller version of the show at a new theatre at Swanage with Jill as the comedienne and Peter Hudson playing all my parts. So for twenty-three mostly happy years, we presented summer shows – twenty-seven in all.

119

12   Pantomime

'From the golden egg of the magic goose the Clown was hatched.'
– Willson Disher

It was at the end of our last summer season at Torquay that we were asked to present our first pantomime. The booking agent for the Pavilion Theatre, Torquay, was in those days Roy Limbert, who also was the director (as successor to Sir Barry Jackson) of the Malvern Festival; and he also became the booking agent for *Summer Masquerade*. Very frequently seasons of plays from the Malvern Festival were presented by Roy Limbert at the Arts Theatre, Cambridge, and through the years he had built up a very valuable relationship with them. Would we do a pantomime at Cambridge? I must say that at that moment I felt we were doing all that our small organization could manage, but Betty, and also Ian Francis, who was my most efficient and valuable 'straight man' at the time, thought differently. Thank goodness their view of the situation prevailed. Betty and I had been a considerable success in the Tom Arnold pantomime at Wimbledon Theatre at Christmas 1945. We had experienced *Dick Whittington* with Harold Dubens in 1946, and I had, with Joan Turner as Aladdin, enjoyed being Wishee Washee for Lew and Leslie Grade in their *Aladdin* in 1947. Of considerable importance, too, Betty had played the name part in *The Sleeping Beauty* for the greatest of all pantomime impresarios, Julian Wylie, at Birmingham before the war, so there was a nucleus of knowledge from which to draw.

We did not own any pantomime costumes or scenery, or even a pantomime script. In the *Stage*, the profession's weekly newspaper, were many advertisements, and the most glowing one was for an *Aladdin* which was for sale complete with costumes and scenery, and was to be seen at Sheffield. Torquay to Sheffield and back on a Sunday and Monday might just have been possible – then, with rationing, strikes and other wartime dislocations not yet righted, we dared not take the risk. Our stage manager at that time was sensible and experienced. The fare and overnight subsistence from Torquay to Sheffield, via London, in those days was a fairly large sum. In effect he went to London, had fun, and returned to Torquay. We did not know this then, of course, and took for truth his glowing account of the pantomime which he described (not having seen it) and bought it. We also paid for it to be stored until we needed it before Christmas. The costumes we had sent to our house at East Grinstead and the scenery straight to the Arts, Cambridge. Betty was in bed with flu when an odd coffin-shaped box arrived. Not even a hamper. Indeed, the size box would not have contained my Widow Twankey finale hat out of our last production of *Aladdin*. 'I'd better undo it,' I thought, 'and see if several more hampers have been lost on the way.' I did undo it. Inside was an inventory and that box contained every costume of a supposedly twelve-scene pantomime. We imagined what the scenery must be like.

I decided to let Betty into my horrific secret at once. One by one and at arms' length, sometimes with my nostrils tightly pinched (we had paid separately for the whole lot to be cleaned, perhaps the stage manager had pocketed the cleaning money too!) I took the entire wardrobe, costume by sorry costume, up to Betty. It didn't take long. She immediately got up and drew designs, rang for seamstresses, got out her machine, and a set of chorus costumes were made that night! In a week all was completed, together with a few costumes from the summer show which fitted in roughly, and the odd set or two purchased separately. One or two of the original lot were included in the final show, and fortunately I had a whole magnificent set of satin personal costumes made by Bobby Roper from my previous year's Wishee Washee when I had supplied my own costumes. In short, a scratch lot – but much better than we could possibly have imagined to start with and better than many a small provincial show. On the way to the theatre I armed myself with several pounds of variously coloured theatrical glitter, and it added a certain air of Eastern magnificence to the sadly sordid scenery.

Norman Higgins, the director of the Arts, Cambridge, was having a year's sabbatical away from the theatre. His wife, Dorothy, sweet and lovable, who became a dear friend through the twenty-five years we presented pantomime at the Arts, was understanding and welcoming. The stage staff were helpful in the extreme, and with judicious lighting, a very good script which Betty conjured out of the air and a good cast, we managed to play to excellent business. When Norman Higgins returned in the spring, we were summoned to that office we began to know so well, with the portrait of Lord Keynes over the fireplace and an absurdly young photograph of George (Dadie) Rylands, who was, and is, the chairman of the Theatre Board, and at seventy plus looks younger than the photograph. Also on the wall was an old playbill – not of the Arts, which began its career in 1936 when I did, but of the very oldest of the Cambridge theatres – the Theatre Royal. The date on the bill is 11 September 1871, and it announces in enormous type a new farce entitled CYRIL'S SUCCESS. I thought this was a good omen, as it proved to be. At the end of our twenty-five years I was presented with this bill, and it hangs framed in my office now alongside a new one printed in the same idiom but informing the public of our latest presentation of *Aladdin*. We opened with it and closed with it.

Norman Higgins then described to us the sort of pantomime he would like us to present at the Arts the next Christmas – up to now they had presented gentler Christmas entertainment such as Clinton Baddeley's *Cinderella*, *Toad of Toad Hall*, *Alice in Wonderland*, but the success of our pantomime pointed in another direction. Could we combine, he asked, first-class ballet and music and singing and décor and story and verse, with the strong slapstick but clean humour which we had managed with *Aladdin*? The result was *Mother Goose*, written and composed by Betty with special arrangements of Old England numbers like 'The Twelve Days of Christmas', 'Ten Green Bottles', etc. There was a strong story line and no variety acts whatsoever. I did not even recite an 'Odd Ode', and resisted the temptation year after year. We had dancers who were just leaving the Royal Ballet School. We had singers who were about to leave the Guildhall School of Music and Drama. We even had a harp in the music accompaniment. Betty designed the costumes, and, most magical of all, the sets were designed by Edward Seago. Ted Seago had been a friend of ours for about seven years, and as his recent biography by Jean Goodman, *The Other Side of the Canvas* (Collins, 1978) says, he loved the colour and the romance of the theatre, the ballet and the circus. Here was a great artist in the Norfolk tradition of Crome and Cotman, considered to be one of the leading landscape painters of his generation, enormously busy with commissions to paint the late King and the Queen Mother; who, because of his friendship for us and love of the theatre, was prepared to paint sixteen exquisite watercolours. It was unbelievably difficult to get him down to practicalities and to curb his imagination. The year following he painted designs for *The Sleeping Beauty*, and after that for *The Queen of Hearts*. Ted even contributed to the attenuated *Aladdin* the previous year – we spent Christmas Day with him at his Dutch House at Ludham (for which Betty made the first curtains and counterpanes) prior to our opening on Boxing Day.

'Have you a canopy to be carried over the Emperor?' he inquired, doubtless thinking of some vast oriental umbrella he had seen at Covent Garden.

'No,' we faltered.

'Impossible to have an Aladdin without,' he said. 'We must make one.'

All of Christmas Day afternoon Ted was painting exotic dragons on circles of canvas and cutting long fringes, and with his deft brush turning lengths of hessian into cloth of gold! The Emperor had his canopy. I sold it with the rest of the scenery two years ago!

Ted Seago was an amusing raconteur who would 'hold forth' at times almost in the Gilbert Harding manner and was equally good value. He would talk either at length in his studio as he painted or after a meal as we all sat round the circular table he himself had painted, decorated and polished; there would be an enormous wood fire blazing in the open hearth and half-way up the wide chimney at the Dutch House. One experience he related he allowed me to use as my contribution to the TV programme, *True or False*. It seems he was invited to a hunt ball – or was it a regimental ball? I cannot remember – his host being either the master of the hunt or the colonel of the regiment. He was to stay the weekend at his host's house – a small manor of some distinction. Ted and other guests were to have cocktails and dinner with his host, and then go on afterwards as a house-party to the ball. When the cocktails were finished they all went in to dinner, somewhat grandly in procession. The dinner was served in some style in a small baronial hall with glinting silver, footmen and a butler.

Ted sat next to a dowager duchess wearing a tiara and a choker of pearls to hold up her sagging aristocratic chins, while on his other side was a clerical potentate, rubicund and well upholstered; a merry man in every way, and physically a pillar of the Church. Soup was served; a thick green-pea soup. Ted had no sooner tasted it than there was a quiet sigh from his left, the sort of sound that is made in late autumn when the last leaf falls exhausted to the ground. As she fell forward, the dowager duchess landed in the green-pea soup – the tiara hit the table with a thud and the false front of crimped grey hair floated on the glutinous green of the soup. No sooner had Ted's appalled gaze 'taken in' the picture of her Grace's sprawling fall, than there was a thud on his right and the pillar of the Church too had fallen, lurching forward into the green-pea sea. Thud followed thud as the guests fell. Ted, who did not drink because of a heart condition, looked aghast at his white-faced host, who too had remained teetotal at the cocktail party. The butler was stretched serenely at his employer's feet.

'What on earth has happened?' Ted inquired.

'My son rang earlier,' said his host, 'and as he is a medical student, and knowing what fun their parties always are, I inquired rather innocently if he had any advice as to how to make a party "go". "Yes," said my son. "Put a teaspoonful of ether in the cocktails."'

'But a teaspoonful of ether,' said Ted, 'could not have caused all this havoc.'

'I put a teaspoonful of ether in each cocktail,' said his host. There around them in various poses lay the flower of the County; unconscious.

'Ring your local doctor,' said Ted.

The doctor, happily at home, said that should there be no heart subjects among the guests, then all would be well and they would more than likely 'come to' in about four hours' time. They were laid in the baronial hall side by side in a long inert row, with cushions under their heads, by Ted, his host and the footmen. Ted, being the artist he was, adjusted the false hair and repaired the make-up where necessary.

'What on earth happened when they woke up?' I asked.

'I never knew,' said Ted. 'I really could not bear to wait and see; I hurried home.'

'True or false?' we asked him.

'Absolutely true,' he said. 'Who could have invented that?'

We spent several of our Christmas weekends with Ted at Ludham. A fellow guest one Christmas was his great friend Field-Marshal Auchinleck. We played wonderfully childish seasonal games, I remember, and had such a happy time as we always did in this quiet backwater of Norfolk, in this ancient house surrounded with beautiful things and lovely pictures of Ted's, and Boudins, and Cotmans, where time stood still and days were as long and sunny as they were in one's childhood. We would often pop into Hall Common, which was where Ted's parents, Bryan and Mabel Seago, lived, with his brother John. Auchinleck, Ted's parents, Ted and his friend and secretary Peter Seymour all came back with us to Cambridge to see the pantomime, and had dinner with us first in the Arts restaurant, as it used to be in Norman's day, with lawn table-cloths, linen napery and excellent menus and wines. Bryan Seago was a little, merry, apple-cheeked man with a wickedly humorous glint in his eye, and Norman Higgins was a dear but eccentric character. He was so wisely chosen by Lord Keynes to launch the new theatre. He had devoted every waking minute to its welfare and had achieved from a standing start a theatre to which every star was glad to come and come again, whose artistic standards were impeccable; and in a city which was not drama-keen, and from a university which, to start with, was but classically minded, he had mined a clientele of devoted theatre-goers.

Norman could not delegate and had to oversee the doing of everything himself, which wore him out and drew his nerves thinly to almost breaking point. This was when he appeared in his most ridiculous guises and, if you knew him, at his most lovable. He had held a somewhat lowly rank in Mesopotamia in the First World War but described to the 'Auk' how a particular battle in which both of them had taken part – the field marshal even in those days being in some kind of command – had been most wrongly planned and executed. Egged on in every way by the wicked Bryan, he then explained for at least half an hour with count-less pepper pots and mustard pots and salt cellars and knives and forks and even the vase of flowers (Brigade Headquarters) how it should have been arranged. What was worrying me was the new battle was only half over when they were calling overtures and beginners and I had to appear in the first scene.

One year we toured *The Sleeping Beauty* for two weeks at the Theatre Royal, Brighton, and then for a final week at the Festival Theatre, Malvern. There was not a great deal of time to set up the scenery for a Monday opening at Malvern after finishing the show on Saturday night at Brighton and there was only a scratch staff at Malvern out of festival time. Norman superintended it all magnificently. Everything was ready; just. He stood by for emergencies, immacu-late in his dinner-jacket. As the show opened, a palace scene flat (i.e. a piece of scenery eighteen feet high and eight feet wide – the size making the moving of it, and the holding of it upright, rather difficult) began to fall forward, on the prompt side of the stage. Norman was there and held it upright in a masterly fashion; as he gazed across the stage, the equivalent flat on the opposite side of the stage then began to fall forward. Norman dashed across behind the sky cloths to hold and steady it, which he did just in time, seeing out of the corner of his eye that his original flat was now slowly on its way falling forward. Like a demented yo-yo, for eight minutes the gallant Norman achieved the impossible and kept the flats upright while other stage hands were standing fascinated, doing nothing. Norman Higgins was gentle and kind and generous, also awk-ward and very touchy and prickly and had a quick temper. But everybody loved him. He was a great man of the theatre. To follow him – with Norman still on the board – needed an exceptional man, and the Arts found him in Commander Andrew Blackwood. He was so good to Norman and so understanding.

The *Guardian* of Tuesday, 22 December 1970, devoted its first-ever colour page to pantomime, and there I was in a coloured picture as Mother Goose – just my face, hat, red-nose and jewellery twelve inches by fifteen inches. They also were kind enough to say:

Cyril Fletcher, however, is an exception, a comic who has never been boxed in. He has for 20 years staged pantomimes with his wife, Betty Astell, frequently at the Arts Theatre, Cambridge. This year at Cambridge, he plays the Dame in *Mother Goose* – a part for which he commissioned a rather chic get-up of ostrich feathers and body-hugger in an attempt to capture the brashness of a nouveau riche old broad who can't come to terms with her first golden egg. He aimed at Danny La Rue, and confessed he ended up with a Barbara Cartland. (In the picture, he wears his finale costume, which indicates that he has given up being pretentious and married the local squire. Some squire.) His pantomimes are played in an intimate theatre, with fine sets, costumes and dancers, and with all the traditional rigmarole of singing to displayed cards, and instantly understood magic. They also have a rather wide-eyed comic who will be quite strange to children reared on television.

David Furnham, a sociologist and pantomaniac who is making a film of Fletcher's *Mother Goose*, sees close parallels between the work of the pop-eyed odd ode author, and that of Grimaldi, the greatest clown of the English pantomime. 'The comic character,' he says, 'flowered in English pantomime with Grimaldi, a master of grimace, and in an age of invention, an inventor unrivalled. In expression his eyes were large, globular, and sparkling, and his mouth seemed fitted to express every physical enjoyment or disgust. You only have to look at Cyril Fletcher to see that there is a similarity in their approach.'

In our programmes we often had this note which I compiled about the history of pantomime:

Pantomime is as English as boiled beef and carrots and Shakespeare and is sometimes as inartistic as the Albert Memorial. It has been evolving in the English theatre for over two hundred years.

Originally it was Italian . . . and not a word was spoken and its principal characters were Harlequin and Columbine and Clown and Pantaloon. As it evolved it has begged and borrowed transformation scenes from the French theatre, and surely that appearance of the Spirit of Evil, be he King Rat, or Abanaza or the Witch in *The Sleeping Beauty* . . . is the Evil One borrowed from the old morality plays that were sponsored originally by the Church.

At one time it consisted wholly of the Harlequinade . . . with Harlequin and Columbine playing the leading and more serious parts. Then Clown began to take over and became the principal . . . and in its heyday at this stage Clown was played by the great Grimaldi.

In early Victorian times the primitive and visual humour of Grimaldi was superseded by the kind of pantomime which sacrificed everything to spectacle, mostly dancing and grandly costumed processions.

The spoken word was eventually brought in and the tales of various nursery rhymes were told. Towards the end of the nineteenth century the music hall began to dominate pantomime and vulgarized it. The music-hall performer's humour was more adult and each performer had his own particular and easily recognized kind of humour. He brought long acts of his own into the show, the music hall speciality acts took up a lot of time, and the fairy-tale story began to get lost and the fight of Good and Evil eventually vanished, or had a token of a few lines at the end.

It was about this time that Julian Wylie, a great pantomime impresario, recalls how he saw a Cinderella who appeared in the kitchen scene dressed in khaki and who sang a patriotic song!

Those of you who have seen our pantomimes before will know that we have tried to recall the most prosperous days of pantomime. We have ballet and singing of a high standard, we endeavour to tell the story and let our spectacle help in its telling and all the time we have the old robust humour of the Clown and the music hall as well. And although it is but a fragment at the end, we do have a Harlequinade.

We are mindful that the Pantomime is the child's first visit to the theatre ... we want to amuse, and enthrall him, and make him laugh to make sure that he will make the theatre a lifetime's habit.

Some nice things have been said about me, and written about me in pantomime. I must say I enjoy playing this oddly grotesque character I have invented and called Dame. I am in no way a woman, or anything like a woman. I feel the fun in pantomime is for the Dame to be quite obviously a man dressed up as a woman and to be a man caricaturing and mocking a woman in everything, especially domestically, that a woman does. Then the children are as amused as the parents. I started off, I suppose as a front-cloth entertainer, reciter and raconteur. In pantomime I am purely and simply a production comedian – revelling and acting in situations which help to tell the story. I get laughs with what I do and how I do it as well as what I say.

After *Mother Goose* at Cambridge we repeated the mixture with *The Sleeping Beauty*. This time not only did Betty compose the music, write book and lyrics and play the Sleeping Princess, but she also set up a wardrobe department and designed and made the costumes. The Garden House at East Grinstead was really too big for a family of three – it was cut into four separate residences when we sold it – so it was very easy to put two of the downstairs rooms completely over to wardrobe and to sleep two seamstresses in the extra bedrooms upstairs. The costumes were made of the best materials obtainable and were very strongly made so that they cleaned well and looked well and were used several times; always being retrimmed and refurbished so that they looked brand new at every opening night. Latterly we purchased a whole opera which Covent Garden had finished with, and we also bought many surplus and glorious costumes from the Glyndebourne wardrobe. Garry Dahms, one of their designers – a man with a great sense of humour as well as artistic flair – made my costumes for the last four of the pantomimes we presented. They were extraordinarily funny and lavish to the nth degree.

Again with designs by Edward Seago, we presented *The Queen of Hearts* at the Arts, Cambridge, and latterly *Cinderella* and a new *Aladdin* – all with me in them.

To vary the Christmas fare of the citizens of Cambridge, we played the various pantomimes which began there at several other venues, we went to the Grand Theatre, Croydon, for two years for Will Hammer and we also played Northampton and Norwich. Because of our artistic and financial success at Croydon, when the new theatre and concert hall, the Fairfield Halls, were built Tom Pyper, the Director of this million and a half pound municipal munificence, asked us to present pantomime there. The result was that Betty and I presented their first eight pantomimes. It was a most happy relationship. We were right for Croydon; Croydon was right for us and was fairly near to Sussex. Although this was to cause us considerable anxiety on our very first appearance there with *Mother Goose*.

The Boxing Day morning of Christmas 1965, prior to our first matinée performance at the Ashcroft, Croydon, dawned with about eighteen inches of snow on the ground. It had not been predicted and in consequence we had not awakened all that early. There is not a great deal of traffic on Boxing Day morning, and even though I was able to get my car to the end of the drive, it was eventually stuck right across the road, which was uphill into the village of High Hurstwood. From the village it was certainly not more than thirty miles to Croydon. We found that the trains were running from Brighton via Haywards Heath and Croydon into London. Haywards Heath was fifteen miles of very snowy roads away from High Hurstwood. I explained the situation to our neighbour, Major Wilkinson, a farmer, who volunteered to get us to Haywards Heath in his Land-Rover. How grateful we were; not only were we playing the leading parts in the show, but we were the producers and presenters and this was our first show at a new theatre.

Slowly but surely we got half-way to Haywards Heath to Scaynes Hill; but there was a bus right across the road, and on either side of it were assembled about twenty cars. It was imperative to move the bus and also jump the queue of all the other cars to get to the station in time. I got out and to my delight a posse of other drivers was already assembled to move the bus. This was done, and I then ran from car to car, briefly explaining to the drivers how urgent it was for my Land-Rover to get through – 'We don't want to disappoint the children who are going to the pantomime, do we?' They were all happy to let me through. In my anxiety to save every second I began to run back the hundred yards or so to the Land-Rover. The road was very icy with packed snow. In my eager haste I fell very heavily on my behind. The occupants of the cars, and I regret to say the Land-Rover, all laughed loudly. I had really hurt myself, and still mindful of the need for speed, I ran again. I fell more heavily this time on my already injured behind. Again a big laugh, and this time in the Land-Rover Betty said to Jill, 'This is no time for him to give an encore!'

We caught the train, which was constantly delayed by snow all along the line, and eventually arrived at the station with two minutes to change and get our make-up on before the curtain rose. Neither of us was in the first scene, so the curtain went up on time and we were ready for our first entrances. I knew that I was in great pain; in the train I had not been able to sit down. But my role was a large one in the show and necessitated a complete change of costume for each entrance – about a dozen in all – and it was not until the show was over that I had a moment to look at the damage, or, for that matter really had a moment to really feel the pain. When one is on stage, especially at a first performance, one is concentrating pretty hard, and in this instance I was dashing about, throwing dough, playing football with it, delivering and receiving custard pies, diving in and out of trick beds, through trick doors, getting children up on to the stage from the audience, singing songs, getting the audience to sing songs: in fact, being a very active comedian. All this dashing about was not only good in that it kept my mind off my injuries, but it kept me mobile too, so that I did not seize up. When the final curtain came down I hobbled back to my dressing room and my dresser removed my finale clothes and I had time for my first review of the damage. The whole of my posterior, when unveiled in front of the brightly lighted dressing room mirror, looked like the behind of those apes on Monkey Hill at the London Zoo; only theirs looked like a black and white TV screen compared to mine in glorious Technicolor. I was thankful that so much agony was producing such a picturesque result. It got bluer and redder and greener and more yellow and purple and more magenta and blacker and more orange with deep shades of gamboge and burnt madder and crimson lake with, here and there, streaks of vermilion. Turner would have been green with envy, Paul Klee frustrated and Salvador Dali nonplussed at the colouring and hues and devastation of my very dead end.

Somehow, now in agony, I managed to perform the second house. A very appreciative audience, a very helpful cast and a very double gin helped me through. The Ashcroft Croydon, is a municipal theatre, a part of the Fairfield Halls complex. Tom Pyper, who had ministered and administrated throughout and been kindness itself, brought round the chairman of the Entertainments Committee to see me. The way the show had gone, the amount of advance booking which looked like a record full-up-for-every-show-for-the-whole-run made the chairman very happy. His name was Alderman Dippy (I can but tell you the truth). In fact, the worthy alderman had so enjoyed himself, and so had his family, that to my mind my injuries were being somewhat overlooked in the euphoria engendered in my dressing room. I decided to mention my fall to the alderman again. He had not noticed anything the matter with my performances, he said, and brushed aside the fact that whereas he was sitting down comfortably in my dressing room, I was unable to. I felt he was not being nearly sympathetic enough. I was in agony. My injuries – or rather the look of them – had 'developed' rather as one develops a film in a darkroom. I decided to show him. With a gesture, the Dame dramatically dropped her drawers. The awful reds and purples of my cheeks shone with theatrical effect into his face. Alderman Dippy fainted.

There are two classic pantomime 'pro' stories I'd like to tell you. One concerns the first day's rehearsal of *Dick Whittington*. The whole cast is assembled for the first reading. The actors are looking each other up and down for the first time. The Principal Boy is thinking that the Principal Girl is not only too pretty, but much too tall as well. The star comedian is seeing how funnily acrobatic and amusing and young the second comedian is – and how inventive. The principal male dancer, mindful of his twice-daily 'lifts', is thinking that the ballerina is fatter and larger and heavier every time he looks at her! The speciality act has seen the size of their names on the bill and is wondering if it's worth while breaking their necks for *that*. The producer is looking at the whole lot and wondering why, when he had the whole profession to choose from at auditions, he chose this graceless and talentless lot . . . when making an impressive entrance, so that as the whole *Dick Whittington* company looks round, comes the only happy and supremely confident member of the cast. ' 'Mornin' all,' he cries. 'I'm Pussy!'

Late in his career that lovable and renowned Dame, Shaun Glanville (the husband of the most wonderful of all Principal Boys, Dorothy Ward), is playing Widow Twankey in *Aladdin*. He has been sleeping off a large lunch in his dressing room when he is hastily called to the stage. Blinking through the glitter of the Emperor of China's Summer Palace, he totters down to the footlights and finds himself alone amidst the oriental splendour. He looks round. He has no idea where he is. 'Where's Goose?' he murmurs.

We were contracted after our first pantomime at Croydon to go back to Cambridge, but Tom Pyper was keen for us to stay on. Norman Higgins in his generous way allowed us to do this, and we even broke our previous year's capacity business record. How this is ever achieved I'll never know, capacity being capacity, but somehow every theatre in the land seems capable of it. I suppose people sit on each other's laps!! On to Cambridge we went with a view to producing *Cinderella* for the first time and bringing it back to Croydon the year afterwards. 'In the meantime,' said Tom Pyper, 'Betty will produce a show here which can then go to Cambridge when you come back to us!' This we achieved three times at Croydon, with five times at Cheltenham's Everyman Theatre to follow.

The alternate show, produced by Betty, usually opened at Cambridge a week before Christmas, so that with a Boxing Day opening for the other show all was possible, the second week of our rehearsal and one opening night taking place during the first week of the second show's rehearsal. With our small production team, this needed a great deal of organization. We would be employing about eighty people; salaries and employment contributions had all to be worked out. The advance bookings for two shows had to be organized with an advance booking manager employed from the last week in September; all the printing and billing with sizes of names according to contracts had to be got out. All the scenery had to be repainted and repaired, or, in the case of a new subject, designed, built and painted. All costumes had to be fitted and altered to fit each new cast together with a new wardrobe for a new subject, and very frequently new costumes for principals. New scripts, new music and orchestrations had to be composed and written.

The subjects we chose for the alternative pantomime were *Dick Whittington*, *Jack and the Beanstalk* and *Cinderella*. The subjects I used to appear in were *Mother Goose*, *Sleeping Beauty*, *Queen of Hearts* and *Aladdin*. Through the years, you can imagine that some of the comedy became quite polished routines with certain and sure laughs in various places. Similarly, the comic visual routines were remembered and repeated, and likewise became regular vehicles of laughter. The production numbers became the right length and the exact mood for their particular place in the plot, and the music, being especially composed for each show, fitted exactly the whole artistic pattern. Betty and I felt at the end of twenty-five years' constant use that these pantomimes were a valuable property for either amateurs or professional companies. Six of the subjects have now been published by Evans Plays and are available to professionals and amateurs alike, and for the last few Christmases have been played at many venues all over the country. So these pantomimes are not just words written on paper, or notes of music printed on staves. They have been seen, heard, applauded and laughed at. They are tried and true vehicles of delight for young and old. They have had the love and care and artistry of my wife breathed into them, and they have been pruned and polished by countless performers and audiences through the years. The comedy business which is so important to the gaiety of child audiences has all been performed and perfected many times. All of this business has been most carefully explained in detail. What is more infuriating when reading a comedy script than those letters 'bus' (the term for stage 'business') – and you have little idea of how this 'bus' goes? Well, one does with these scripts, and they can be performed with the confidence of knowing they are not an author's airy whim. They have all been part of successful professional shows.

In our alternate shows we starred Jim Dale, Kenneth Connor, Jess Conrad, Jimmy Thompson and Peter Goodwright. Peter Goodwright especially flowered in pantomime under Betty's direction. He was not just the impressionist we all applaud, but became a most lovable clown with a touch of genius that all the children loved. Some impresario should go and see Peter in pantomime and nurture him to become a top star comedian.

Doing two pantomimes at once did open up the possibility of certain adventures such as me and Alderman Dippy or Betty and the organist.

Organists were never very easy to find for the pantomimes – they needed to be able to play not only rhythm numbers, but also semi-classical music, including concerto-like pieces which Betty composed for the ballets. One particular year had been particularly difficult, but at last Betty received a telephone call.

'I understand you still need an organist for your pantomime at Croydon.' Would he audition? 'Yes, delighted to do so.'

Betty went to Boosey & Hawkes, and there she met this gentle giant of a man who played like an angel – 'Yes, anything, classical, or jazz.' He was booked – rehearsals went magnificently – he was so good she couldn't think why he had been without a booking so late in the season. He had just come home from a tour in Canada, he said. Dress rehearsal went very well, the pianist for the show was young and inexperienced but good, and under the guidance and help of Betty and the organist, all went smoothly. The production was *Jack and the Beanstalk*, a new show which Betty wrote for that year. It starred Jim Dale as Jack, and naturally he was to do a musical solo spot towards the end of the show. Quite apart from that, there was a very full musical score.

The show was due to open on Boxing Day and, as always, the company was called for noon. This was done to ensure that everyone was back from their Christmas trip 'home' – wherever that might be. Everyone was gathered on the stage for a final briefing by Betty when the organist arrived – rosy-faced and extremely cheerful. He bent down from his great height to kiss Betty on the cheek. It nearly knocked her over – it was patently obvious that he had been at more than the wine gums. Still, she thought, it's Boxing Day, he'll be all right by the time the curtain is due to go up. As soon as she had finished her chat, she sent everyone off for coffee. The pub opposite the theatre had an excellent coffee bar, and she especially made it clear to the man-mountain that strong coffee was the only thing he was to drink. Alas, her instructions fell upon deaf ears. Certainly he went to the bar – but . . .

He staggered back at 2.15 for a curtain rise at 2.30. Betty saw him. 'Well,' she comforted herself, 'some musicians become veritable geniuses when they are tanked up.'

The theatre was totally packed for the first performance.

From here on this is how Betty tells the story.

'I'll go into the orchestra pit myself and take my baton in case I need to conduct to keep everything together. I think it may help. Even then I had the gravest misgivings. I alerted Jim Dale that the music might be just a trifle "umpty" here and there and went into the pit, where I sat on a small stool next to the organ. The musicians came in – the pianist pale and rather nervous, the drummer unconcerned and the organist as happy as a sandboy; it was time to start the overture; after the first fanfare I knew what I was in for. All my drunken friend could do was to flop his vast jelly-like hands anywhere on the keyboard, and his huge feet played two or three booming bass notes at the same time and the cacophony was appalling. The pianist gazed at me in panic. "Play" I hissed. "Not you," I said to the organist. "S'fine, s'fine," he burbled, making an unbelievably rude noise by half falling across the instrument. "Shut up," I said, thwacking him really hard across the knuckles with my baton. The curtain rose on the first scene and the astonished chorus tried to find something they could recognize from the musicians. On my hands and knees, hopefully out of sight of the audience, I crawled under the piano. "Listen," I said, "play all the tunes as simply and as loudly as you can – I'll try to keep him in order but ignore us, just play." Back I crawled. For a while I sat next to the monster, hitting him hard across the knuckles with my baton when he insisted on making these dreadful discordant noises. "I must stop him somehow," I thought. So, once again, I crawled on hands and knees towards the piano, the electric switch for the organ was there somewhere. It had to be, there was little light down there, but after searching carefully, I found it. In triumph I pulled the plug out, and plunged the entire orchestra pit into darkness. The piano stopped, the organ stopped, and, for what seemed like an hour, every sound stopped. In fact it was only a split second – the singers had merely drawn breath, which was more than I had. Frantically, I switched on again to be greeted by a long-drawn-out growling sound; my fat friend had fallen right across the keyboard. I crawled back and with superhuman strength managed to drag him off the keyboard, and then, oh joy of joys, I found the right switch and turned off the current to the organ.

'This had all taken quite a considerable time, and I was now able to tell the pianist to play for all he was worth, while I set about the problem of how I was going to get that great bulk out of the pit as soon as the interval came without it being obvious to all and sundry that we had a great drunken lump sitting there. "Sleep," I thought. "If he has a bit of a snooze we may be able to wake him up slightly more sober." He slept, and, oh hell, he snored; all through the ballet, a very weird accompaniment I can tell you. Most Boxing Day audiences are full of Christmas pudding, and this one was no exception. They were not unduly critical, and such was the great virtue of my cast, and Jim Dale in particular, that they were thoroughly enjoying themselves, and if they thought it odd to have just a piano and drums in the music department, it meant little or nothing to them. Meanwhile, my hair was going more grey by the moment. The interval came, the curtain fell on the ballet: beautiful wood nymphs speeding Jack on his way up the beanstalk, and honking noises from the organist in time to the drum rolls and cymbal crashes of the dramatic musical climax, applause; applause and a muffled yelp, for I chose the applause to dig my baton very sharply into the ribs of old Rip van Winkle; he shambled to his feet, gave me a bleary smile and said, "Tha's alright – goo show," and to my relief began to stagger out of the pit. Having once got him into the band room, I rose to my full 5 feet 2 inches and confronting this 6 foot 4 inch jelly told him to get out of the theatre. "Gotter play show," he said – "Gotter get out and fast," I replied, "and come in tomorrow and apologize," I yelled. He departed. I went back, switched on the organ – which I had never played before – had a quick look at the keyboards, and during the second half of the show the numbers were sketchily accompanied by me, as well as the pianist, and every one had a good loud chord at the end. We got by, and we replaced the man for, by a great stroke of luck, someone who had worked for me before, but who had retired, came to the rescue; though I have to say he charged us twice the usual rate for the job.

'I mention the name of neither musician for obvious reasons.

'The next day a very contrite organist arrived filled with apologies and promises, neither of which were accepted. Long afterwards I learned that he always behaved in this fashion, and by changing his name every so often he would be booked by some poor unsuspecting idiot like me. Poor man – he was such a good musician too.'

Do you remember when those small bicycles first became popular about twelve years ago? 'We'll give you one if you use it in the pantomime,' they said. 'All right,' I said. 'It will make quite a topical and funny entrance.' Then they sent round one of those very persuasive young photographers. His wonderful idea was that I should, dressed as Widow Twankey, ride through the High Street of Croydon on the bicycle, and he would take a picture of me by some traffic lights sandwiched in between a bus and a car. 'All right,' I said. I get a little light-headed during pantomime rehearsals.

So I dressed up in full fig: the clothes that Widow Twankey wore in the laundry scene – woollen stockings striped red and yellow, a very bright red, yellow and green spotted dress, with a multi-coloured woollen shawl and a white apron, my red pantomime wig, parted in the middle and with curls on either side topped by a mad woollen hat with an outsize bobble. I also wore gold high-heeled shoes. I was really quite shy of appearing in the outside busy High Street like this with my red nose and ruddy cheeks. I need not have been; not a single soul stared, no child called out, nobody even nudged anybody. I stopped at a traffic light. I looked very meaningfully into the faces of several occupants of the bus. I put my tongue out at one child on a lady's knee. No reaction at all. They just returned my quizzical stare with a bovine one. They either thought that a lot of old ladies rode about on bikes like that, or they may have said to themselves, 'It's some stunt for the telly.' I don't know what they thought, but if ever you, dear reader, should be worried about cycling round Croydon dressed as Widow Twankey – think nothing of it.

One of the most enjoyable events of the Christmas season was always the pantomime church service, usually held on the first Sunday after Christmas Day. At Cambridge, Norman Higgins would read one lesson, I would read another, and a few of the superb voices from the chorus – usually from the Guildhall School of Music and Drama – would sing various solo items. The church would always be packed for this, and Betty and I would be humbly proud of the soloists, who invariably proved each time that in no way were they chorus material. On one occasion it was a darkish morning and there was an electric light attached to the lectern as I read the lesson. As I finished and began to walk back to my pew, the lectern's enormous brass eagle began to follow me down the aisle as if intending to roost on my shoulder. I had caught my foot inextricably in the electric flex. Jill and Betty were in the front row, grinning up at me in the most irreligious way. I managed to release my foot while still walking just as the lectern reached the top of the chancel steps. I heard the congregation sigh with relief as I achieved the miracle.

Gyles Brandreth, who is the director of the British Pantomime Association, of which I am the president, wrote in one of our programmes an article 'Panto Past and Present'. Here is his last paragraph:

Over the years panto has certainly changed. All the same, it remains a joy. Just 110 years ago Andrew Halliday wrote the very first history of pantomime and in it he declared: 'Wise men of all ages have affirmed that laughter is a good thing. It clears the lungs, shakes up the diaphragm and loosens the fetters of the brain. How then shall we get a good hearty laugh? If we want a good roar, if we want to make our lungs crow like a chanticleer, we must go and see a Christmas pantomime. There is no fun like it after all.

13   Films

'It's one of those mammoth biblical epics where
Noah has eight of everything.' – Betty Astell

To suggest that I have had any sort of film career is an hilarious beginning for a chapter. I have been in three films only. The last one obviously a bad picture, because it has not yet been shown on television; and plenty of bad, indeed, excruciatingly bad films have now been shown several times!

Fairly early on in the war Betty and I were invited to a reception to be given by a Mr Spyros Skouras at Claridge's. It seemed that he was the executive head of 20th Century-Fox and it would be a very grand affair. Anna Neagle was the only other artist there, and she was there only because her husband, Herbert Wilcox, was one of the leading British film directors and producers of the day. The reception was held in a pillared room of large proportions, and one advanced a long way over a chequered marble floor to meet the great man, who was seated at an imposing buhl table at the other end of the room. There was a large contingent of press present, and the whole of the British film industry was suitably represented from the direction, production and distribution side. No artists except us. This made a lot of the press boys clamour round us, and I'm sure even Spyros Skouras was very impressed by the fuss. We didn't know who *he* was either. Betty and I got a little giggly, and it was quite obvious that we had been invited completely by mistake. Why are you here? the press kept asking us. A lot of them clamoured for exclusive interviews. 'Oh, we are off to Hollywood to make films,' airily we lied. Totally unbelievable and consequently believed! We enjoyed ourselves hugely. I must say I was most proud of the way Betty looked. She was wearing a champagne-coloured velvet dress with a small model hat of the same material and a Russian ermine fur coat which had been my wedding present to her. She certainly looked a film star.

This reception took place in the afternoon. In the morning we had been very busy in the garden at Welwyn; remember that we kept chickens, rabbits and geese and we were producing as many vegetables as we could to help out with food rationing, so we worked very hard and longer than we meant to; a quick hurried change of clothes and we were in London to be bewildered by Hollywood's hospitality. After the reception at Claridge's Betty and I went out to entertain the RAF at Northwood Air Station. We met the rest of the show's artistes at the ENSA theatre, and went to the changing rooms – one for the chaps, one for the girls. Peals of hilarious mirth came from the girls' room. Betty was obviously telling them of our Claridge's adventure. It couldn't be as funny as all that, I thought. What I didn't know was that as Betty began to change she realized that in her great hurry she had slipped the champagne-coloured velvet dress on over the top of a very old tweed gardening skirt covered in mud, which was showing a good six inches below the hem of her dress. No wonder Spyros had stared.

In Anna Neagle's starring vehicle *Yellow Canary*, produced by Herbert Wilcox, I played myself, doing my act in a cabaret – in the middle of an Odd Ode someone was murdered. The part was small, but Betty and I benefited from it enormously. From then on Anna and Herbert became dear friends and Anna was kind enough to become Jill's godmother. Herbert, then obviously very ill and only a few weeks before his death, was sweet enough to honour me by his presence at my *This is Your Life* programme. It was a brave and generous gesture. Anna, happily, is still with us, as lovable and glamorous as ever.

Sir Michael Balcon then invited me to play the part of Mantalini in Charles Dickens's *Nicholas Nickleby*. I enjoyed this immensely. Fay Compton, one of the great ladies of the theatre, was Mrs Mantalini, and there was an all-star cast headed by Sir Cedric Hardwicke, with Stanley Holloway, Sybil Thorndike, Bernard Miles, Cathleen Nesbitt, Alfred Drayton and Sir Michael's daughter, the velvet-voiced Jill Balcon, in her first film part. Cavalcanti was the director. We did six comedy sequences as the Mantalinis, and sometimes we had to retake some of them because the technicians on the set laughed out loud. The film was over-long; the only scenes not closely involved with the story were the Mantalini comedy sequences. Only one half of one of the sequences was left in the film. While I was making this film at Ealing – shooting our scenes took a fortnight – I was appearing with Betty in our road show, *Odes and Ends*, at Chiswick Empire and Golders Green Hippodrome. There was a heatwave and we were playing twice nightly. An awful lot of effort went into those funny sequences left on the cutting-room floor.

However, Sir Michael was instrumental in Betty and me being included in a scheme of J. Arthur Rank's to exploit new talent in some well-made but not too expensive new film ventures. We were to star in a film of *The Venus Touch* by F. Anstey. It was a most acceptable comic idea, and six weeks were set aside out of our busy music-hall schedule to make it. There was a hitch over getting the film rights of the story; Mary Pickford had acquired them many years previously to make a musical film of the story, but she had not made it. Rank were confident that they would be able to buy her options on the story. They couldn't. She decided to make the film after all. Cyril and Betty had reminded her of her valuable property! By now we were very near to the six weeks set aside to make the film, and we were, of course, under contract to Rank to make it. We were summoned, Betty and I, to Mr John Davis's office, and he told us that the film and our contracts were cancelled. There have been times in our careers when we have stood out for our rights, and though we sympathized very much with the dilemma in which Rank found itself, we stood to lose a great deal if we didn't make the film; not only had it already been publicized that we were to make it, but we would lose six weeks of very high music-hall salaries. It was nine o'clock in the morning and Mr Davis was quite annoyed. Much heat was generated his side of the desk. He shouted and bullied us quite a lot. I always get very quiet under these circumstances, and so does Betty.

'We shall make a film for you at the scheduled time,' I said, rather firmly.

'And if necessary,' said Betty, 'we will find a story for you.'

We left. In the car on the way home I said to Betty, 'Where on earth are you going to find another story?'

'I shall write it myself,' she said, and she did.

The film was called *A Piece of Cake*, and had it been given the necessary time for production and the necessary finance, and also an experienced director, it might have proved a good film. Betty's fundamental idea was an excellent one, and she wrote a very good story. I was to write an Odd Ode about a rather nasty character who came to life and endeavoured to wreak all kinds of awful vengeance on us for having invented him. This part of a minor Prince of Darkness was played by Laurence Naismith, who was excellent. John Croydon was the producer, and also wrote the actual screenplay. As a producer he could not have worked harder for the good of the film, and he stretched the tiny budget in a most imaginative and admirable way. He needed a lighter touch as a writer, and the script needed smarter, crisper dialogue. One of the wonderful things he did, however, was to commission Edward Burra to design some horrendous surrealistic caves for a dream sequence. Some of these designs were offered to us at the end of the picture for most reasonable sums, like £50 or so. We thought they were too macabre to hang on the walls of our home to become familiar friends, to be looked at day by day, and we refused the offer. Had we accepted they would today be worth tens of thousands of pounds.

When Betty was writing the sequence of the chasing of us by the devil character from the Odd Ode in these caves, I kept trying to restrain her imaginative pen. '*We* have got to *do* all these things,' I kept saying. 'And I've got a horror of heights!'

'Do not worry' she said. 'A lot of this can be done by flying on a Kirby wire as they do in pantomimes, and the really difficult stuff will be done by stunt-men doubles.'

I was not entirely convinced. Betty as a child actress and ballet dancer had appeared in Maeterlinck's *Blue Bird* and had worked on a wire. On one occasion they had let her in supposedly to the ground so that they could unhook her and she could remove the harness and run to the dressing room for a quick change; when, in effect, they let her in to about three inches from the stage, dangling helplessly in full view of the audience.

When the filming began, Betty had eventually to fly about thirty feet above ground on to a precipitous ledge of rock where there was a gallery of tiny caves in the big cave. As the wire was hooked to the harness in the centre of her back, she was left at studio roof height with nothing at all to hold on to. She was all right for the first two or three takes, but eventually fainted. In the next shot I had to dangle in a kind of gigantic netball net over a den of roaring, hungry lions. There were no real lions on the set; this was to be a 'wild shot' edited in later, so there was no danger there. But I did, with my very real fear of heights, have to get on to a girder about twenty-five feet up and jump perhaps ten feet into this net, which was still suspended fifteen feet above the ground.

'Why isn't the stunt man going to do this?' I said, pointing to a very muscular chap dressed in identical clothing to mine who was looking on.

'It would be so much better if you did it – it would save us time and money and we are already overspent,' said the director. I thought to myself, 'If I have the courage to get up to the required height and then edge along the girder twenty-five feet up, I will have the courage to do the jump. Especially as I will have to edge my way all the way back if I don't jump and I am being watched by about fifty technicians on the floor.' I got up to the girder, sweating profusely. I edged my way, fearfully and carefully, along it to where I had to be in order to jump into the net, which would hold me suspended over the lions; but I was too afraid to jump. The longer I stayed up there contemplating the drop, the more fearful I became, and, indeed, the more strongly the thought came into my mind that it would be quite wrong for me to jump into the net. Imagine then my humiliation in front of everybody – especially Betty, who had done her piece so bravely – when I edged my way back along the girder. The experienced stunt man then walked along the girder in a most nonchalant way (I had edged along inch by inch, sitting down), and jumped superbly into the net. It promptly collapsed; he fell fifteen feet and broke his leg.

Rank changed their policy and did not make any more of these experimental films which were to provide them with new stars. It may have been *A Piece of Cake* which caused the change in policy! I've not made a single film since.

14   Odd Abodes

'Someday we'll build a home on a hill top high
You and I.'

           – 'The Folks Who Live on a Hill'.

Betty and I are both country-loving people. We had always wanted to live in the country, and so, on marrying, we were able to fulfil our ambitions. And since then we have continued to do so, in five different houses.

Our first home in 1941 was a thatched one at Welwyn – Old Welwyn in Hertfordshire – about five miles from the Garden City. It was on a hillside, facing south, in twenty acres of ground surrounded by woodland. Quite near to the A1 road from Welwyn to Stevenage, but sufficiently off it to be quiet, and there were few houses near. It was approached by a drive lined with enormous trees of *Cupressus macrocarpa* – the golden frost-resistant ones – and Lombardy poplars. It was largely a wooden structure, having been built in the 1920s, and was thatched with reed. It was a beautiful little house with a balcony running the length of our bedroom, which was large, and over a larger drawing room with polished pine floors. The hall was square, with an open fireplace, and this we made into a dining room so that the actual dining room housed our desks and books and became the study. This had a veranda leading to the garden and was much lived in. Upstairs there were three bedrooms. It wasn't a large house, but it was fairly spacious.

We lived there for three years – happy, sunny years, in a garden with masses of shrubs and roses, a great deal of grass to mow, a hard tennis court and a herbaceous border one hundred yards long, which I ordered from Bakers of Codsall and planted with the help of Betty's mother, who then, I suppose, was over sixty and who thought nothing, when over eighty, of flying to Paris to lecture, or to take an initiation ceremony for the Co-Freemasonic Order. 'I'm flying to Ireland tomorrow,' she'd say, as she waved good-bye. 'It's so much quicker.' We never forgave her for dying quite gracefully at the age of eighty-two, she was too merry and useful.

It was difficult to get furniture at that time. New furniture was not being made and was largely sold out. In any case, antique furniture was really what we needed. We managed to get some of the last white Malabar carpets there were – and with old and new, and Betty's considerable decorative flair, we managed a reasonably graceful home. The war helped in some ways, as the grand piano we purchased – a Playel – had been brought over by a French concert pianist and reluctantly sold. We treasure it now, and one of the best-remembered days at Welwyn was when Richard Tauber came out and played on it, and accompanied himself on it, for us to be the first to hear his lovely musical show *Old Chelsea*.

One morning I awakened to see a little man in a bowler hat knocking stakes into the bottom of our field. I was very much monarch of all I surveyed – one is when one first purchases a piece of one's native land. And so, picking up the bowler hat I had kept as a memento of my insurance days, and regardless of the fact that it might look a little incongruous with my bright-red pyjamas, I marched through the dew-drenched grass to 'tell off' the intruder. (Sometimes small boys would collect sweet chestnuts from our woods in sacks, and we would go down, having waited until they had laboured hard enough to fill the sacks, and confiscate them.)

'What on earth do you think you are up to in our field?' the irate landowner demanded.

'Aar,' said the man, 'this is where the Stevenage by-pass will run through.'

The landowner became immediately aware of the power of bureaucracy and his feet felt suddenly cold and the bowler hat lost its jaunty angle. 'I'll get dressed,' I said, 'and you can tell me all about it.'

He did, of course, tell me all about it. We decided to sell immediately in a great panic, and the road was opened exactly twenty-one years after we sold. When we sold it to Mr and Mrs Charles Forsythe of Forsythe, Seaman and Farrell, a top-line Canadian variety act of the time they converted it into a hotel and had caravans in the field with a restaurant and club where Charlie Forsythe proudly displayed his talents at cookery.

There began a search for the next house. It was a little difficult, as we were on tour with one of our road shows all over the country, but we would search the Sunday papers; find anything likely and try to see them at weekends. We were at the Mumbles Hotel near Swanage one Sunday when I read out to Betty the particulars – rather glowing particulars as I remember – of a property which was exactly what we wanted at exactly the price we wanted to pay. I rang the agent next morning with an offer – it was an advertisement to sell our very own house at Welwyn.

We always wanted to live in Sussex, so we tried a lot of places there, only to find that 'belt of woodland between house and road' would become a few wisps of rank privet and some decrepit *Rhododendron ponticum*. We saw at least fifty houses, and one day we went to see, at East Grinstead, what looked from the particulars to be not at all what we wanted. We were not to know that the Edwardian house would be a rather attractive attempt by the Edwardian architect to pretend he was building a long, low Tudor house; we were not to know that the garden, which was hardly mentioned, was on the side of a south-facing hill and overlooked miles and miles of Ashdown Forest and glorious sweeps of the Weald of Sussex. There were lovely mature trees – forty-foot high glaucous cedars, a tulip tree the same height, mammoth magnolias, gigantic cypresses and tall, tapering junipers. There were terraces and stone steps and balustrades, little secret walks between high stone walls, the scent of ancient box hedges and golden yews. There were tiny ponds and large ponds, and hidden rivulets of water. A long pergola, heavy with roses and clematis, led you to a wild garden of mature oaks and beeches where the sun shone through on fifteen feet high and fifteen feet across bushes of every possible kind of rhododendron, pink and yellow, white and red, some orchid-like in sheer beauty. Through a little glade you came upon the tiny cottage I described earlier. There were separate rose gardens, a peach house, seven other greenhouses, a trog-like potting shed. A dream of a garden, most beautifully kept, except for one spacious lawn on which an enormous defence work of steel poles and barbed wire was erected – a defence work, part of England's brave last-ditch defence, already mouldering like a Martello tower.

It also needed a ten-ton truck of anthracite to heat the house! Imagine the cost today! And the cost also of the two gardeners (full time, one resident in the lodge cottage), the cook, the house parlour-maid, the two dailies and the Norland nurse for Jilly, and the secretary who lived in the chauffeur's cottage! I was thirty-two years old and must have been a millionaire.

The house, you gather, was vast. It was on the ground floor that we had a large entrance hall about fourteen feet by ten, a study leading off into a conservatory, a dining room, a very large drawing room, which was originally a billiard room and was rather grand with a great open fireplace, and an entrance from a gallery down some steps. There was a downstairs nursery and a servants' sitting room, and a labyrinth of kitchens and butlers' pantries. Upstairs there were eight bedrooms and two bathrooms. All decorating at that time was only allowed by licence from the local authority. Our licence for so large a house was derisory. We decided to do much of it ourselves. When an irate inspector arrived to see if we were exceeding our quota, he found the glamorous actress Betty astride the bath painting the bathroom ceiling. Our licence was immediately enlarged, but this was in effect our first effort at decorating. Always there were staff troubles. Our first domestic as such seemed to be an Old English sheepdog in maid's uniform, who needed to keep her feet up as much as possible. We didn't please her and she left.

Her complete opposite came and did for us. She was a companion house-keeper. Had once done for the Dean of Windsor and had left, we imagined, because of all those turret stairs. She was quite fun and a superb cook after being primed with a couple of gins. Because of petrol rationing we used to travel into London by train. The last train back which we had to catch for our theatrical engagements did not have first-class carriages, as the train we used to take into London was always so full we had to stand; anyway we saw no sense in the extra expense of travelling first, so we travelled third – we used to say goodbye to her on the platform while she got into her first-class compartment and we travelled third. When we moved from Welwyn to Sussex we sent her on holiday to Bristol for fear she would get in the way. So we did the entire move. We got everything exactly in place as it had been at the old house, carpets down, pictures hung, curtains up, furniture in place, and very contentedly travelled, after this hectic weekend, to the New Theatre at Cardiff where we played our two houses of variety. After having done two shows, we decided to ring her up at home (she had crossed with us in our journey to Cardiff and hers from Bristol to Sussex) to see what she thought of it all. She had had a holiday. We had put the house straight and done two performances and a band call in a variety theatre. Her journey was a little shorter than ours.

'Oh,' said her weak, tired voice over the phone, 'I've had such a ghastly journey.'

'But what d'you think of it all?' we excitedly said.

'Well – after my ghastly journey, I arrived here, and what d'you think . . . no cake!'

A gardener we had at Welwyn was a dear pixilated man, and he didn't feel very well one winter's day. I thought he looked very ill indeed, so I decided to use some of my precious petrol ration to take him home in my car. He used to cycle home. It took him some ten minutes. I wasn't exactly sure where he lived and asked him to direct me. After we had been motoring quite quickly for at least twenty minutes I said that indeed he lived a very long way away. 'Oh no,' he said, 'this is the long way round. I thought the drive would do me good.'

The posh lady was followed by 'a married couple', Maria and Henry. They were curiously late for their interview, but seemed suitable and had impeccable references, it seemed, from half the names in *Debrett*. I was recovering from jaundice when they came, and to cheer myself up, and also to cheer up Betty's Aunt Diddy, who was also convalescent and staying with us for a holiday, I would do the odd little comic turn. Always as I finished one of these comic gems, the immobile face of Henry would suddenly be there, like the Cheshire Cat – but there was no smile on the face of the tiger, only a blank disapproving stare. He never walked anywhere – he silently glided. It was Betty's Aunt Diddy, some years later, when she was in her late eighties, who was discovered by Betty playing football in her bedroom with some rolled-up socks with her sister, Betty's mother, who was in her early eighties. Betty said, in mock disapproval, 'How dare you at your age?', Betty's mother said, 'Well, you're only old once!'

Now Maria proved to be a dream of a cook. Succulent masterpieces followed in Lucullan splendour. We could not believe our luck. *Debrett* had been right. Perhaps the richness of the food was bad for my recovery – like all jaundice sufferers, I became very irritable, and when a whole lot of banging of doors started one afternoon I rang for Henry and demanded an explanation. He seemed oddly flustered. He would see that it didn't happen again. More doors were banged, which shook this extremely solid house. I decided to go and investigate. Jaundice leaves one curiously weak and I tottered out into the kitchen. There was a demented Maria, hair all about her shoulders, eyes very bloodshot, shouting like a fishwife at Henry. I thought she had gone mad. Actually, she was drunk. On seeing me she seized our enormous butcher's knife and made towards me with it, yelling with blood-curdling screams the while. Henry shut himself rather smartly into a broom cupboard. Maria and I were alone. She was now advancing on me and I was moving round the kitchen table. The odd lunge at me was made across the table, the large knife embedding itself in the scrubbed white deal. It took all of Maria's strength to pull it out each time and this delayed her progress a little. With my jaundiced weakness I was not retreating very fast, and it was obvious that she was gaining. What on earth was I to do? I have a large voice. Large enough to fill the Albert Hall; or empty it. At its most stentorian and dramatically Shakespearian, I turned it on her.

'Woman!' I thundered. 'Woman, go to your room!'

She immediately put the knife down like a zombie and went wailing up to her bedroom. Henry shot out of the broom cupboard like a racing greyhound as the gate goes up, dashed after her and turned the key in the lock.

'It has been like this for years,' he explained to me. 'The reason why we were late for our interview was that Maria got into the pub at the end of the High Street and I had to sober her up before we could see you.'

'Why do you not get her into a home?' I said. 'Or get her some treatment?'

'I love her,' he said, simply. 'And as long as we can we must stay together.'

That night the gardener insisted on sleeping on a mattress in the corridor outside her bedroom with a truncheon under his pillow. They packed their bags the next morning. The week after we were playing the Hippodrome, Brighton, with one of our road shows. As we went through the stage door on the Monday night, there were Henry and Maria, arm in arm. 'May we have a couple of tickets for tonight?' he said. We gave them a box – there were no other seats to be had. Most graciously she waved her programme at us as the curtain came down.

One of our dearest friends, Frances, followed Maria and Henry. She came as a house parlour-maid and after a succession of disastrous cooks, Betty – who is in the Cordon Bleu class (which is why my dewlaps and stomach are pendulous) – taught her how to cook. Frances then entered the Cordon Bleu class and stayed with us for many, many years. She was Irish and Catholic. We were English and Protestant. From some of our houses later the Roman Catholic churches were fairly distant; Frances used to cycle, and if the weather was very bad and I was at home I would drop her at her church and then, so as not to waste the petrol, I would go to early-morning service at my church. We both worshipped the same God, but in a slightly different way. Frances respected my difference and I respected hers. We lived happily and amicably under the same roof tree until one of her sisters had a stroke and Frances had to return to Ireland to take care of her as her other sister was sadly bedridden. By then Frances was well into her sixties, and is still there leading her good cheerful life. We miss her terribly, not only for her help in the house, but for her smile and her way of life and sense of humour. We write and keep each other up to date with our news. One of her sadnesses is that the dogs she knew and doted on have now died. She loved her 'petties' and the three cats too, which we had while she was with us. However, we have told her all about their successors and she has had photos of them and they are inquired after as members of the family, which, of course, they are. We can never thank Frances enough for sharing so many years of our life so gently and so helpfully.

We sold the house at East Grinstead as it was getting almost suburban in that part of the town, and we bought in 1950 the Water Mill at Colemans Hatch; Newbridge Mill mentioned in Domesday (which, of course, is where I get my jokes from!). We bought it from Margaret Eason, who was the widow of Sir Herbert Eason, a medical mogul, I believe, of Guy's Hospital. She loved her husband dearly and was quite bereft when he died; selling the house was a wrench too, and as she lived in a nearby cottage which they also owned, she decided she would be our secretary. She would answer the phone, saying, 'This is Lady Eason here, Cyril Fletcher's secretary,' and as these were the snob days at the BBC it got me a lot of work! She was immensely tall and thin with huge feet and a nose of similar proportions. It's ungallant of me to mention this large embellishment to her merry face, but she too would make fun of it. I always had trouble in getting shoes large enough (men's size nine) for my Dame in pantomime; very expensively, I had them especially made.

'Why not go to the Tall Gel?' said Margaret.

'Who is she?' said I.

'A shop,' said Margaret, 'where I get my enormous shoes.'

So I went one day to the Tall Girl off Piccadilly and asked for some court shoes, size equivalent to size nine men's, and the girl went away and brought some. She was about to wrap them up, my having approved the style, when I said, 'Don't wrap them up yet. I must try them on.' The girl went very red and disappeared into the inner sanctum of the shop and came back rather hurriedly and flustered with the manager and an alsatian dog. I explained that I was playing Dame in pantomime and all was well.

Margaret Eason told us, when she sold us Newbridge Mill, that it did not flood. It did, pretty regularly. She had this very much on her conscience, and every time there was a storm, or rain for several days, she would put her nose round the door and say, 'Any anxiety?' It is difficult for me to give you the accent in print, but her anxiety was stretched from here to Roedean and back again, with an upward inflection of inquiry sounding like 'anx-aht-teh'. We hated the Mill because of its propensity to flood, but so funny was this constant question and the way Margaret uttered it that we dissolved our fears frequently in laughter. One of her daughters at that time was married to the principal tutor at King's College, Cambridge, and when we were in pantomime there Margaret too would come up. One day she advanced down the passageway through the stage door at the Arts Theatre, having evaded the stage-door keeper, right on to the side of the stage. On she went into the wings, and was about to step on to the brightly lighted stage, preceded by her nose, saying, 'What's going on here? Anything interesting?' when luckily I fielded her just as she was about to make her incongruous entrance. At all costs she had to be stopped. She would have got a bigger laugh than me. I am able to write like this about her because she was so amused at herself, and so lovable.

The Mill, though mentioned in Domesday, was largely Tudor. It was known as the Hammer of the Forest in old records, and was an ironmaster's house. Nearby was a row of cottages built to accommodate workers in the armaments drive at the time of the Armada. Ashdown Forest, with its wood and charcoal furnaces and its iron ore, was very industrial then. Many is the time I would move a 'stone' out of the river bed and find it was almost solid iron. The water ran very rustily red in places. *Winnie the Pooh* was written up the road, and Christopher Fry lived at the Mill for a time.

The first autumn we lived there was very wet indeed, and the mill house and the mill building were, in effect, on an island, mill pond one side and weir, then the stream flowing by the front of the house and under a bridge. (This was too low and held the flow of water.) If it rained a lot and we were on tour, we would ask to speak to Jill on the phone, who was between the ages of five and seven. She would then give us a picture of the state of watery siege. 'It's three bricks high on the bridge, Daddy – there is one leaf out of the weir' (the water being controlled by the putting in or pulling out of pieces of wood – known as leaves – over the weir) 'and we have two planks in over the wheel.' Then I would be able to visualize the amount of flow of the water and asking the local weather forecast (instructions were given never to miss it) be able, even two hundred miles away, to give instructions for Frances or the gardener to adjust, with the putting in or pulling out of leaves in the weir, the amount of water, and thus avert a flood. It was only Jilly, child though she was, who could give us the exact picture. Sometimes I would come home late at night from some cabaret performance, at the Savoy perhaps, at two in the morning. I would get out of my car and hear the thunder of the water over the wheel. If it had a certain 'ring' to it I would know that I would have to get my rubber boots on, climb on to the wheel – about twelve feet above the surging torrent below – and, standing in a similar surging torrent above, by the light of a torch held in my mouth, ease out with a spade a piece of wood the size, weight and thickness of an old wooden railway sleeper. I would have to do this with one arm while I anchored myself firmly with the other; for, once the sleeper of wood was raised, the rush of water would try and send me with the weighty piece of wood flying down the stream two or three fields away to be retrieved in the morning.

At great expense I had the river widened and the banks raised. All to no avail. Mill dwellers will know that there is not a mill in the kingdom that does not, or has not, flooded at some time. After three years of 'anx-aht-teh', we decided to sell, and quite truthfully we could say to prospective buyers that the Mill had not yet flooded. Damn near it; but never quite in our time. We sold, the contracts were exchanged, the new house was bought, but we were still living at the Mill. It was a beautiful June morning; albeit clouds were gathering fast. Betty's mother, and my mother and father were there to lunch; the rest of the household were Jill, her governess, Frances, and a housemaid, who was French. There was a cloudburst. This over-filled a lake up the valley, which burst its banks, and the whole valley flooded very quickly. Dead cows and poultry floated by. Cyclists were swept off the road into the stream and were rescued by firemen. With fascinated horror, faces glued to the window, we watched the water rise. We were certainly going to flood.

We took as many books as we could upstairs. We lugged as many of our white Malabar carpets as we could upstairs. I was quite sure it would be the stream at the back of the house that would overflow, held, as it was, by the bridge. (That bridge beneath which we often caught trout for the table. Don't tell anyone, but we scooped them out of the stream in a wastepaper basket. So sporting!) In great haste and with a deal of energy, I cut three flood boards to fit the back door. I fitted and held them in position and caulked where they met the jambs of the door with Jilly's plasticine. The water rose, I held the boards against the flood; I was smiling triumphantly as I stooped there. The water would go down and we would be saved. Suddenly my behind was gripped by ice. The water had flooded from the pond, had entered the front door and was swirling round my frozen buttocks. It rose to four feet, having come in over the cess pit.

We had the only grand piano in Sussex to grow its own watercress, and our TV set was bobbing on the flood from room to room. Frances was trying to save a water rat from the dogs. My parents and Betty's mother and Jill and her governess were upstairs. This is when great forest trees floated by, and mindful of the fact that the house was ancient – an oak frame house with brick and wattle walls – might it not give way under the great pressure of the water, and might we not be all swept away with the dead cows, sheep and poultry? There was an ancient stone wall surrounding the north of the house by the river and connecting the house to the bridge. I put Jilly on my shoulders and, holding hard to the stone wall, I edged my slippery way to the bridge and safety. I knew that, should I slip, Jill would be washed away and drowned. I am six feet tall, fairly heavily built; in 1953, I was exactly forty years old, and it was all I could do to remain upright against the weight of water.

I landed Jill and came back for Betty, who is five foot three inches at the most, and very slight; arm-in-arm we waded along by the wall – it was as much as we could do to stay upright. 'This is June,' I said to myself, 'in Sussex, on a Sunday afternoon. Anyone would think we were fighting for survival in the Rockies!' Back I went to the house. The governess was standing by with the first of the dogs for me to carry across!! 'Not on your Nelly!' cried the hero of the house. In an hour the water had gone down to unfrightening proportions. In another half an hour, with the aid of a couple of duckboards over the deepest puddles, we were able to get my parents out. They were so keen to go. My mother inferred that we had flooded the whole valley on purpose and that we would be hearing from her in no uncertain terms.

'Stay behind and help dry the books?' we suggested. (We lost over 1,000 of them.)

'Stay behind? But we have fifty miles to motor home!'

I have never seen my immobile mother so mobile. She was an active sixty-seven at the time. Frances, Betty, Jill, the governess and Betty's seventy-four-year-old mother and I then bailed out this stinking water. It took us eight hours. We had one respite; when my mother rang.

'We had quite a sunny drive home,' she said. 'Hardly any traffic and no rain.'

We owned eleven acres of grazing at the Mill, and this we let, as Lady Eason had done before us, to a charming family – a sort of English hillbilly family – who kept a pet horse. It was thin and old and ugly and 'had broken my brother's arm', said one of the family. 'We only keep him as a pet.' Well, one very cold winter's day the pet horse fell into the stream, and it looked sadly as if the thin gaunt beast would never get itself out of its watery dilemma. It is extraordinary how large and bony and obstinate an elderly horse can be, especially if it is virtually upside down in icy water, grinning at death with its long yellow teeth. 'Will you come and help us?' the elderly brothers said. You will remember my horror of horses, inherited from my mother. I made encouraging noises and, indeed, very bravely I went up to the horse and pulled it and pushed at it; but my heart was not in the job. I kept reminding myself of the brother's broken arm. The poor beast was lurching less, and its smile had no humour in it at all. The two brothers were pushing astern. I was pulling at a bridle we had put round its head and neck. The brothers' sister was weeping copiously on the bank. It was obvious something had to be done.

If they had owned a tractor we might have pulled him out, but they only had a bull-nose Morris. Then I had a brain-wave. I dashed back into the Mill House, and remember this was under the Socialist régime in 1950, when everything was rationed or on the black market; particularly whisky, which was like gold. I got the only bottle of whisky for miles around from my cupboard and dashed back to the horse. In all fairness I ought to explain to you that gin is the only spirit I can drink without harm. Whisky gives me terrible stomach pains: but I do keep it for my friends. The poor pet horse was gasping its last as I shoved the whisky bottle between the long yellow teeth amid the slimy yellow foam issuing from its mouth. I emptied half the bottle down the thin aged throat. Both the brothers started to cry now, as well as the sister. They were fond of whisky and had not seen any for years. I told you the horse was grinning at death. Now slowly, and almost imperceptibly, this harrowing grin became a seraphic smile; the horse almost laughed. It almost danced. Its feet flayed about; it tried anew as the whisky coursed through its veins, and it practically jumped out of its watery and icy grave on to the side of the stream. Lurching forward so quickly, so successfully and so suddenly, it saved its life, but with the same great leap broke the brother's other arm. I gave him the other half of the whisky, and greeny foam or not around the bottle's mouth, he took a great swig and with his arm hanging limply at his side staggered off with his brother and sister; all three, and the horse, grinning with their long yellow teeth.

The house we bought next was a stone Georgian house belonging to a retired admiral, which had a hand grenade in the best bedroom and a derelict air and a derelict garden. The 'before and after' pictures are reproduced in this book. The house was charming and it was exactly the right size; small but gracious and well proportioned. We were very happy with it, and it was almost the perfect house, though its view did not spread far. I did not make a lot of the garden here, but we had a good peach house and extensive kitchen garden; we grew all that was needed for our own food, with plenty over for the assortment of gardeners we employed.

When we brought the Mill we decided to add a couple of bedrooms and an extra bathroom and more spacious kitchen quarters to the old building. You will understand that to copy a Tudor building is difficult and needs artistry and flair; qualities not found frequently among builders. I did know, however, of a Sussex firm, Lions Green Works, belonging to a Colonel Tuppen, who had created and built many a pseudo-Sussex farmhouse with ancient atmospheres. Greatrex Newman's partner, George Royle, had bought one at Cross-in-Hand, and we had played tennis here weekend after weekend while playing *Fol-de-Rol* summer seasons at Hastings. Allan Perry had been a frequent visitor to these tennis parties and had employed Lions Green Works to build him a thatched house in a wood at Brookmans Park as his home when he got married. This house, too, was delightfully done, so I had a great deal of confidence in letting Colonel Tuppen build an extra wing to a house mentioned in Domesday. You would never have known that an addition has been made, and even had you known, you would have found difficulty in knowing where the addition began. His foreman for this work was Fred Russell, a delightful craftsman, Sussex born and bred, a good builder and artistic with it.

One day while living at High Hurstwood in the Dove House – the Georgian one – we were televising a documentary programme from the Marshes near Rye, and on our way there Betty read in the local paper of a Georgian cottage near Ringmer in a third of an acre of ground. It was priced at £1,000. This, even then in the late 1950s, was absurdly cheap.

'We'll buy it,' I said.

'Without even seeing it?' said Betty.

'Well,' I said, 'even if it's condemned, a Georgian cottage in a third of an acre of ground near Ringmer, which is also near to Glyndebourne, must be worth that.'

So I stopped the car and rang the agent and bought the Old Black Cottage, Potatoe Lane, Ringmer. It *was* condemned! After endless chats with the local planners, and in spite of endless entreaties by them to pull it down and build a nice modern bungalow on the third of an acre, we eventually – with the aid of Fred Russell and some mates of his working in their spare time – turned it into a pink-washed little Georgian enchantment, with a new kitchen, new drainage and cess pit, new bathroom and Betty's decorating and furnishings, calling it Nightingale Cottage, Potato Lane, Ringmer. Two tiny bedrooms it had upstairs, two tiny reception rooms downstairs, but the Georgian proportions and windows were exactly right, and, enhanced by Betty's swagged curtains, period fabrics and wallpapers, it was a dream of an adult's doll's house. What to do with it? You may well ask. I shall come back with the answer later, but before I do so I would like to mention the enormously hard work Betty put into it. She not only made the curtains and hung the wallpaper – she painted

147

all the woodwork and ceilings (with my help), but she upholstered furniture, did odd carpentry jobs and, in short, by immense labour transformed the place. She even fitted and laid all the carpets. Oh, and I put a fireplace in.

Jilly, you will remember, went to Battle Abbey School. And on Sundays when we went to meet her out of school, on the road between Buxted and Battle, was this unbelievable view of twelve miles of unspoilt Sussex, finishing with the sea. 'If only our lovely Georgian house at High Hurstwood had that view,' we said every Sunday for several years.

Now, of course, it does, and we are still living there! One day we saw a house for sale – a decayed piece of hideous Victoriana – with no garden but a lovely avenue of beech trees up to and away from the house. The very view we wanted, and the whole standing on an island site of thirty-three acres. We knocked it down and built a replica, with all those little amendments we wished we had had before at the High Hurstwood house. As we could not afford stone – it would have cost the earth – we built in brick, and because we took the outside measurements of the old house at High Hurstwood, our new one is two feet or so larger all round inside. I was, in effect, the builder, and Betty the architect. Fred Russell engaged and paid the workmen and bought the materials. I paid him each week. There were frequent delays; some windows had to be remade, the staircase arrived like a child's playground chute and had to be completely rebuilt. Little chimneys were built instead of the extra wide ones needed to accommodate the Adam grates and Georgian mantels, some of which we already owned, and some of which we purchased in Brighton, and these had to be altered. I think it worth recording that in the Dove House the bedrooms had enchanting duck's-nest grates in them – we wanted so much to repeat these at the new house (even though they would be purely for decorative purposes, as we did not make actual chimneys for the bedrooms) but search as we might, there seemed to be none available. One day, on going over to get something from our scenery store at the Dove House, we noted a pile of rubble on which sat two of these beautiful duck's-nest grates. 'May we have them?' we asked the new owners. 'If you want them,' they said. 'We don't like the blessed things.' So, in triumph, we brought them home, where they grace the bedrooms, but I must remember, if ever we sell this house, to tell the buyers there are no chimneys!

There were plenty of dramas. The result is exactly what we wanted and, out of our five homes through the years, the only new one. Betty, as I said, drew up the plans, and being a replica, many visits and measurements had to be made to the old house. We were playing pantomime at the time and a lot of the plan-drawing was done by Betty between songs at the Ashcroft Theatre in her dressing room. Not only did Betty do the planning, but when the house was built she decorated it. She hung every piece of wallpaper; some of it period flock-wallpaper; and, of course, made every single pair of swagged curtains, every bedspread and, indeed, quite a lot of the upholstery. As an amusement I have asked her to calculate how many pairs of curtains she has made since we were married, and the result is – you'll never believe it – 245 pairs! All of them lined and interlined, and some of them with the most elaborate swags. It was when we were in the theatre that things would go wrong behind our backs. The new house grew so slowly that when we had to move out of the Dove House, it being sold on a certain date, the new house was nowhere near ready. So our address became Nightingale Cottage, Potatoe Lane, Ringmer, for three months. It was so tiny that the beagle and the bulldog would scrap together under the table in the tiny dining room and Betty would get bitten trying to part them. She has a way with dogs!

It was to Dartmouth that we went one day when we were playing a week's variety one Whitsun at the Princes Theatre, Torquay. Edmund Hockridge was on the bill. We had made an offer for him to be with us in our first summer show when we heard him sing in a Canadian Air Force show broadcast (in which we were guests but which he had to turn down because the Canadian Air Force would not release him). Quite out of the blue and in Above Town we saw for sale a Georgian house called Castle View. (It looked up the river to the college and down river to the castle.) It was on three storeys and had beautifully proportioned rooms. 'Let's look at it,' Betty said. We did and we could see the sense of converting it into a top flat to be entered up a few steps from Above Town, and the two remaining floors into a maisonette to be entered from the tiny garden from Chapel Steps. Before we left that week for home we had purchased Castle View and it became our first property venture.

Betty hung the wallpaper assisted by Peter Hudson (a merry tenor from our summer show whom we turned through the years into a very good comedian). She also made all the curtains with Georgian pelmets, and fitted the carpets. I made some working services and helped with the painting. We attended auction sales: at the first auction sale, as we walked in someone bid £3 for Lot 35. So for fun, and to make Betty laugh, I bid £3.50. I'd no idea what Lot 35 was but I soon found out, for bidding stopped at £3.50. It was a magnificent genuine Georgian sofa. The flats were soon furnished and were really a picture. We used to let the maisonette to surgeon commanders from the Naval College; keeping the top flat for ourselves. We never had time to get down there and enjoy this top flat so we let it to a rather sad lady who kept getting very behindhand with her rent. She did a moonlight flit eventually and when we did her flat over, I opened a cupboard and a great avalanche of racing newspapers enveloped me. Then we let it to a butcher who kept watering his window boxes and the surgeon commander's lady's best Ascot hats. She in turn had a whippet that watered our new carpets. We owned this property for about five years and got very fond of it and the people of Dartmouth too.

Now I am writing this from a penthouse flat we own at the back of Torquay above Lincombe Woods with a view right across the bay to Brixham and Dartmouth with, to the right, the harbour at Torquay and behind that the moors. A fabulous view it is of one of our most favourite parts of this lovely country. When we had the summer show at the Pavilion we would take the dogs every day through Lincombe Woods and worry about where we would place the summer show next year, whether we would be able to clinch that radio series, and where could we do pantomime the year afterwards! Always worrying about the future and keeping all our plates spinning like a juggler with a view to an affluent old age. There were reverses as well as successes always and here we now are (if only we could have looked into the future) perched above that very walk in Lincombe Woods in one of the most handsome of all Torquay's penthouses. Furnished too, and decorated so artistically and comfortably by Betty's fair, sure hand.

Castle View, Above Town, Dartmouth, was the first of our properties, then came Nightingale Cottage at Ringmer. After that we really got the 'bug'. Bess of Hardwicke had nothing on Betty Astell!

What with presenting so many pantomimes at Cambridge, we had often stayed in hotels and then Frances, with whom we always left the dogs, was called hurriedly to Ireland. This meant we had to take furnished rooms in Cambridge so that we could take the dogs with us. For two successive years we took different flats from a local lady doctor who dabbled in lettings and property, and we realized what a demand there was, and also what a dearth there was of well-furnished and imaginatively decorated flats in the city. We decided to help Cambridge out! We purchased a large Victorian house on four floors on Mid-Summer Common, which was used as undergraduates' lodgings and kept by an elderly couple who fed and looked after the students. We converted this into four flats, Betty once again working out where the bathrooms would go, where we could find room for small kitchens and so on. Plans were passed very quickly and Fred Russell supervised a gang of Cambridge builders, who again took for ever and did not once complete on time. With outdoor work the weather can sometimes delay (though this surely could be allowed for!), but indoor work surely should be to schedule.

We once arranged with a Devon builder to do certain work in Castle View before we went down on holiday – a precious fortnight kept clear of bookings – to do the decorations. When we arrived, weeks after work should have been completed, the builder had not even begun! I would love to arrange that the opening performance, on Boxing Day afternoon, of one of our pantomimes, should be completely sold out – the whole house – to some confederation of builders and their wives and families. They would all arrive on Boxing Day afternoon at 2.30 prompt, full of cold Christmas pudding, and they would wait with beaming, expectant faces for the pantomime to begin. I would not even bother to dress up as Widow Twankey or Mother Goose – in my dressing gown, at approximately three o'clock, having kept them waiting only half an hour, I would saunter through the curtains to that house sold out completely to builders and their families and say, 'Sorry we are a bit late. As a matter of fact, we've had a bit of bother getting the right timber and the right canvas for the scenery. Some of our costumes are not finished yet; but I tell you what, if you all come back at Easter we'll do a pantomime for you. Good afternoon!'

The theatre curtain always goes up on time; even during the bombs it was seldom late. If one industry can do it, why cannot another?

Betty then decorated these four flats in Cambridge and furnished them, and they were all immediately let. When we asked the bank for the necessary finance for this operation they were over-generous, and actually suggested that we should have some more; so we bought two completely new flats in another part of Cambridge. These we decorated and furnished and let. We owned them for some years, and only once were we taken to the Rent Tribunal by one of our lodgers for a reduction in rent. The tribunal raised it! What was so nice was that a whole lot of married students, sometimes Americans or Canadians, would take the flats immediately after their weddings. Our flats were their first homes. We are still getting sentimental letters from some of them; we still have some of the pot plants that many of them would leave us at the end of a tenancy!! As our little property empire became a going concern we decided to be even more daring and we bought a completely new block of six flats, each with two bedrooms, sitting room, and all conveniences. These Betty furnished most beautifully and quite expensively in a modern idiom, and they all let very quickly to Americans who were there for research for three-year stints. Indeed, we provided accommodation for an Arab prince for two years.

Even under a Conservative government a private landlord had many difficulties and restrictions. As soon as a Socialist government came into power, 'landlord' became almost a dirty word. In our limited experience we found that the saying 'Good landlords make good tenants' is true – because we went out of our way to try and make them not only comfortable but happy. Betty kept in close personal touch with them at all times, and it was a totally rewarding experience. So we sold the lot. We were delighted with our little capitalist spree, but sometimes Betty, scrubbing out a flat at change-over time, would look up at me and say, 'And they call this UNEARNED income!'

Let us now go back to Nightingale Cottage, Potatoe Lane, Ringmer. The dilettante's doll's house, remember? At this time Polly Elwes invited us to a party. A fellow guest was not only a property millionaire, but he loved opera, especially at Glyndebourne. 'Come to tea,' I said. This cheerful man and his family came to see the cottage on their way to Glyndebourne. He really could not put it down. He went from room to room. 'May I go upstairs again?' he said. He revelled in Betty's colour schemes; he appreciated the way it had all been accomplished with economy. (After all, he was a millionaire!) The result was that he told Betty of a very expensive block of flats he had in Kensington which, empty, would not let. Decorated as Betty might decorate them, and furnished as Betty might furnish them, they would. They did. They let so quickly that he was always breathing down Betty's neck wanting the next one done. It is impossible today to get immediate delivery of certain expensive furnishings. It was almost impossible then to get them at all, and Betty was sometimes running to keep up with the inexorable pressure. So she stopped, but she greatly enjoyed this creative spasm while it lasted. One day our property millionaire and his charming family were to come down to us in Sussex for the day. His secretary rang about eleven in the morning. The poor man had had a stroke in his bathroom that Sunday and had died immediately. He was a kindly and ebullient man, whose loving family must miss him terribly. So that is the end of our Odd Abode adventures at the moment, but like Bess of Hardwicke, we have been badly bitten by the bug and Betty might break out again at any moment. When you have such creative and inventive and artistic flair, it is a pity not to use it.

15   Associated Speakers

'Many of the Nobility kept a fool or two, like the motleys of our court, in the days of Elizabeth, but like in name alone; for their wit, if they ever had any, is swallowed up by indolence. Savoury sauce and rich repasts swell their bodies to the most disgusting size; and, lying about the corners of some splendid saloon, they sleep profoundly till awakened by the command of their lord to amuse the company. Shaking their enormous bulk, they rise from their trance, and supporting their unwieldy trunks against the wall, drawl out their heavy nonsense with as much grace as the motions of a sloth in the hands of a reptile fancier.' – W. J. Thoms, *Anecdotes and Traditions*

Some nine years ago I began giving lunch-time talks about my adventures in showbusiness, early radio and the beginnings of television to ladies' luncheon clubs, and, similarly, talks to libraries and arts societies and theatre clubs. This I did for Maurice Frost, who for some twenty years owned and ran from a small office in Wardour Street the largest and longest-established lecture agency in the country. He was a quiet, charming man in his late sixties (I would guess), and he had worked up the whole flourishing concern from nothing. Apart from Anona Winn and Isobel Barnett, I was the only showbusiness name on the list. There were other well-known names, of course, like Sir Bernard Lovell (whose fee did not include taking his telescope with him!), A. L. Rowse, the historian and writer or the Duke of Bedford. It was most enjoyable work, and as most of it was at lunch time, one could invariably return to London for cabaret; so that although the fees were not the same as those for cabaret, it was, as it were, extra bunce! The ladies and their hospitality were delightfully welcoming and their response was warm and jocund.

For two or three seasons I did many of these talks, and then Maurice Frost sent to all his speakers and his clients a letter which was a positive bombshell. He was giving up; the agency was to close. I felt it was a pity that these small but delicious little jobs where one was paid and fed to enjoy oneself (talking about *oneself* is always enjoyable) would no longer happen. Now, Betty and I always mull over the morning post while Betty is in the bath! Sometimes she makes an emphatic point by hitting the water with the flat of her hand with devastating effect to the bathroom decorations. Before Betty was dry I had phoned Maurice Frost and had purchased the agency.

Suddenly we were the owners of the largest and most flourishing lecture agency in the country and didn't quite know what to do with it. I was very busily engaged all over the place in cabaret, radio, TV and personal appearances, as well as presenting annually, with Betty, two pantomimes and appearing in one of them. It was quite obvious that the day-to-day running of the agency, with thousands of separate bookings a year for 300 or so lecturers, was beyond the capacity of our small production office.

When Bob Monkhouse and Denis Goodwin began in partnership as writers (I had used them from their very beginnings), they had a very active and energetic young manager named Tony Davis ('Dabber' Davis to all and sundry). Not only did they have a scriptwriting business, but they also became artistes' managers and agents. They became mine for radio and TV and some separate shows (though not my own productions, such as summer shows and pantomime). So, in effect, 'Dabber' Davis became my radio and TV manager and agent. Monkhouse and Goodwin parted. Later Goodwin died. I stayed on with Tony Davis, and so did one or two other artistes, but he was not as busy as he had been. I also knew that his wife Paddy Davis, having been a hospital ward sister, was a very efficient lady. I thought with Dabber part time and Paddy whole time, and with his long and valuable experience as a theatrical agent, they would be ideal to work the agency. Dabber was ill in hospital at this crucial moment. Indeed, had been very ill for some months. Paddy agreed to take it on. This she did from their home, where we were later to build a sumptuous office. A typist and telephonist were engaged and we were in business.

The Maurice Frost Lecture Agency could have become the Cyril Fletcher Lecture Agency, but I was keen that the theatrical profession should still think of me primarily as a performer and comedian, and there was a danger that it might be generally supposed that I (already in production for summer show and pantomime) might be management only. So it was decided to call it Associated Speakers. It runs exactly as a theatrical or variety agency would, licensed annually, with the one exception that we have an annual luncheon and conference at the Dorchester Hotel, Park Lane.

The conference is held in the morning, when perhaps 300 of our clients come and discuss the new speakers, when we listen to any complaints, gloat over our successes, and explain any new business procedures which we have decided upon to improve the working of the agency for the coming year. A new catalogue is published to coincide with the conference when new speakers are included, and the whole list of speakers brought up to date. Fees are not included in the catalogue, but they are revealed to the delegates and discussed. The success of the speakers during the year is also discussed, and invariably the great success of the season for Society X is the greatest failure of the season for Club Y.

After the conference the delegates then mix with about a hundred or so of the speakers for drinks before luncheon. This procedure was once described by David Jacobs as 'the cattle market', but it does give the clients a chance to assess whether the personality of a particular speaker is likely to appeal to their particular audience. Luncheon takes place about one o'clock at small, round tables of ten with two speakers at each table. Again a good chance for clients to fraternize with speakers. Later, about a dozen speakers address the conference for three minutes each.

The list of subjects talked about is most comprehensive, ranging from ballooning to spying, taxi-driving and stage-door keeping at the Palladium, to heraldry, caravanning, music, wigs and fashion and unidentified flying objects. You name the subject you want, and we are bound to have it on our list of speakers; should you require a specialist authority on an obscure subject, we will doubtless find you the very distinguished authority you need. Among our famous speakers we have Lady Barnett, Joan Bakewell, Basil Boothroyd, Lieutenant-Colonel Blashford Snell, Frank Bough, Julia Clements, Sidney Harrison, Rachael Heyhoe, Edmund Hockridge, Anthony Hopkins, David Jacobs, Lord Longford, Edgar Lustgarten, Christopher Mayhew, Sir Bernard Miles, Robert Morley, Sheridan Morley, Ted Moult, Bob Price, Anna Raeburn, Jean Rook, Stanford Robinson, A. L. Rowse, Sheila Scott, Semprini, Ginette Spanier, Ariana Stassinopoulos, Godfrey Talbot, Geoffrey Wheeler, Desmond Wilcox, Dorian Williams, Ted Willis and Anona Winn. Add to this illustrious list a couple of hundred experts who are all renowned and competent speakers, and you have an array of speakers whom we are very proud to represent. For the snobbish among you, we represent a couple of earls, a countess, several life peers, a baroness and Rouge Croix pursuivant – and a Plantagenet who finishes his speech by walking out on his hands.

Gyles Brandreth has a splendid talk on prisons, but when he hit the headlines as the young member on Lord Longford's pornographic commission in Denmark, while he would still be booked for his other titles by the ladies' luncheon clubs, when he got there he would be taken behind a potted palm by the secretary, who would say, 'I suppose you couldn't talk to us about pornography, Mr Brandreth, could you?' Life can be difficult. At one Round Table Rally I was preceded by six speeches – and because I was the guest of honour, each speaker recited an ode – one of which was three typed pages of foolscap long – all of them unbelievably blue and impossible for a professional comedian to follow. When I got up to contribute my little mite at half past midnight with the admonition to, 'Keep it short – we're running very late,' I was delighted to oblige. On another occasion, an old gentleman assailed me after one of my lunch-time speeches with, 'I thought your material was very rude. Quite disgusting!'

'Which, sir, were the jokes which offended you?' I asked.

'I couldn't tell you. You see, I'm very deaf and they were laughing very loudly!'

One of the objects of the agency is to supply a very necessary service should one of our speakers be ill – or unable to appear for any other reason. Strikes and weather sometimes interfere. Our best performances to date are when we were able to supply a speaker at Preston at half an hour's notice; and at Slough, when an American luncheon of businessmen at a conference were tired of listening to themselves and wanted a professional speaker – this decision being made as they sat down to luncheon. So they got on to Associated Speakers. While the coffee was being served, Frank Bough walked in the room to speak, and as usual, was received with acclaim.

The late Godfrey Winn was one of our most successful speakers. He died suddenly while playing tennis one Sunday. He had several engagements for us at the time, one on the Monday. Paddy Davis rang up the secretary.

'You may have seen in the paper that Mr Godfrey Winn died yesterday and will be unable to speak for you. Would you like us to send you a replacement?'

'Oh dear!' said the lady at the other end of the phone. 'This is not good enough – I'm afraid he'll have to come. We have his name printed on our programme!'

'No,' said Paddy. 'I don't think you heard what I said.' And she then repeated the sad news.

'I'm afraid he'll just *have* to come,' said the lady. 'What are you going to do about it?'

'I suppose we could arrange a séance,' Paddy said.

Paddy and Tony Davis through the years have run Associated Speakers, not only efficiently but with a great deal of personal charm, and it grows from strength to strength; their loyalty and friendship is a warm and important part of our lives.

'Are you from Assorted Speakers?' one secretary asked, and I think that describes us all very well.

16   After Dinner with Cyril Fletcher

'A mélange of melody, merriment, melodrama, mummery and memories' – Ipswich Arts Theatre programme

I am not inviting you to coffee and liqueurs. The title of the chapter is the title of my one-man entertainment, which I first unveiled to an astonished world in 1966 and have been performing frequently, at irregular intervals, ever since.

Like so many events in this business it began by accident. I was invited to take the chair at a morning lecture on opera by Anthony Besch, as part of Bexhill Music Festival in the De la Warr Pavilion. He was late, and it was decided to start the proceedings without him – 'Do a ten minute introduction, Cyril, I'm sure he'll be along by then. He's only coming from London and he is a most reliable man.' I was still on the stage over an hour after the initial ten minutes, and to my delight it was not proving a nightmare – in fact, I was rather enjoying it. Anthony Besch arrived in time to prove that he was still alive and spoke for a few minutes – it was lunchtime by then. As I performed I had realized that here were the bones of a one-man show – it just needed rearrangement. It needed carefully prepared crescendos of laughter and quiet serious pieces here and there. It would also require the extra colour that a pianist and a possible change of costume would provide.

As I received no fee for presiding over the lecture – 'It will only require a few words, Mr Fletcher, and after all, you live locally!' – I felt that the management at Bexhill owed me something, and, indeed, before I left the theatre that day I told him that I expected a date for my one-man show in return for having held the fort. This was arranged and our faithful Francis Haynes, musical director and organist of many of our summer shows and pantomimes, rehearsed with me a couple of times and all was set.

My parents at that time were living at Bexhill. My father had retired. We had tea with them and I bought them two stalls in the front row. After the rehearsal and setting up the lighting it was almost time for the curtain-up, so I went back to my parents' house.

'Come on,' I said, 'time to go to the show.'

My mother came out into the hall. 'We have been thinking it over,' she said. 'Your father and I have come to the conclusion that we couldn't possibly sit through two hours of you!'

The show went quite happily that night, and I see from my diary that I played it another sixty times during its first year at several theatres all over the country, and the Belgrade, Coventry, was rash enough to book me for a whole week. The press has never been very effusive about my performances throughout my career as a whole, but for my one-man show they have been very kind indeed. Is it that they think there is an especial skill in a solo artist able to entertain an audience for two hours or so? In some ways it is easier. You have time to get to know the audience, and they have time to get to know you. Over the two hours you are together you can explore each other. I can find out during the first half what shape I am going to give my show in the second half. Being in front of this audience with only a pianist for your first hour – and knowing we are going to be together for an hour – I can plan things slowly. I have got to make them decidedly mine in the first five minutes if we are both going to really enjoy ourselves for those two hours; sometimes it takes longer; on occasion it has taken the whole of the first half, although this is rare (he said, boastfully), but they are still sitting there when I come back for the second spasm after the interval. A solo performance of this kind has an advantage in that one does not have to bother about cues from other performers. One does not have to bother about exact positionings on stage, and one can rearrange one's material as one goes along to suit each individual audience. The only exhausting drawback is that you have to concentrate every second of the time you are there. Every laugh must be timed exactly, every movement, every raising of an eyebrow. You cannot rest, you are the one thing they are looking at and to which they are paying attention. At the end of two hours, one is exhausted.

A one-man show is useful in that it can be played in large theatres or small. Village halls are not too small a venue; so long as the seat prices are high enough! Arts and music festivals are frequently held all over the country, and for such occasions it is ideal, especially if some of the other events are very classical and a little heavy and if there is no light relief to split them up. May I be permitted to quote from a notice I had for one of my smallest venues? I include it in all modesty, not because of the kind things the reviewer says, but because it does give a little of the content and a little of the flavour of my performance. So here is a notice of my performance in a village hall at Cookham, Berkshire, which was part of their Arts Festival:

Cyril Fletcher sent his audience home with red eyes. From laughing until we cried. He worked a packed Pinder Hall up to such a pitch that a mere lift of the eyebrow or searching glance had us slapping our thighs with renewed mirth.

It was quite an achievement. For nearly two hours Fletcher kept an audience of all ages and interests in the palm of his hand. When he joked we roared; when he recited a piece from *Henry V* we were so quiet that the ticking of the clock was an intrusion.

He joked about fêtes, faux pas, politics, parrots, toothless old women, the Church. He teased us for being arty, embarrassed late-comers, made mileage out of a (deliberately?) empty front row seat, parried interruptions.

Veterans say he hasn't changed a bit over the decades – except to get funnier.

In turn velvet-voiced, tender, worldly, twinkling, and gently rude, he was every inch the professional. Thursday night's performance is the sort that makes Cookham Festival a name for its one-man shows. And the charming part was that Fletcher seemed to enjoy himself as much as his audience.

And the *Buxton Advertiser and Herald and High Peak News* said, among other things:

Mr Fletcher has, as well as native wit, two main talents: a three-manual organ of a voice, with a glorious deep diapason stop, a speciality in a range which includes also a strident trumpet; and a meaningful look which, unlike most comedians nowadays, is not a leer with strong sexual suggestion. In fact, there was hardly a sex joke all night, and still the audience – a most intelligent one – was in tucks of laughter, which goes to show that occasionally we CAN do without it – and survive.

While the *Bucks Examiner* said:

At the end of the concert, when a hot night must have left him feeling exhausted, he returned to the stage, raised his hands to calm the vociferous applause, and paid a most handsome tribute to the Chiltern Festival (for which he had already given time and services without reserve).

He begged the audience to make sure that they brought friends to the later events, and seemed particularly anxious that artists such as Dorothy Tutin and Irene Handl would get a full house when they appeared at the festival. He was obviously far more concerned with their reception than with the fact that he had travelled all day from Milford Haven to entertain us at Chesham.

Enough of tributes from the 'National' Press at such important artistic events!!

It was not always easy for Francis Haynes to accompany me because he lives in Hampshire and the journeys were not always possible. I was performing at Henley, and Francis's deputy for the show was Richard Brown. Richard is twenty-five and has long hair, a large black beard and horn-rimmed glasses; there is very little face, as such, showing. What does show mostly are gleaming white teeth, because he is a merry man and always laughing. Richard is going to be even a bigger success than he is now. He is a very good pianist. (He plays mostly for a section of the Royal Ballet.) He is a good all-round musician in great demand for session playing, orchestration, and TV and radio accompaniment. He is a delightful companion as well, and makes an expert co-driver when we have long journeys. Richard lives with his wife in the country near Esher, in an ex-lodge cottage called the Turrets.

Sometimes we drive 250 miles and then rehearse and then do a two-hour show. When I say Richard helps with the driving and laughs a lot, these attributes both help a great deal when we get lost, as we frequently do.

I find I am always terribly interested in the faces of the people from whom I ask the way. I get totally mesmerized by a wart, or an outsized mole of unusual shape, or an unwanted nose. Then I'm always amused when I see a look of recognition steal over the unusual features: 'Oh, of course, this man is Arthur Warner or Jack Askey – no, no, no, how silly of me, it's that man who recites those Odd Odes in the Esmé Ralston programme!'

I was glad that Richard was playing for the ballet once when I got myself involved in a charity show. He sent his 'Royal Ballet' deputy to help me on this particular occasion. I find, sometimes, if you say you will give your services for a charity show – knowing that they have you for nothing and there is therefore nothing to lose – some organizers will not bother overmuch to publicize the show and sell the tickets, and you find yourself doing a performance which could perhaps have benefited the charity by twice as much money for the same amount of effort. I have a scheme to combat this. I say to the organizers I will come for no fee provided that you will pay me £1 for every vacant seat. Consequently they sell out and the charity benefits to the full.

For this particular show we arrived at quite a large hall with a circle containing about a hundred extra seats.

'Full up and sold out?' I inquired.

'No,' said the lady, 'only downstairs, we decided not to bother with the gallery.'

'You remember our arrangement?' I said.

'Oh yes, in detail,' was her rejoinder. 'But we are going to pretend the gallery isn't there! Would you like me to show you your dressing room?'

We had come quite a long way and were still in our lounge suits and had to change into our dinner-jackets. She ushered us into a room, a small room containing two lavatories of the sit-down kind, each in a little box room of its own leading off our small room, which contained a wash-basin and two large plastic dustbins with domed lids. All right, we have all dressed in worse places than that, and there was, after all, a lavatory each, a dustbin each, and a wash-basin. No soap or towel and no lock or bolt on the door. The audience by now were coming in, and our sheltered nook turned out to be the only lavatory in the building and the audience kept barging in and out the whole time we were trying to change. Even the mayor came in at the interval. 'Not three chains to flush,' I murmured; a poor joke, but we were helpless with mirth by then. The only surfaces for our make-up were the domed lids of the dustbins. There was nowhere to hang our clothes, and certainly nowhere to leave our effects and properties during the performance. When one is giving one's services for charity, it's usual at the end of the show for someone to give a little speech of thanks. Sometimes one is told how much one has earned for the charity. I never expect more than that, but sometimes if they are very kind one gets perhaps a bottle presented to one. If it's wrapped, it's sherry.

At this concert the organizing lady staggered on with an enormous cardboard box, and it was heavy, too. 'What *are* they giving me?' I thought. 'A settee and two armchairs?' I could hardly wait to get my present to the 'dressing room'. The mayor had beaten me to it. He was just finishing. I opened the box. It was full of dropped apples.

A one-man entertainment is good for all kinds of charity shows as it's self-contained and does not have any props. I get lots of requests for it. Here is one the humour quite unintentional, I'm sure:

We have just under 200 beds in the hospital of which about 90 are for geriatric patients and the rest are for our mentally handicapped adults. I'm sure that both sections of our hospital would look forward to, and enjoy tremendously, being entertained by you!

In *After Dinner with Cyril Fletcher* I recite a piece of Shakespeare, a poem by Crosbie Garstin and two poems from my favourite poet John Masefield. I won the Elocution Prize at the Guildhall School of Music with two Masefield poems, and when I left the Scottish Union and National Insurance Company, my fellow office boys clubbed together (and on their salaries they could ill-afford it) to present me with a leather-bound volume of his collected works. After some of my religious broadcasts for *Ten to Eight*, Jill recited several poems of Masefield's which fitted the mood and content of my text. There were two end-products to this. One was a sweet letter from John Masefield's daughter Judith, sending me a postcard view of Herefordshire which was on his writing desk when he died. The other was a birthday celebration, when Ledbury held a Flower and Masefield Festival in the parish church, a vast ancient church of red sandstone. 'Would you and your daughter,' the organizers wrote, 'give a recital in the church of some of his poetry?' We were delighted and honoured, and enjoyed doing so. We chose 'King Cole', as it has a religious and a showbusiness story. Two of John Masefield's sisters were there, both in their late eighties. 'We enjoyed it very much, Mr Fletcher,' they said. 'But do excuse us, we are motoring back to Surrey.' And they had motored up that morning too.

We were doing *After Dinner with Cyril Fletcher* at Leigh near Manchester in a pleasant room in the library – a new building – for the Northern Arts Society. The room was also used as an art gallery – there was a pleasant exhibition on and I had decided to buy one of the pictures. I was discussing this with a member of the hanging committee at the bar at the back of the hall when a charming elderly couple came up to me, and the wife said, 'Oh, Mr Fletcher, it's so nice meeting a celebrity. We've only ever met one celebrity before and that was Mr Stanley Holloway at Blackpool on our holiday three years ago. It were luvly meeting 'im. He stood just where you're standing and he were sooch a nice man!'

'Nay,' said her husband. ' 'Twern't Blackpool three years ago, 'twer Cliftonville.'

'Yer reight,' said his wife, 'yer reight. It were Cliftonville. In that case it were Jack Warner. He lives at Cliftonville. It were luvly meeting him. He stood there, just where you're standing, and he were sooch a nice man!'

'Eedie!' said her husband. 'Three year ago we were on holiday at Eastbourne. That's where we were on holiday three year ago!'

'In that case,' said Edie, 'it were not Jack Warner, it were Sandy Powell. It were luvly meeting him. He stood there just where you're standing and he were sooch a nice man. It were a thrill meeting him.'

Nice One Cyril

Then I was called away. I wonder who they said they had been talking to in the bar at Leigh, near Manchester.

Richard and I have had many adventures as we have toured the countryside with *After Dinner with Cyril Fletcher*. In some weird and wonderful way, fate seems determined to entertain me. It will be impossible for me to give the correct venue for this particular adventure; I must simply say we were to entertain in the north-east; it was not the south-west either, and though highly improbable it is true.

We were met and taken to the theatre by a delightful lady of late middle age, considerable presence, well dressed and without a trace of local accent: 'an admirable member of the Local Bench' would describe her. We rehearsed and adjusted the lighting, gave cues to the stage manager and were taken to our hostess's house to rest before the show. One of the hazards of being an itinerant jester is that sometimes if you are performing, shall we say, for a ladies' luncheon club evening function, it is difficult to get out of what is called by the booking agent 'local hospitality'. This means that instead of the society paying for your board and lodging at a local hotel, you are entertained by a leading member of the committee. This leads sometimes to meeting very charming people and being entertained in anything ranging from a most comfortable cottage to a cold and draughty stately home or vice versa. One is often tired after the two-hour show, and sometimes one finds to one's horror that a party has been arranged by one's hostess, and even if not expected to actually perform at it, one is very much the star attraction and has to be the life and soul of the party. To put it bluntly, it is an imposition, but usually so unknowingly, being arranged as an honour and as added generous hospitality.

The house we arrived at was in a cathedral close. It was a beautiful small Georgian house of lovely proportions, full of period furniture. We each had four-poster beds in our bedrooms, I remember, each with an enormous Union Jack as a counterpane, but nothing was quite as it should have been. In the hall was a beautiful yew sofa table over which was hung an ornately carved gilt Italian mirror. On it there was a large Chinese ceramic bowl in which reposed car keys, a single cycle trouser clip, an old toothbrush, a dead African Violet in a pot and an old-fashioned rubber-tubed enema. Stacks of copies of *Country Life* were under chairs, some chairs – doubtless Chippendale – had pieces of carving missing and horsehair showing through faded, torn and stained upholstery. Some of the paintings, oils of distant ancestors, were hanging, not just a little crooked, but positively askew. A curtain pelmet was half-down over one Georgian window, through which one caught glimpses of dark conifers and long, faded, weedy overgrown rosebeds. We forgot about this scene of sadly genteel desolation as we returned to the theatre and played to a happy and vociferous audience.

Our hostess and her husband (who was a retired shipping factor) came to collect us from our dressing rooms. He was sober and with impeccable manners; she was rather merry. Her husband helped her into the house and we were taken immediately into the dining room. He prepared drinks for all of us; she insisted on a double. It was obvious from the carefully laid table – great silver candle-sticks and rose bowl, and period silver cutlery – that our hostess had prepared all beforehand, and Richard and I looked forward to some cold collation with relish, provided we could get it over quickly and away to the quiet of our rooms. The double doors from the dining room led off straight into a spacious kitchen, from which appetizing aromas arose, but which in the distance looked even more dirty, bedraggled and neglected than the hall or the rest of the dining room. Here, indeed, wallpaper hung in festoons, and a filthy but distinguished chandelier threatened – dare I say drunkenly? – to fall crashing to the table. None of this really came into view other than as the background to our host and hostess, and our attention was riveted on a large green and red and blue parrot, which flew unrestrainedly around and about the room. Here it alighted on a chair, there it pecked at a bread roll on the table, and where it had flown and alighted, and as it flew to and fro, the bird – and it was the largest parrot I had ever seen – never ceased to 'decorate' the table, the carpet and indeed the food with what my grandmother used to call Jo's 'little messages'. Only parrot's 'little messages' are much larger than those of canaries.

The husband, taking over, poured out an appetizing soup. She hardly touched it. We three were sitting down and she hovered to and fro, sometimes bumping against the table, sometimes peering closely into our faces, and at times striking at the parrot; a little like the Duchess in *Alice* struck out at the baby. But she insisted on serving the next course. Out in the kitchen she began to sing loudly, accompanied by culinary bangings. Our host told us at some length and in some detail of his last round of golf, of the last round before that and the one before that, in such detail it took even longer than the preparation of the next course by his wife. Eventually she glided in, one plate per journey, each plate piled high like a school dinner with *bœuf bourgignon* and an assortment of vegetables, all covered with a glutinous gravy, shining with rainbow colours like oil on a wet road. The parrot in the meantime flew to and fro, over the stove and in and out of the dining room, swooping in low parabolas over his mistress's head, screeching and laughing. She had stopped singing.

The meal was before us. Richard was sitting opposite me, and although we both were amused, we were simultaneously sad at the whole situation which, from the husband's resigned air and the house's air of dilapidation and neglect, was not by any means a once-nighter. But we were much dismayed at the fact that we would have to eat the (dare I?) befowled food. Here providence was helpful. Our hostess had forgotten the wine. It was warming on the Aga; and in spite of her husband's protestations that he would get the bottle for her, such was her eagerness for it that she moved this time quite quickly, but her speed was her undoing. In turning quickly she lost her footing and fell across a food trolley about waist-high. It is difficult to imagine how she did it – but she had thrown herself, a shortish, fattish person, upon the empty top shelf of the trolley, which took off like a gigantic skateboard and at what seemed like breakneck speed, across the kitchen and into the gloomy depths of the scullery, where it met a pile of saucepans and crockery and finally came to a thudding halt against and partly through a glass back door. The noise and speed of the whole operation was breathtaking. It was like a film cartoon.

Our host had to leave us to rescue his wife. I got up and shut the doors to the kitchen. We could not bear to watch. And this will show how quick-thinking and practical musicians are. Richard began to feed some of his dinner to the parrot. The parrot was hungry and voracious. It ate mine as well. By the time they both came back, we found ourselves saying, 'We do hope you didn't mind our finishing our meal, we were so hungry *et al.*' Some stiff black coffee followed all round and we were soon in bed.

In the morning our hostess was her usual sunny self. She looked the impeccable magistrate she possibly was. She had even picked me a bunch of a particular rose I had admired when we first arrived. 'We did so enjoy *your* performance last night,' she said, 'but I must tell you my husband and I are rather sad this morning. The parrot died in the night.'

So I'm grateful to Bexhill Entertainments Director for asking me to chair the lecture for the music festival. I have many dates for *After Dinner with Cyril Fletcher* in my diary ahead as I write.

> 'Tis true, alas, I have been here and there
> And made myself a motley to the view,'
> said – William Shakespeare.

17　Gardening

> 'Of all things from which gain is obtained, there is nothing better than agriculture, nothing more productive, nothing sweeter, nothing more becoming to a man.' – Cicero

Gardening has always been my hobby. On 23 February 1933, when I was almost twenty and an insurance clerk with no prospects whatsoever of fame or fortune, I wrote this rather oddly prophetic piece in a sort of diary which I kept for some years:

> Amidst glorious, pastoral and beautiful country; small part left remnant of Old England; nestling between hills, yet not too far from the great, old city there was a cottage. Built 20, 30, no 40 years ago; but when built it was an imitation of the archaic, so that now with its aura of honeysuckle and old roses of forgotten names, covered as it is with the tracery of branches and leaves, and the scent of wisteria and the dark glossy sleekness of ivy; now it appears really old, an ancient among houses. Instead of being a gem set in gold, the setting is of gems. The garden is more beautiful than any jeweller's art. No man alone could make this garden, and yet one man and time and the grace of God combined to make it; to make its long lush lawns, its tall conifer clumps, its red, old clumsy walls with their mosses and lichens and fruit trees, to make its banks of glorious flowers, its quiet quaint nooks, its cool spattering pond and its mellowness and age and unusual statuary.
>
> This garden was a man's life's leisure, full of loving moments of pleasure when perhaps there was only time for some dead heads to be clipped off or other more unpleasant moments in wind, winter's whistling wind and autumn's cold wet blast.
>
> *
>
> A youth, a tall youth, discovered this garden in all its fresh June glory and he marvelled at it. He marvelled at the size of it, the plan of it and the artistry of it, and he loved it. He loved the small snugness of the cottage, the coolness of the conifers and the lawns and the contentedness of the birds' songs; so that he entered it.
>
> He entered under the brick archway, through the old-style wrought iron gates, along the flat flower-strewn York stone of the pathways and his heart

lifted and swelled and reverberated with the glory of the garden and the sky and life, sweet life itself. And as he turned a corner (the garden had many odd corners; a trick which enabled you to see vista after vista, fresh and different so that there was always change and variety there) he came across an old man who was tall, lank, withered and aged; eighty he might easily be, whilst before him was his ancient dog, a Scots dog grizzled and very grey.

The old man was idly pottering away with a trowel, putting precious stalks straight and laying roots right and he seemed to be almost the spirit of the earth himself for he loved gardens and the earth very much indeed. As the youth looked up the old man said, 'Why do you come here in my sanctuary, my hermitage? I do not mind, indeed, I'm pleased you admire my handiwork; I am pleased that you too who are young love a garden; I am pleased that the love of beauty, the love of the beauty and fruits of labour is not yet dead.' And he stopped for breath more than anything else and surveyed his intruder with a shrewd, wise and strangely young brown eye. Age had not crabbed the old man, he had a young heart. A heart which leapt at each spring and reaped a harvest of experience each autumn. 'What is your name?' asked the youth, as he fondled the ears of the Scottish terrier. 'My name is Cyril Fletcher,' the old man said. 'I know it not,' said the youth. The old man smiled quietly and resumed his work, and there was a great scent from the lavender bushes nearby and the last few forget-me-nots matched the June sky with their bright blue.

When I wrote that I'm sure I had never yet read a book on gardening, and I'm sure I had never visited any large garden, but I have described in this entry of my diary when I was twenty a lot of this garden that I look out at now that I am sixty-four. My house is the one we built twelve years ago as an exact replica of a Georgian house we lived in for thirteen years. We have walls and wrought-iron gates, we have nooks and hidden vistas, and old roses with forgotten names. And in twenty years' time, when I have reached the age of the old gardener, no one will have heard of me. (Odd decayed and dog-eared copies of this book will by then have reached the White Elephant Stall at the local fête, marked 1p to clear!)

An Englishman cannot help making a garden. And an Englishwoman cannot help tending it for him and with him.

The English and the Chinese are supposed to have brought the art of gardening to its ultimate artistic success. To this I can hear Le Nôtre snorting in the shades and the Japanese smoothing out yet another area of sand, and the Dutch, those horticultural wizards, ready to pelt us with Edam cheeses. But this seems to be the accepted fact.

Gardening as we know it started in Rome. Pliny in his letters describes in A.D. 62 his ancient gardens with topiary work, trees and shrubs trained to cover walls with groves of ilex, pine and cypress and myrtle as settings for his statuary. There were rose nurseries, too, with roses imported from Persia.

The first English gardens were around the great monastic houses, and the fifteenth-century illuminated manuscripts show us walled gardens and fountains, courtyards and arbours and beds of plants and rows of fruit trees. And pleached alleys.

In my gardening book, *Cyril Fletcher's Gardening Book* (Luscombe, 1974), on creating a garden with the reader I say:

We are setting out on an adventure. An exciting adventure. What could be more exciting than creating a work of art? And that is what we are about to do. We are going, Reader, you and I, to create a garden together.

And no matter how small, how modest, this garden will be a work of art. It may not be entirely successful, or indeed all that beautiful because, as with painters and sculptors and musicians, there will be degrees in our expertise. Some of us will be masters and some of us will be very modest 'trial by error' types as it were – Primitive painters. Also, the material we have to work with may be very inferior. We may have thick clay or salt-laden breezes, or sooty city fogs. We can be on top of a hill, deep in a frost hole, in the shade of great trees, or on arid sand; we may be trying to create a Versailles in a draughty corridor between two suburban houses. But wherever we are or whatever our advantages or disadvantages, a garden will result and because we have had fun doing it, and satisfaction out of our achievement, the result, no matter how unsuccessful, will be of a kind, a work of art. For a moment and very frequently (let's be honest) by accident we may create something exquisite – a minor work of art, but, and this is the delicious factor in gardening, we shall have to repeat it every year.

Not only are we just to paint a picture. We have to satisfy the mysterious demands of our aesthetic taste. Let us have a romantic garden which will perhaps look overgrown. Gertrude Jekyll calls it 'a beneficence of overgrowth'. The amount of material we have to choose from is bewildering and we must use restraint. We must have colour – and colour through the whole spectrum of the seasons, not, I implore you, 'a blaze of colour' as the gardening magazines demand or the seed packets insist. There must be contrasting foliage, both in colour and texture, and some of the foliage will be deciduous and will be gloriously different in spring and autumn, and some of the foliage will be evergreen and will furnish the garden and give us interest in the depths of winter.

The shapes of everything will matter: a low group of shrubs here, and there a coniferous exclamation mark. There will be formal hedges and flowering hedges and vast expanses of lawn and tiny enclosed gardens. Secret gardens, lakes, formal ponds – different levels. You will even, if you are a really artistic gardener, worry about and contrive tricks of sunlight – shafts of light coming through woods and avenues and hedges to enhance foliage of differing colours or jets of animated water. Here is the sort of subtlety I mean: on your west wall, or a west-facing slope or some westering portion of your garden you will have copper maples and russet-barked pines, and dark red roses, and pink camellias, and peonies and berberis and dusky dahlias to catch the red rays of the setting sun, which will give such a magic luminosity to those shades of red you will stay out in this enchanted place until the near-dark will send you inside, and on the way in, the tobacco plants and night-scented stocks will remind you that there is even an added dimension to your garden: that of the scented darkness. If you do not smoke, your sense of smell will be enhanced and will be especially satisfied in a garden. There are plants which look well in themselves: grey plants, for instance, or plants with variegated foliage. There are others which you'll have only for the flowers, like lilac, which you will put up with for a whole year – an uninteresting, dark bush – until, phoenix-like, it flowers and perfumes for a generous week or two. But best of all, like the lavenders, santolinas, some rhododendrons, many Mediterranean shrubs – you will have the foliage, the flowers and then their glorious aromas: an aroma all the year round from the leaves. This aroma comes from the volatile oils within the plant and is released by sunshine – this oil is called by some gardeners ethereal, a picturesque word indeed.

As a gardener you will renew yourself in some strange way as the garden does each spring. You must realize that the gardener himself is part of a design, and that you are using, as a gardener, beautiful living things which you do not own, but which are in your safe keeping for a time. You must realize this and give a good account of your stewardship.

And when you have made your garden, you have not necessarily made it for yourself. It will gladden and refresh the eye and the soul of the passer-by. You will have made it for some unborn child to enjoy and to shelter as a grown man under some vast tree you planted as a sapling. Time will do wonders with your garden – parts of it will become gigantic, and lichens and mosses will turn your garden stones and statuary to gold, and climbing roses and descending tendrils and weeping trees will make a wonderland for a sleeping princess.

I'm sorry I have run on so about gardens, but, you see, not only is it my principal hobby, but it has now become a part of my professional performing life.

Some of you who live in the Midlands, or Scotland, or Northern Ireland will know that every week for the last six years, together with an expert gardener, Bob Price, I, the keen amateur, have a television gardening programme. Those of you in London won't know anything about it, but will know that on Capital Radio every Monday my dulcet tones are heard expounding gardening wisdom (I hope), and once a month on this programme you can test my gardening wisdom by ringing me up and asking me a question. Occasionally I also write for the gardening press.

This is how it came about. Francis Essex, you will remember, knew us first of all when he was a BBC Producer of Variety and Musical shows, and became Programme Controller for ATV. He was about to include a gardening programme in his schedule: he had a most able producer and director for his programme, Donald Shingler, and he had a very knowledgeable expert – Bob Price – who had performed in many gardening programmes on both TV and radio. But he was searching for some different angle – one might almost say gimmick – for the programme. The very morning on which he had to make a decision my face fell through his letterbox! I contribute the odd article or two to *Popular Gardening*

– the excellent weekly paper for amateurs – and that particular week, there I was on the cover, and Francis suddenly thought of me as his gimmick. He had been to several of our houses as a guest, and was a keen amateur gardener of great knowledge and expertise himself; he knew several of my gardens well. So it was that I was engaged for an original six programmes, and we are now in our sixth year.

In the winter we record the programme once a week because there is not enough daylight to do two, and in the summer we record one in the morning and one in the afternoon, and these we do once a fortnight. We started our own ATV garden in a derelict corner of Kings Heath Park, Birmingham. The first autumnal day we worked there it was like the Mons battlefield. Rain fell down, we fell down and two mechanical diggers we were demonstrating sank almost without trace. Since this first broadcast, levity has crept in a great deal. Bob is not only a wonderfully knowledgeable gardener, but he has a very merry laugh and a great sense of humour. I wrote a preface to his book, *Today's Guide to Greenhouse Gardening*, in which I said:

> Bob and I find, when we do our gardening programmes for ATV *Gardening Today*, that each time we schedule a recording in the greenhouse there is a heat-wave – even in December – but when we are outside in 'blazing June' then there is a blizzard. But we, unlike your good selves, are not our own masters. We have to obey the Producer and the planned positions of the cameramen, the lights, the microphones and what have you.
>
> It is under such conditions as war, a revolution, or making a gardening programme, that one finds the sort of person of whom one can make a friend. These conditions stretch a man. With Bob it doesn't show that he's stretched – he looks roughly the same length always – but you realize that here is dependability (like the weather), here is a fund of knowledge which is so firmly based that no crisis will allow him to forget or falter. He is a man of sterling worth who knows his job. But one of the best things about Bob Price is that he is such good company. You will find ample proof of this in his book. He will share his knowledge with you pleasantly and with charm. As you learn from him you will be in good company. Here is your chance to get to know him now. I have known and worked closely with him for over six years and enjoyed every minute of our time together.

The fan mail for the gardening programme is prodigious and it contained this little gem the other day. Here it is, with my reply:

Leicester.
August 4th 1977

Dear Mr Fletcher,

I am very displeased with the way that you often interrupt what information that Mr Price is trying to impart.

I thought it the very limit in tonight's programme when you were both in the greenhouse discussing earwigs climbing into stalks of straw which had been stuffed into an upturned pot, you then made a facetious remark and Bob Price put the pot away saying that was one of the old remedies. But I should like to ask: WHAT IS? WHAT DO YOU DO when all the earwigs are inside the stalks of straw; that question was never answered on the programme.

I am very sorry if this letter sounds rather strong but this is not the first time it has happened and I feel that it should be pointed out to you.

Yours sincerely,
D. Delves

Sussex
17th August 1977

Dear Ms Delves,

I'm sorry you do not like my interruptions. That, of course, is why I'm there and thankfully is the reason for an enormous fan mail of delighted viewers who *do* like my interruptions.

I have been a comedian for 41 years and have made a practice of *never* explaining my jokes. Where would *you* have put the straw full of ear-wigs? . . .

Please do not be too serious with your gardening – it is great fun.

Yours sincerely,
Cyril Fletcher

We were at a banquet at the Savoy; one of those grand charity occasions. The Lord Chief Justice (at the time it was Lord Parker) had just made his speech and sat down when Lady Parker, an American lady of great charm, leaned across the table and said to Betty, 'I've got you in my bed.' Betty, thinking she could not have heard aright, looked blankly at her for a moment. Lady Parker explained: it transpired that she was a keen gardener and had a bed full of Betty Astell lupins. Bakers of Codsell named a beautiful pink Russell lupin after Betty which won many prizes. She is a Michaelmas daisy, too.

It was eighteen months ago that Capital Radio invited me to do a weekly chat on what to do currently in the London garden, week by week, every Monday. We call it *Down to Earth with Cyril Fletcher*, and once a month I do a 'phone-in' as well, when the whole of London rings me up and asks me what to do with this or that and I tell them! I was terrified at the idea of facing a phone-in audience on my own – after all, I am but a keen amateur and no professional gardener and there is no time whatsoever to look things up, it is all off-the-cuff question and answer, so I invited Fred Nutbeam, the Head Gardener at Buckingham Palace, to help me out. This he did in his enchanting and very knowledgeable way. I've also been joined by Jock Davidson of Rochfords, the nation's largest suppliers of indoor plants, when we have queries about indoor plants, but I usually manage the sessions on my own now with sometimes a hundred eager inquirers waiting to be answered in a busy hour.

They ring me up and say: 'I've got this plant.'

ME: What kind of plant?
THEM: Oh, I've no idea, but it looks dead.

170

ME: Then how can I help?

THEM: I want you to tell me what to do with it!

It is an enticing moment!

But usually they are sensible queries and it is a very happy hour listening to gardeners' keen questions and sometimes learning from the questioners themselves.

I certainly have learned a lot from Capital Radio. You will remember I have been broadcasting for over forty years and that when I began the BBC was smaller and merrier. Capital Radio is smaller and merrier. They do so much broadcasting all the time with a twenty-four-hour service that they now do it with a nonchalant expertise that makes me quite nervous – not only for myself but for them: sometimes we do not go into the studio until a minute before we are on the air.

In addition to the TV gardening programme and the Capital Radio programme and my gardening book, I have made six gardening cassettes for Polydor. Imagine me talking to you as you weed and plant and so forth.

Because of all these horticultural pursuits, I have also sponsored various gardening products. I was at Chelsea Flower Show in 1977 for Sandvik Gardening Tools; behind me on the stand in letters about two feet high was the legend: 'Cyril Fletcher says are your tools Sandvik sharp?' An old girl came up to me and said, 'Excuse me, are you Cyril Fletcher?' to which I replied that I was, which seemed to annoy her. 'There now!' she said. 'My friend said you were a man made up to look like him!'

Another member of the public approached me, this time a man. 'Work your leg,' he said. I didn't think I had heard aright. 'Do what?' I said. 'Work your leg,' he repeated. I said I didn't understand him. He then stood with military precision, working right arm and right leg like scissors in the way that Harry Worth does at the opening of his television programme!

In 1978, at the Royal Horticultural Show, Chelsea, I designed a garden sponsored by London's Capital Radio and the *Evening News*. On my brochure I described it thus:

Mindful of the economic realities of the day here is a small garden which will grow flowers, fruit, herbs and vegetables. The vegetables and fruit being grown amongst the flowers in an orderly riot. I have endeavoured to accentuate colour in four schemes – and I have varied the textures of foliage and the shapes of plants to give as much possible interest in so small an area. Immediately stepping from the house one is on a terrace made of simulated York paving. The lawn is surrounded by borders which are roughly in four sections:

A. Plants and shrubs of coppery red and blue.

B. Plants and shrubs of white with white and yellow variegations, and yellow flowers and foliage and silver foliage.

C. Plants and shrubs of mauve and blue.

D. Plants and shrubs of red and yellow.

Use is made of all boundaries of wall and fencing with cordon apples, espalier cherries and plums, loganberries and boysen berries.

And to my immense surprise the Royal Horticultural Society awarded me the Flora Silver Medal for it.

Gardening is the most delightful hobby, because you never stop learning. You never stop experimenting, and in spite of how fumble-fingered you may be, nature never stops enchanting you with all sorts of delightful surprises.

18   That's Life

'Who sayes that fictions onely and false hair
Become a verse? Is there in truth no beautie?
Is all good structure in a winding stair?
May no lines passe, except they do their dutie
   Not to a true, but painted chair?'
                              – George Herbert

Nearly all the good things that have happened to me in my career have come like a bolt from the blue. As President of the Pantomime Society I was present at a reception given at Foyle's on a Saturday morning to launch a collection of pantomime books by my friend Gyles Brandreth, the secretary of the society. It was a merry occasion and part of the merriment was caused by meeting, for the first time, a Miss Esther Rantzen, who was armed with a tape recorder and wanted an interview for her late-night BBC sound programme. We went behind a bookcase far from the madding crowd and a somewhat frivolous interview was recorded. We found we laughed at each other's jokes. The following Monday I was to be in the morning radio programme, *Start the Week*, with Richard Baker, and, of course, Esther was there again. I had not heard one of these programmes before; it was fairly early on in its long and entertaining career and I rather had it in mind that one was interviewed. I did not know, and had not been told, that one wrote a short dissertation and then joined in the general conversation about one's own piece.

So there I was without my set piece about Odd Odes and me; and while the other guests were nattering about their particular subjects, I sat down and wrote 500 words, and as some of the jokes in the 500 words were some good old and previously successful material, it was received well. Esther was watching; very little escapes her notice; and at the end of the show she was telling me all about *That's Life* and how she was to produce and present it and she was looking for a slightly comic and avuncular figure to add balance to the youth and charm of the rest of the team. Would I like to join? We were to do twelve.

Over the last three years we have done a hundred shows and, at the end of the last series, *That's Life* was at the top of the Jictar ratings with an audience of over 17 million viewers. So by now Betty and I have known Esther for four years or so.

Nice One Cyril

It would seem we have known her for ever. You, the readers of this book, will know her; this is one of the joys of television, we come right into your homes. (And with the flick of your wrist we can so easily go right out again!) Because you, too, know her I need not describe her to you, or tell you of her wit, charm and erudition. I need not tell you of how she has become the knight in shining armour who fights the causes of many downtrodden people. People who come to her as a last resort, either for her to sort out some bureaucratic tangle and scandal; or for her to bring to book the perpetrators of some rather nasty hidden skullduggery and law breaking from which the public have suffered. This she does most thoroughly, and at the end of each series she has been able, with justifiable pride, to remind the audience of her many successes. Many wrongs have been righted and many rogues have been stopped in their nefarious activities. Not only has she given a much-needed service in airing these cases, but she frequently manages to do it with wit and humour, and the show in its entirety becomes an original entertainment. I do not think it is generally known that Esther is the producer as well as the presenter, and as such is responsible for the content of the programme, and also for the programme's personnel, both in front of and behind the screen. This calls for brilliance and originality, both of which she possesses in abundance.

This brings me to Glyn Worsnip and Kieran Prendiville. Such original and unforgettable names. Glyn, the dark, straight-haired one, always has, in the scripts, to play the villains of the piece. He comes both from journalism and the theatre, having done some distinguished work in musical shows – he is a delightful singer and off stage has a most acid and witty humour which is so funny that one could never take offence. Keiran is the curly-haired one; the youngest of the team, and wholly from journalism. He is very good company as well, and all three of them, cooped up as they are, working under great pressure to get items written, films shot, interviews done (sometimes at great distances), knotty legal points ironed out, are always laughing and joking and making work seem like fun. One day Glyn and Keiran, having fallen on good times, will enlarge their political outlook and become happily and paunchily content with success and its bourgeois trappings.

When the programme gets under way there is a postbag of several thousand letters a week; and you know how some of them are addressed!!! Every letter is read and sorted; some become *causes célèbres*, others are just funny misprints for Cyril.

Once the material is assembled and scripted – all three of them work on this with help from backroom boys as well; Esther as producer, arranging content and actually writing a whole lot of the scripts herself. Then it is all assembled, and the running order – with 'funnies' sandwiched between very serious and sometimes heart-rending material – is of the utmost importance. Some of the items have been filmed during the week – you will recall the talented pets, the motor mower race and, of course, the walkabouts or 'vox-pops' as we call them, which precede each programme, sometimes featuring that remarkable teetotaller octogenarian Annie Mizzen. Esther works the whole week through, and with scripts now written and printed we arrive at the studio to rehearse and record the programme the same day that you see it. Rehearsals begin at 10.30 and by lunchtime we will have gone through it once and the editor of the programme – (we have had several), who is in charge of production on the day, comes down from the control room and tells us we are over-running by fifteen minutes! Then the cutting, tightening and rearranging begins. This is often done during the music rehearsal of the vocal act, which arrives after lunch. One or two more run-throughs and we are ready for the audience. Make-up and changing into the clothes we are to wear then Esther and I 'warm them up'. This really consists of welcoming them. I do a few gags and an odd ode – always the same jokes and Odd Ode, because this way I can gauge for Esther whether they are a receptive audience or not. Sometimes they may have been outside in the wet or the cold and need warming up literally. Then I introduce Esther and she explains the programme to them. She explains various pieces of TV equipment and gets as many, if not more, laughs as I do. After about twenty minutes we are ready to record.

A lot of the runthrough rehearsals have been not only for us, but also for the cameramen and other technicians. The speed sometimes in which the director will cut away from one picture to another (all of which is explained in detail in the script) is most adroitly done and means a great deal to the success of the whole show.

In the first series I would be given a funny situation, and then I would write an Odd Ode about it. For instance a couple were complaining because the law demands only that a warning notice should be put up on one side of a low bridge and not on both sides so that a high vehicle entering the tunnel as it were from the unwarning side would receive quite a jolt. A couple who lived in a bus had found it very annoying.

> *Freddie Fuss*
> *This is the tale of Freddie Fuss*
> *Who bought a double decker bus*
> *And to his wife, one known as Kate,*
> *Said 'This will do to live in mate.*
> *No rent to pay – not even fares,*
> *So 'op on quick – get up them stairs.'*
> *They bought wallpaper, paste and paint,*
> *They made it look like what it ain't.*
> *With Tudor beams and plaster pink*
> *All mod cons plus kitchen sink.*
> *No 'Mon Repos' upon the gate*
> *They had a destination plate.*
> *And Mrs Fred would lounge in bed*
> *With 'Do not Spit' above her head.*
> *One day when Kate was in her bath,*
> *She thought – 'I'll do it for a larf'*

And with abandon – sad to tell
Stretched up her arm and rang the bell.
Her husband in the driving seat.
Drove at fifty down the street.
With Katie yelling 'Stop you beast!'
And soap suds round her Aldgate East.
But on it rushed as buses do
Until a low bridge hove in view.
'Twas thus that Kate and Freddie Fuss
Came to own a top-less bus.
In other words at one fell blow
Their bus became a bungalow.
Whilst Katie, nude, without much hope
Tried to camouflage herself with soap.
Yelling to Fred, 'Now you've gone too far
Where d'you suggest I put the loo-fah?'
A passing postman, somewhat coarse,
Said 'If she's Godiva – where's 'er 'orse?'
Fred cried, 'Here's my boob for all to see
And with yours uncovered that makes three!'
A boy on a push-bike started shrieking,
'Cor! Look at that there lady – streaking.'
The latest news is Freddie Fuss
Now owns a single-decker bus
Whilst Mrs Fuss – his better half
Wears a bikini in her barf.

The next series it was decided that the audience should write their own Odd Odes. This idea emanated from a *Blue Peter* programme where we had an Odd Ode competition with the children sending in their poems. The standard was remarkably high. So, indeed, it was for us, and I would sometimes rewrite the odd line or two. Having exploited Odd Odes for about forty programmes, Esther decided to ring the changes and I do each week a group of either misprints, oddities or quaint items ranging from menus in supposed English from the Greek or Japanese to wonderful gobbledegook out of some bemused government department.

I have now moved from the settee of the first series to the opulent leather armchair with the Victorian ferns behind it, tickling my lughole. The fact that I am always sitting down leads the audience to think I am even more senile than I look. Very old ladies at luncheon clubs are apt to totter up to me and through their geriatric gums to murmur, 'Oh, you are able to get about still, I see!' This chair also led to this poem, for the *Radio Times*:

Now viewers all, I will lay bare
The confessions of a TV chair.
I'd love a real home, loving, kind,

When I'd get to know well each behind.
Instead I've got this job inferior,
A home for anyone's posterior.
I have one consolation though:
Every Sunday night I know
That Cyril Fletcher's slim, small seat,
Clothed by Savile Row so neat
Will sit and laugh at Esther's pun
And amuse the nation with his fun.
In the meantime, here I stop –
A popular BBC TV prop.

It also leads stage directors to ransack every town and village for one when I appear in my *After Dinner with Cyril Fletcher* show. I think I shall have to be buried sitting up in one, it now seems to be so much part of my image.

You will remember the captions for one series of *That's Life* consisted of a band and small contingent of guardsmen in red uniforms and bearskins marching up and down Shepherd's Bush Market. We bore enormous placards proclaiming *That's Life*, and many of the guardsmen had *That's Life* placards pinned to their chests. One woman passer-by yelled out 'Oh look! It's the teabags!'

Later that afternoon the same 'brigade of guards' was marched to and fro across Westminster Bridge in the pouring rain: rather thin, flat-chested men with bandy legs and knock-knees – film-extra material, and not exactly splendid athletic soldiers as those required by the Guards; and accoutred in uniforms rather hastily gathered from a flustered wardrobe department at short notice, an epaulette missing here, the wrong belt there – in short, Fred Karno's army with the elderly Fletcher bringing up the rear, bespectacled, double-chinned and with a brewer's stomach. (I might have mustered for a retired colonel, but not the regimental sergeant my stripes proclaimed me to be.) Outside the Houses of Parliament we stopped exhausted to lean at all angles against the castellated wall when the filming had stopped, and very glad we were of the rest, when a party of Japanese tourists came and took many photographs of us. They thought – as doubtless many, many Japanese back home thought – that we were a magnificent band of the Queen's defenders of the realm. You see, to the Japanese we all look the same.

Esther's sense of humour is very alive, as is that of Desmond Wilcox, her husband; to be with them is always delightful and full of fun.

In some ways both Esther and Desmond are the acme of sophistication; but they are not brittle people. They are warm and sensitive. To see Esther with her new daughter Emily Alice shows a very different side to her. To see Betty and Esther discuss fabrics and furniture and pictures and antiques; to go, all four of us, for an excursion to Sissinghurst Gardens when they are our guests in the country is to see two very human and unsophisticated and artistic people, whose friendship means a great deal to us both.

Nice One Cyril

On the way to the last-night party of the last series of *That's Life* to be held at a Kensington Hotel, I parked my car a few hundred yards away and Betty and I, both in evening dress, were walking towards the hotel when we saw two Jack Russell terriers playing in a garden. In the garden also was a fat jolly lady hosing down a paved area with a very strong jet of water from a hosepipe. One of the dogs looked very like our Henry, so we stopped and admired them playing. The woman looked up, recognized me and said, 'Oh, Mr Fletcher, I would love to have your autograph for my little boy!' In her surprise at realizing I was real, she forgot the presence of the hosepipe and pointed the jet of water straight at us. We very quickly jumped out of the way. In her excitement she then dropped the hosepipe, but such was the pressure of the water rushing through it that the pipe leapt about like a snake and ricocheted off one of the terriers, got between her legs and pointed up her skirts, causing shrieks of dismay for what seemed a long time as she was transfixed by the icy horror of it. Finally she smiled a wan smile, endeavouring the while to remove the Niagara from her knickers. With perfectly straight faces Betty and I signed her sopping-wet autograph book. Ah well, *That's Life!*

19   A Day in the Life of . . .

'Doing jobs like that (i.e. being an insurance clerk) is just working
to be paid. Being an entertainer you have fun and get paid for it.'
– Tom Jones, the pop star

When you are my age and are not appearing regularly on television in a
series, the public either thinks you are dead, or they say, 'You've retired,
of course.' Well one does not expect the public to know of all you are doing
when a whole lot of them are private shows all over the country – some, like
my gardening TV shows, only shown in certain areas, and some, perhaps,
on radio, which is now listened to selectively and at certain peak times.

Here at random from my diary is a typical week:

Monday	*Morning*. London. Judge Comic Verse Competition for Trident Assurance. *Afternoon*. Record some Odd Odes for Safety for the C.O.I. for Radio. *Evening*. Capital Radio broadcast 'Down to Earth with Cyril Fletcher' – weekly gardening talk. Drive to Oxford to stay night preparatory to
Tuesday	Recording of two Gardening TV half hour programmes in rose gardens at Oxford. *3.30. p.m.* Personal appearance at Selfridges, St Ebbs Street, Oxford.
Wednesday	Book signing at Jarrolds Store, Norwich of 'Odd Odes and Oddities' between 11 a.m. and 1 p.m. *3.0. p.m.* Rehearse and record interview for Anglia TV, Norwich
Thursday	*1.30. a.m.* Radio Brighton *3–4. p.m.* Book signing session at W. H. Smith, Bognor Regis.
Friday	*3. p.m.* BBC Radio Nottingham *Evening*. Speech at Dinner of B.M.A. at Grand Hotel, Leicester.

Nice One Cyril

Saturday   *Morning and afternoon.* Opening of Gardening Centre at Derby.

Sunday   *10.30. a.m.* Rehearsal of 'That's Life'.
    8.30. p.m. Recording of 'That's Life'.

So, you see, one is hardly retired. Dead? Well, not exactly; after all that – almost! But in between all this one does the occasional – sometimes frequent – appearances for charity. One is sometimes expected to do a charity show; one is sometimes expected to do a show for patients who are ill or convalescent, or sometimes one is expected to 'go round' an institution, workshop, hospital or whatever. Here is an example of this sort of thing: some notes I made in the train on the way home after one of these visits:

October 3rd I was asked last night if I would visit a home for spastics in
1974   Scunthorpe near to the hotel. In cowardly fashion I tried to get
    out of it – a script to write, I faltered. I was being invited by a
    large friendly dark-haired lady who had sat in the front row last
    night and had laughed a lot. Her merry face fell at my excuses.
    Suddenly I realized that if it meant as much as this to her;
    perhaps someone of hers was in the home. 'They'll love seeing
    you,' she said. 'They'll be so thrilled.' So I went knowing that I
    would carry away sad – unbelievably sad – cameo pictures
    which would haunt me for the rest of my life.
    I was asked to be there at 12. This turned out to be their
    lunch hour – and like all lunch times precious and not to be
    disturbed, especially as many of these people worked in a
    workshop on piecework.
    One or two were hounded out into the corridor to meet
    me in between the courses. First of all a young man of perhaps
    twenty (he was twenty-nine) tall, dark with a handsome smile
    of perfect teeth and very smartly dressed – a young bank
    official perhaps – he knew all about me. He had his autograph
    book to the fore – he even remembered *Workers' Playtimes*
    he had heard as a child. His sentences were sensible and
    well constructed, his conversation was charming and intelligent.
    His speech had that back-of-the-throat sound – not quite a
    cleft-palate sound, but similar – which most spastics have. The
    ugly ones, the cruelly distorted ones are sad enough, but it
    seemed sadder still to see this young man and also a sweet-
    faced beautiful blonde girl with tinted glasses and also in the
    prime of her young womanhood so nearly whole but not quite.
    How too additionally sad for them to spend their young lives
    among some of the more horrific cases by which they were
    surrounded. 'I like you,' yelled out a fat happy youth in a wheel
    chair with several chins and glasses and a look of Billy Bunter.

180

'But I think Esther Rantzen's smashing!' They all laughed
making their sad distorted sounds. By now I was in
the dining room and talking to each one separately. I am
slightly deaf (through the mastoid operation) so that it was
difficult to understand some of them with their broad Scunthorpe accents as well as their speech disabilities. They didn't
mind how many times they repeated what they said. The pretty
blonde girl was feeding banana fritters by spoon into the mouth
of a cruelly crippled man of about thirty-five in a wheel chair
with his tiny distorted arms held together in a suppliant gesture
like a squirrel holding a nut. I took over. He liked that. He
beamed with pleasure and ate the rest of his fritters for me. He
couldn't say anything. One old tiny soul was crouched in his/her
wheel chair against a wall, his/her head so awry one could
not see the face. There were about forty in all. Each one with
his active mind imprisoned for all time in his shapeless body
that he could not control. Some of them so happy for a
minute to see in the flesh an elderly comedian they had
laughed at for a moment on the telly. And then as I came out
of the dining room one chair propelled at quite a speed – faster
than we were walking, trundled past us through the wide door
and I saw then the emaciated, tiny warped body working so
hard to move the wheels and swaying to and fro in a sort of
demented triumph to get past us. The poor little body in its red
sweater was so small and helpless and vulnerable. I will never
not see it. How would I feel if it were me? How would I feel
if it were my son?

20   Cancel Tomorrow

'Smile at us, pay us, pass us
But do not quite forget.'
  – the caption to a picture of a clown by Edward Seago, from
  a poem by G. K. Chesterton.

I have no idea of how to finish this book. I had very little idea of how to begin it. Come to think of it, there are very few ideas in the middle.

Many events that shape our lives are beyond our control. Somerset Maugham said, 'You cannot change your essential nature, all that you can do is to make the most of your limitations.' From this wisdom I gather the more the limitations, then the more likelihood of making a career! I might, in my instance, say that I have stretched a thin talent as much as possible over a very long period. For the British public's stamina I am grateful. As I write I am commencing a new series of Esther Rantzen's *That's Life*; I am continuing my sixth year of *Gardening Today* for ATV's weekly programme, and I have just signed a contract for BBC sound radio for a sixteen-week serial as compère and presenter of the *History of the Minstrels*. In my diary, stretching ahead, are innumerable private shows, separate cabarets and appearances in my one-man show. After forty-two years I am thankful there is still a reasonable demand for my 'talent to amuse'.

As well as loving my work, I love the people I work with and the public I work for.

I have great attachment for the English landscape and the English countryside. That my friend Allan Perry gave his life defending England makes it even more dear to me. I love my village here and the people, the two ancient churches (my land is in two parishes), the pubs and, of course, the view. We do not farm; we sell the hay as a standing crop and we have sheep in the fields in the winter. We do not have any sprays or artificial fertilizers, but are wholly organic and I try not to kill things. I wonder if I might be considered a yeoman – one definition reads 'a small landowner'. But being a yeoman means more than that. It means to me that, as well as owning a piece of the country, my heart beats with it and for it.

I like what Max Wall, that droll genius, wrote at the end of his autobiography, *The Fool on the Hill*: 'If my life has been a training for being an idiot, perhaps I will succeed at last.'

There is one thing I have found amusing through the years and that is the attitudes of the public to a comedian. They do not think you can ever hurt yourself, and if you do really hurt yourself, it is a cause for great merriment. When opening a fête I once stepped from a platform on to a box-crate placed there for me. The crate was rotten, my foot and leg went right through it, and not only did I slit an expensive trouser leg and thus ruin a costly suit, I had a very painfully lacerated and bleeding leg full of dirty old splinters. Up to that moment, with my verbal jokes and my endeavour to make merry with declaring the fête open, I had found them an unresponsive audience. Once my foot went through the rotten wood, they roared. When somebody talks of what has apparently been a most successful show, when you have had the audience rolling with laughter in the aisles, they will themselves never admit to laughing at you. It's always, 'My husband roared with laughter.' 'My daughter was so amused.' To be perfectly truthful, there are some who say, 'I *had* to laugh! I really could *not* stop myself', as if some great internal struggle had gone on to suppress all risibility! Then there are those, when you are appearing in pantomime, who only ever want a copy of an ode for their children, or only want an autograph for their children – or, 'My children would never miss you on the telly' – all said with a superior air as if one's efforts at entertaining are only suitable for the appreciation of the simple or the very young. Another observation I would like to make is that it has taken me a jolly sight longer to review this platitudinous pageant of my life than the half-hour that Eamonn Andrews took in *This is Your Life*. It occurred to me then that one's whole life is supposed to pass through your mind as you drown; perhaps a few seconds only. *This is Your Life* is like drowning for half an hour!

I would also like to recall this observation of one of our late speakers. 'I don't care what anyone says about God,' wrote Godfrey Winn, 'He's been awfully sweet to me.' I too am grateful.

I am assembling a magnificent cast to help me with this last chapter. Somerset Maugham, Max Wall, Godfrey Winn and now Evelyn Waugh moving into the limelight. He wrote: 'Only when one has lost all curiosity about the future has one reached the age to write an autobiography.' I have not lost all curiosity, or enthusiasm. Every new day to me is an excitement and a wonder. Every new day goes by so quickly because there is so much to do. That great war-time radio star, Bebe Daniels, was heard to murmur as she hurried underneath a bed in an appalling air-raid: 'Not now, please God, I've got so much to do!'

Before one writes a last chapter one is inclined to read the previous ones. Let us admit it: although I am a household name, like Whiskas or Chum, I have achieved very little. I've had a lot of fun achieving my niche in the enter-tainment scene. It has been especial fun because I have had the companionship and the intense love and loyalty of Betty to help me on the way. There is in the English prayerbook a phrase about living a life of good report. I have tried to do this. And in my meanderings through life (I prefer that expression to the more pompous one of career), I hope sincerely that I've not harmed anyone or spoilt anything for anybody on the way.

Last evening I walked slowly down my avenue of newly green beech trees on a quiet, sunny, May evening: 'Walking one low lit evening in the whispering wood.' And because of this book my mind was in the past. I realized what a chancy business life is. I thought of my old school chum Allan Perry; we had left school and both entered the City together. We met at lunchtimes, we spent our holidays together. I was best man at his wedding; he was best man at mine. Our minds chimed harmoniously, and we dreamed our dreams of success together. We were two men with equal opportunities, similar education and background, and similar likes, dislikes and capabilities. Suddenly there was a war and Allan was killed in the RAF. All his journeying came to an end; mine went on. Life is very odd. It is impossible to understand the pattern or the design.

As I came through the wood, dimly lit with the white light of the lamps of late narcissus, I reached the corner of the house and said to myself with Tennyson's voice:

> Good Lord how sweetly smells the honeysuckle
> In the hushed night as if the world were one
> Of utter peace and love and gentleness.

Some of it is, but not enough.

I'm going to finish with my favourite poet, however, John Masefield:

> *Prologue*
> I am a pilgrim come from many lands,
> With stories gather'd about many fires,
> Some, when the moon rose above Asian sands,
> Some, when the sun set over English shires.
>
> How often have I told these tales before
> To you, the listening pilgrims, who anon
> Set out towards the wells you thirsted for
> Across the desert, while the planet shone?
>
> Often, perhaps; and often may re-tell,
> In distant lands and times, as daylight fails,
> When you, the pilgrims, camp beside the well,
> And I, the pilgrim, recollect the tales.

Thank you for being an attentive audience while I have recollected my tales.

Index of Persons

Entries marked with an asterisk indicate inclusion in the photographic section of this book.

185

Index of Persons